THERE'S NO GOING BACK

THERE'S NO GOING BACK

The Life and Work of
JONATHAN DEMME

David M. Stewart

Foreword by
Joseph B. Atkins

A note to the reader: Some of the quotations printed in this volume contain insensitive language, including homophobic slurs. The original terminology is retained here for the purpose of historical accuracy. Discretion is advised.

Copyright © 2025 by The University Press of Kentucky

Scholarly publisher for the Commonwealth, serving Bellarmine University, Berea College, Centre College of Kentucky, Eastern Kentucky University, The Filson Historical Society, Georgetown College, Kentucky Historical Society, Kentucky State University, Morehead State University, Murray State University, Northern Kentucky University, Spalding University, Transylvania University, University of Kentucky, University of Louisville, University of Pikeville, and Western Kentucky University.
All rights reserved.

Editorial and Sales Offices: The University Press of Kentucky
663 South Limestone Street, Lexington, Kentucky 40508-4008
www.kentuckypress.com

Cataloging-in-Publication data available from the Library of Congress

ISBN 978-1-9859-0265-7 (hardcover)
ISBN 978-1-9859-0266-4 (pdf)
ISBN 978-1-9859-0267-1 (epub)

Member of the Association
of University Presses

To Bud and Dot

Contents

Foreword by Joseph B. Atkins   ix
Preface: Angelic Greetings (November 2023)   xiii

1. Monsieur Demme's Holidays (1944–1959)   1
2. The Animal Lover and the *Alligator* (1959–1967)   6
3. A Road Scholar (1968–1970)   12
4. A New World (1970–1973)   20
5. Girls, Guns, and *Shampoo* (1974–1976)   25
6. Frequency Issues (1977–1979)   36
7. Easy Street (1979–1981)   47
8. Shift in the Breeze (1982–1983)   56
9. Juggling Act (1983–1984)   67
10. Something New (1985–1986)   75
11. Second Chances (1987–1989)   84
12. Dinner with Friends (1990–1992)   97
13. Angels Crowding Heaven (1992–1995)   110
14. Subways, Galleries, and Storefronts (1996–1997)   124
15. Ghosts at the Door (1997–2000)   131
16. Losing Control (2000–2004)   144
17. Heavy Winds (2005–2006)   156

Contents

18. A Creative Marriage (2007–2009)   166
19. Burning Desires (2010–2013)   176
20. Flash and Dance (2014–2015)   185
21. Eagles and Condors (2016–2022)   191

Acknowledgments   199
Notes   203
Index   229

Illustrations follow page 130

Foreword

Director and producer Jonathan Demme liked to tell young filmmakers, "All you need is a camera and a story to tell"—simple advice that likely helped many Demme protégés get started. What the famed filmmaker left out, however, was the hard work, plus the years and years of honing one's craft, and the inevitable ups and downs even when you're at the top of your game.

Along with his camera and story, Demme gave his films an "inner lyricism," his fellow filmmaker Martin Scorsese once said. Film producer Mike Medavoy saw something else in Jonathan Demme: "You can't be in a room with Jonathan and not get excited because he's got this excitement and this vision."

The lyricism, excitement, and vision are evident throughout David M. Stewart's *There's No Going Back: The Life and Work of Jonathan Demme*. You feel it in Oscar-winning Demme-directed films like *The Silence of the Lambs* (1991), *Philadelphia* (1993), and *Melvin and Howard* (1980). They make a nice list of classics even if they weren't always recognized as such when first released.

Demme, who died in 2017 at the age of seventy-three, left behind a formidable body of work that ranged from major feature films and documentaries to live theater. He was a producer as well as a director, and his films are imbued with his lifelong love of music and commitment to social issues, whether it be women's rights, civil rights, protests against war, or solidarity with those who are poor and marginalized.

He had the rebellious heart of an independent filmmaker even though he had to labor long within the confines of Hollywood's big studios with all their strictures imposed for the sake of the bottom line. He acknowledged the reality of working the system if a filmmaker is to get the funding and distribution needed to reach a wide audience. Even so, Demme's long-stated goal was to be a "bearded Trojan horse" within the system.

As Stewart details with impressive research, Demme's career sometimes resembled a roller-coaster ride. Alongside grand critical and box office successes such as *The Silence of the Lambs* and *Married to the Mob* (1988) were dismal bombs like *The Truth about Charlie* (2002), which grossed a mere seven million dollars worldwide on a sixty-million-dollar budget.

Even his successes sometimes came with sharp criticism. Gay organizations protested the depictions of cross-dressing in *The Silence of the Lambs,* which film critic Pauline Kael dismissed as "pulp material treated as art . . . a bit of a fraud." Demme heard those protests and devoted his next major film, *Philadelphia,* to the then-raging AIDs issue. Once again, he couldn't please everybody. The film got five Academy Award nominations and won for Best Song (Bruce Springsteen's "The Streets of Philadelphia") and Best Actor (Tom Hanks), but Larry Kramer of the *Chicago Reader* panned it, saying the film "doesn't have anything to do with the AIDs I know. Or the gay world I know."

You need resilience in show business, whether in the face of downright failures or when great successes (*Philadelphia* was a huge box office hit) get panned by the very people they were supposed to reach. Resilience is something learned over a lifetime.

Author Stewart traces Demme's life from his youth on Long Island and in Florida and New York City through his early career as a film critic and press agent before picking up the camera on his own. For all Demme's talent and drive, his life is also a testament to the importance of connections. His father, who did public relations for the Fontainebleau Hotel in Miami, helped get him a meeting with film mogul Joseph E. Levine, who then helped land the young Demme a job with Embassy Pictures in New York City. Later in New York, Demme got work chauffeuring French New Wave pioneer

François Truffaut, who encouraged the young man to pursue film as a career.

Later connections with folks like legendary filmmaker Roger Corman gave Demme an appreciation of the helping hand and of loyalty. This is demonstrated again and again in the list of mentors, colleagues, friends, and family members populating the roll of credits at the end of his films.

Demme didn't let Hollywood pressures deter him from interests that engaged him his entire life, such as music—seen in his documentaries on musicians such as Neil Young, Justin Timberlake, and the Talking Heads—as well as Haitian art and culture—as seen in his 1988 documentary *Haiti Dreams of Democracy*. He was an avowed feminist and supporter of issues important to women—he saw *The Silence of the Lambs* as a feminist film—yet it didn't prevent him from having major dust-ups with Goldie Hawn on the set of *Swing Shift* (1984) and Oprah Winfrey during the filming of *Beloved* (1998).

This wonderfully detailed book doesn't just provide deep insight into the making of Jonathan Demme's films and the personality of the man who made them. It also offers a unique, behind-the-scenes look at Hollywood and the inevitable tensions in a hardcore capitalist industry that depends on free-spirited artists to feed the bottom line.

Jonathan Demme walked that tightrope as a big studio director under the scrutiny of the moguls and as an independent with his own production company. What resulted were several of the seminal films of the late twentieth and early twenty-first centuries. He was indeed a "Trojan horse" who fought hard for his art and his vision. His was a commitment in which "there's no going back," as author Stewart tells us in his book's title.

Joseph B. Atkins

Joseph B. Atkins is a veteran writer and professor emeritus of journalism at the University of Mississippi. His books include Harry Dean Stanton: Hollywood's Zen Rebel (*University Press of Kentucky, 2020*) *and the novel* Casey's Last Chance (*Sartoris Literary Group, 2015*).

Preface

Angelic Greetings (November 2023)

Apple cider and laughter warmed up the cold November evening in Nyack. People lined up across the northwest corner of Broadway and Depew Avenue anticipating the heat and music flowing through the archway of the former church converted into a community center. Beyond the smiles from local artisans, mulled wine, and baked goods, a movie screen displayed a series of music videos from New Order, UB40 with Chrissie Hynde, and Artists against Apartheid before showing a montage of close-ups of Anthony Hopkins's Hannibal Lecter from *The Silence of the Lambs*, Tom Hanks in *Philadelphia*, and Oprah Winfrey in *Beloved*. Rockland County and the Rivertown Film Society came together to honor one of their loyal friends and artists, Jonathan Demme.

A framed photo of the director is perched on a table in the center of the stage with a lit candle and a series of walking sticks on display. Presiding over the ceremony was Brooklyn Demme, Jonathan's son, a local filmmaker and activist, welcoming those in attendance with a smile that bore an uncanny resemblance to his father. Following the salutations, Jonathan's music supervisor Suzana Peric, production designer Kristi Zea, and cinematographer Declan Quinn regaled audiences with anecdotes about working with Jonathan on some of his notable films like *Something Wild*, *Married to the Mob*, and *Ricki and the Flash*.

Preface

In between the conversations about Jonathan's upbeat energy on set and in the editing room, a video made by Brooklyn featured those who couldn't fly out to Nyack commemorating Demme. Roger Corman, who passed away six months later in May 2024, delightfully talked about being recognized as the secretary of state in Demme's 2004 remake of *The Manchurian Candidate*. Julie Corman, Roger's wife and producer, recalled sharing the list of fifties jukebox tunes with Jonathan while making his second film, *Crazy Mama*. Tony Award–winning choreographer and family friend Annie-B Parson warmly reflected on being with Demme's family during the filming of *Philadelphia*.

Rocklanders chimed in, sharing their memories of Demme when he riffed with them after screenings held at the Jacob Burns Film Center. From the shared excitement of what was seen on the screen to tips for aspiring filmmakers, Jonathan Demme was never short on answers, and his love of film, music, and humanity left one question I wanted to answer throughout the course of writing this book: Where did that love come from?

In his worn-out sneakers, camouflage pants, concert T-shirt, and multicolored beads, Jonathan Demme was a cultural magpie who collected stories to bring back to his proverbial nest before sharing them with his worldwide audience. In a career that spanned nearly five decades, Demme championed stories about strong women and characters who resisted bigotry and racism. He also had an uncanny knack for capturing the essence of musicians in live performance. His inherently eager nature became a central part of his life, which revolved around the art of storytelling.

This book is not a definitive biography as so many people have their stories about Jonathan and are the respected keepers of the flame. This is an investigative labor of love that hopes to honor and understand Jonathan Demme as a filmmaker and humanist whose work served as a beacon of hope in troubled times.

1

Monsieur Demme's Holidays (1944–1959)

Jonathan's parents were distinguished citizens of Long Island, and their activities were reported in the society pages of local papers. Robert Eugene Demme was born in Cedarhurst on May 13, 1910. As a teenager, Robert worked on the floor of the New York Stock Exchange as a runner, and he enrolled at Duke University in 1931, studying business administration.[1] His grades and inherited business acumen earned him a spot in the Alpha Kappa Psi fraternity. Standing at five feet, nine inches with brown hair and brown eyes, Robert Demme had an uncanny resemblance to Cary Grant, and his charming personality was infectious.[2] Moxley Arnold, Duke's undergraduate dean, saw ambition in Demme and encouraged him to join the Key Club, a nontraditional fraternity focusing on merging with Beta Theta Psi.[3] Sadly, Demme lost his mentor when Dean Arnold died in a car crash in 1934.[4] Building connections was what Robert thrived on, and after Arnold's passing, the young Key Club member decided to unlock the doors of opportunity to something he was passionate about: writing.

Robert's first foray in journalism began when he started writing for the *Duke Chronicle*. Although his name is listed along with the other members of the school-run newspaper, no record of Robert's collegiate reportage was found in the *Duke Chronicle*'s digital archive. During this period, Robert flew to Chicago to look at prospective business opportunities before graduating. He was invited to a dinner party hosted by William Tracy Alden, the former president of the Chicago Bar Association and general solicitor for the United States Fuel Administration during World War I. Alden's wife, Marjorie Edwards, introduced Robert to her niece, a young artist named Dorothy "Dodie" Louise Rogers, who was studying at Mount Vernon Seminary.[5]

Born in Chicago, Illinois, on March 21, 1914, Dodie came from a long line of revolutionaries. The Rogers family is purportedly associated with the bloodline of Jonathan Edwards, the New England theologian and missionary who spearheaded the Great Awakening movement in the eighteenth century with his sermon "Sinners in the Hands of an Angry God."[6] In understanding the cultural and historical notes of America through her ancestors, Dodie learned about the importance of goodwill toward others and keeping a diary, advice she would pass along to Jonathan and her other sons years later.

Dodie married Robert Demme in 1935. Longing for a change from the Midwest and hoping to channel her aspirations toward life as an artist, she left Chicago with him that same year, settling in Oceanside, Long Island. They had their first child, Frederick "Rick" Alexander Demme, in 1937. To bring money into the Demme household, Robert worked as a reporter for a local newspaper and then landed his first published article, "Salt Water Safari," in *Motor Boating* magazine in December 1938. Demme's travelogue captures the sun-drenched splendor of an island in the Bahamas ten miles south of Bimini, the Cat Cays.[7] The publication put him up at Manor House, a clubhouse converted into a hotel with Tudor-style lodgings shrouded by palm trees. Demme reported on local fishermen catching nimrods and marlins, whose group of recreational anglers included Errol Flynn—fresh in the minds of filmgoers from his titular performance in Michael Curtiz and William Keighley's *The Adventures of Robin Hood* (1938).

Returning to New York was bittersweet for Robert Demme, who wanted to make traveling his living at any cost, but another opportunity had him flying back to the Bahamas in May 1939. Demme covered the annual Cat Cay Tuna Tournament in his only syndicated newspaper article, "Deep Sea Game Hunting Paradise." In the article, he portrays himself pining over his typewriter with a briar pipe, like Melville's Ishmael, introducing "the tale of a mighty fish."[8] Citing tuna and blue marlin fishing as "a man's job," the penultimate paragraph gives a nod to Mary Sears, wife of the New York Yacht Club commodore Henry Sears, who had hooked a 730-pound blue marlin. "Pardon me," Demme wrote. "You just can't keep the women out of the conversation no matter how you try."

Demme's joie de vivre landed him an advertising job on Madison Avenue with the Erwin Wasely Company. While there, he became part of a group of fellow journalists and publicists who met during lunch at the Hotel Delmonico and formed the Publicity Club of New York. In response to Hitler's invasion of Poland on September 1, 1939, and the propaganda campaign launched by Joseph Goebbels, the Publicity Club offered support to America and its Allies. As reported in the August 9, 1941, issue of *Billboard*, the group of publicists "have been in contact with government officials in Washington, working out an angle whereby the boys and girls might make themselves useful for propaganda purposes."[9]

Meanwhile, Robert's mother, Edie Castle, signed up to work at Grumman Aircraft in Bethpage, Long Island. Working from 4 p.m. to midnight, Edie was on the assembly line with hundreds of other women making sure the F6F Hellcats could withstand combat with the enemy. James A. Forrestal, undersecretary of the navy, would claim that "Grumman saved Guadalcanal."[10]

Robert was inspired by his mother's effort at Grumman Aircraft. In December 1943, while he was working as an assistant editor for *Skyways*, the magazine ran his article "Evolution of the Hellcat." Demme covered the Hellcat and its earliest incarnation, the XFF1, with meticulous detail: from the .50 caliber machine guns down to the landing gears. Three months later, he landed a public relations position at Pan American Airlines (at that time known as American Export Airlines); however, the big news in Robert's life was the birth of his second son.

Robert Jonathan Demme was born at Mercy Hospital on February 22, 1944. Nicknamed "Jobee" by his brother Rick, Jonathan had a big smile and brown eyes always searching for excitement.

Jonathan's world was enlivened by Robert's travel stories and grandmother Edie's tales of working at Grumman Aircraft, doing her part for the war effort. Jonathan watched his mother, Dodie, put charcoal to paper, still harboring now-dampened hopes for her artwork, which left an indelible mark on him. "I grew up being the subject of generosity and nurturing from different women," Demme said. "I got early on two things: relative superiority of women's sensibilities apropos men and this extra dimension of difficulty that confronts women when they go forth to accomplish whatever goals they set for themselves."[11]

In December 1949, Dodie and Robert had their third child, Peter Castle Demme. Soon after, the family moved to 27 Lorenz Avenue in Baldwin, Long Island.[12] As Dodie doted over her newborn, five-year-old Jonathan searched constantly for something to stimulate his active mind. Brother Rick would be the general of his toy soldier army as they recreated World War II in the basement. Jonathan tagged along behind his big brother, walking to and from Coolidge Elementary School, so much so that Rick's childhood girlfriend, Sylvia Strumpf, could recall how "Jobee would glom on to us and tag along. Rick would say, 'Jobee, get lost!'"[13]

Jonathan was mesmerized when his father brought home a television set. Along with children in the other 3.8 million American households that owned televisions, Jonathan would don his cowboy hat like William Boyd, watching episodes of the NBC western series *Hopalong Cassidy* (1952–1954). Ernest B. Schoedsack's titular Gorilla thriller *Mighty Joe Young* (1949) and Michael Curtiz's musical *Yankee Doodle Dandy* (1942) were the Million Dollar Movies Demme tuned in to see as channel WOR-TV 9 competed with the box office fare of mid-fifties cinema.

On Thursday evenings, the Demmes would go to the movies; it was a communal experience that had an impact on young Jonathan. From the attack of giant killer ants in Gordon Douglas's *Them!* (1954) to the film noir of German expat Fritz Lang's *The Big Heat* (1953), movies became Jonathan's refuge from this self-described period of loneliness.[14] He would travel by bus around Long Island to movie theaters in Jamaica, Queens. His mother took note of her son's growing enthusiasm and encouraged him to write about everything he watched. Jonathan savored the taste of international cinema through the humor of Jacques Tati's *Monsieur Hulot's Holiday* (1953) and danced to the grooves of Marcel Camus's *Black Orpheus* (1959). He got a notebook and started on a new path of not just watching but also analyzing the moving image to uncover the secrets behind the magic. Demme said years later, "Once you start seeing movies for free, there is no going back."[15]

Robert Demme had been working at InterContinental Hotels Corporation, a subsidiary of Pan Am, traveling extensively on assignment for the company magazine *Clipper*, his suitcase now adorned with stickers and luggage tags from Europe and South America. He had always had the knack of mixing work and pleasure, and he parlayed that into a series of publicity and account executive jobs, then a position as manager at the Miami offices of a budding ad agency, Communications Counselors.[16] These career moves would bring Robert Demme's family to Miami and a whole new panorama of life-changing experiences for Jonathan.

2

The Animal Lover and the *Alligator* (1959–1967)

The American beech trees and white oaks gave way to black olives and cypresses as the Demmes made their way from Long Island to Florida. It was 1959 when Jonathan and his family arrived in the Sunshine State, and in 1964, Robert Demme was offered a job as the publicist for the Fontainebleau Hotel, the premiere hotel for the likes of Frank Sinatra and Elvis Presley.[1] Jerry Lewis used the hotel as the setting for his comedy *The Bellboy* (1960), as would Guy Hamilton when he shot the third film in the James Bond series, *Goldfinger* (1964).

In Florida, Jonathan was able to further explore his growing passion for animals, a parallel obsession to movies. While still in Long Island, he had taken to birdwatching. With his autographed copy of Roger Tory Peterson's *A Field Guide to Birds*, he sought out the flocks that circled Nassau County and joined the American Ornithologists Union.[2] While in high school, Demme saw himself as a veterinarian.[3] He applied for a position cleaning kennels, which led to assisting the vets in acquiring greyhound blood for transfusions. A pint of greyhound blood went for seventy-five dollars.[4] It wasn't long until Jonathan got attached to the dying and sedated greyhounds as the blood drained from their bodies. When Jonathan saw Jojo, a sprightly greyhound, howling as he bled into the bottle, he made a call to a farmer asking if he wanted the best dog in the hospital. The next day, the veterinarian fired Demme and threatened to call the police for kidnapping Jojo. A tear-filled Demme yelled, "Fuck you! Call the cops!" as he stormed out of the hospital.[5] Jonathan wasn't interested in profiting off the blood of greyhounds—only saving animals. It was a wake-up call for the aspiring veterinarian.

Trying to maintain his rationality during bouts of rage was a balancing act Jonathan would exercise throughout the course of his life. Days passed before the veterinarian called his former assistant; he had been demoted to kennel cleaner: "You'll never be a vet, but you can be a good damn kennel man."[6]

"Thank God, my family moved to Miami," Demme said in 2016. "Things opened up for me, working with black people, hanging out with them, going to clubs and churches with black friends in segregated Florida."[7] Overtown and Coconut Grove were homes to Miami's thriving Black community and dubbed the "Harlem of the South" (at the time, the racist and politically unsound "Colored Town" was also used).[8] When Jonathan attended Sunday mass with his parents, his ears perked up at the sounds of the music and communal energy. Memories of the rich culture of Overtown would crystallize and emerge in his later movies and documentaries.

Jonathan also spent time driving through Coral Gables on his Vespa scooter to watch first-run movies at the Miracle movie theater. He built a circle of friends who shared his devotion to the cinema, like fellow cineast Julian "Buzz" Kilman.[9] Their weekends were spent at theaters like the Dixie and the Rio and at drive-ins, cracking nickel beers and watching westerns. Even when they took girls to the movie theater, the boys were more focused on the double bill of Ralph Nelson's *Father Goose* (1964) and Vincente Minnelli's *Goodbye Charlie* (1964) and their smuggled beers than on making out with their dates.[10]

Demme kept up with his film fix, parking cars at the Riviera Theatre before being promoted to usher. This unlimited access to the movies was his passport to a world of storytelling, a reprieve from the paranoia that surrounded Miami of the early to mid-sixties—if it wasn't the threat of nuclear war during the Cuban Missile Crisis, then it was the assassination of President John F. Kennedy in November 1963.

THERE'S NO GOING BACK

After graduation, Demme briefly served in the Air Force Reserve, a period he barely touched on in interviews.[11] Although military service ran through the Demme bloodline, Jonathan's derring-do patriotism was undercut by the regimented lifestyle of military life. Like his grandfather during World War I, Demme signed on for six months in the military, and he managed to fulfill his service before the Vietnam War. The conflict struck fear into an entire generation, and many would question the validity of America's involvement in the affairs of Southeast Asia. On his discharge from the air force, Demme dealt with personal conflicts at home.

As the sun fell on the Fontainebleau Hotel, the eleven-story crescent-styled North Tower would light up as a beacon for the high-profile clientele who once flooded the neighboring Roney Plaza Hotel. It was at the Roney where Robert Demme met Lillian Yaniz. A former Miss Cuba, she was working as a sales director at the time. During her eventful life, she had moved back and forth between Cuba and the United States and had fled communist rule after her first husband, a US naval officer, died, leaving Yaniz to raise their two children alone.[12]

Dodie was kept out of the conversation. She had started drinking heavily while still in Long Island, finding herself standing in the shadow of Robert Demme's patronizing social climbing and constant travel. After thirty years of marriage, Robert divorced Dodie in April 1965 and married Lillian Yaniz the following month.[13] As far as Jonathan was concerned, this made him the man of the house. His brother Rick was back on Long Island with Gail Kern, raising two children, which left Jonathan to look after his mother and little brother.

In the fall of 1964, Jonathan enrolled in veterinary studies at the University of Florida in Gainesville. During this period, Dodie attended AA meetings, went back to her wood carvings, and helped finance Jonathan's college education. "I had saved up money for college and my mother pulled out a couple of hundred bucks so I could stay up in Gainesville for a trimester," Demme said.[14] His empathetic nature and dedication to saving animals did nothing to bolster his grades, though, and the scientific context of being a veterinarian

The Animal Lover and the *Alligator* (1959–1967)

went over Demme's head. However, one animal Jonathan still had his eyes on was the *Alligator*—the university's newspaper.

"After I failed chemistry," Demme said, "I realized that there were no movie reviews in *The Florida Alligator* . . . so to feed my moviegoing habit, I offered them my services."[15] When asked by the editor for a sample of his work, Demme rushed off campus and looked at the State Theatre marquee to see what was playing: the Peter Sellers courtroom comedy *Trial and Error* (1962). Rather than going to the movie, he went to the library and looked up reviews of the same film in *Time* and *Newsweek*. Demme confessed in 1991, "I got a sense of the film and rushed back to my editor and gave him a review and he said I could be the film critic."[16]

Jonathan made his debut in the *Alligator* on February 24, 1965. He gives a rundown on a series of film screenings throughout Gainesville, including a glowing review of the Marx Brothers' *The Cocoanuts* (1929), which was playing on campus. He then proceeds to give a mixed review of *Trial and Error*: "*Trial*, I'm afraid, is no *A Shot in the Dark* [referring to the 1964 Blake Edwards comedy starring Sellers as the bumbling, yet iconic, Detective Clouseau] . . . action is at a minimum with an overabundance of lengthy dialogue. This combination makes for a pleasant but dull bit of nonsense."[17]

Demme and his high school friend Buzz Kilman were determined to channel their mutual obsession with cinema and share it with the rest of Florida. After attending a foreign film series at the University of Miami, they proposed a summer series of screening 16 mm films twice a week at the Studio M Playhouse on 208 Bird Road, an abandoned car garage that had been featuring local theater productions and screenings since 1952. There were fire hazards that concerned the city commission, but Demme and Kilman got support from the locals when fellow Miami moviegoers rushed to their defense via the editorial board of the *Coral Gables Times*. "Using the Planning and Zoning Board's argument," an anonymous reader wrote, "can these be as bad as some of the trash—the undulating fannies of those fleshy beach party films—available to children today? And since when did age serve as a criteria for enterprise? If these young men meet the requirements of the law, they ought to have the same chance to make their mark and money in the world like anyone else."[18] But the Studio M plan was short-lived, and the planning and zoning board turned down their proposal. Studio M closed for good in September 1967.

The *Coral Gables Times*, however, took note of the young men's pluck and determination, and in November 1965, Demme and Kilman were hired as arts and entertainment critics for the paper. Demme's first high-praise review was of Sidney Lumet's World War II prison drama *The Hill* (1965), warning readers that the film will "smash you in the guts with the force of a task sergeant's boot."[19]

Jonathan then found an unlikely ally in his father, who had recently befriended the latest guest at the Fontainebleau Hotel, Joseph E. Levine. Levine was a showman of the highest degree—stocky, brash, and passionate about films. He founded Embassy Pictures in 1938 to huge success, and in 1963 was offered a thirty-million-dollar deal with Paramount Pictures to work his magic. Robert introduced Levine to his son, the fledgling film critic, who had just given a glowing review to Levine's latest smash, *Zulu*. "You've got good taste. Want a job?" Levine asked the timid University of Florida dropout and offered him a job in the publicity department of Embassy Pictures.[20] But what looked like the offer of a lifetime was more of a detour.

Jonathan spent only a year in New York and then returned to Miami when his money ran out. There, he idled, going back to the animal hospital and writing the odd movie review. Still, he made a valuable connection with Stuart Byron, who was working publicity at Embassy the same year as Jonathan. Demme struck up a correspondence with the future *Village Voice* critic, pouring out his frustrations at his dead-end life in Miami and giving the first hint at his desire to get behind the camera. He told Byron that he had written the local International Alliance of Theatrical Stage Employees office "with the hope of getting a union card and thereby a shot at learning the cameraman's chores."[21]

In later interviews, Demme would give the impression that his career consisted of a series of seamless stepping stones from one

The Animal Lover and the *Alligator* (1959–1967)

opportunity to the next. While still in Miami, he came close to working publicity on the Sinatra vehicle *Tony Rome* (1967), which was being shot at the Fontainebleau, but it turned out to be empty promises from his father, who had by then left Dodie and married Lillian Yaniz. Before Jonathan could get back on track by working in New York, he stayed a spell with his mother, who had moved back to Long Island after the divorce.

3

A Road Scholar (1968–1970)

In the fall of 1967, fortune smiled on Demme when a position opened at the New York offices of United Artists. Jonathan leaped at the opportunity to go back to Manhattan. He clicked with Larry Kaplan, publicity manager, who hired Jonathan to work at the offices located between Forty-Ninth Street and Seventh Ave. "I was just a kid," Kaplan said. "They had fired the head of publicity and they put me in the job. I hired Jonathan and we hit it off immediately."[1] Around the same time, Demme covered the New York Film Festival. Demme's political sensibilities were heightened as he sat in on a screening of the documentary *Far from Vietnam* (1967), made up of vignettes focused on the social and political interpretations of the Vietnam War and directed by a sextet of filmmakers (Jean-Luc Godard, Alain Resnais, Agnes Varda, William Klein, Joris Ivens, and Claude Lelouch).

In Resnais's segment, actor Bernard Fresson portrays French leftist intellectual Claude Ridder delivering a monologue on the harrowing and existential elements the war played in his life. "That fifteen-minute episode utterly turned my head around," Demme told journalist and filmmaker Mark Cousins. "Discussing their confusion about how they used to love Americans because Americans had liberated Paris from the Nazis. But now, in Vietnam, it was the Americans who were the Nazis and the oppressors, and the Vietnamese needed liberation."[2] Demme reacted to the film by taking the bus to Washington, DC, in

A Road Scholar (1968–1970)

October 1967 to protest with 100,000 others marching to the Pentagon and attempting to levitate the building.[3]

Soon after, Demme found his own apartment downtown and started filling his bookshelf with texts such as Eldridge Cleaver's *Soul on Fire* and *The Autobiography of Malcolm X* as enlightening tools for his perception of race relations in America in the wake of the race riots in Watts, Los Angeles; Detroit, Michigan; and Trenton, New Jersey. Additionally, Demme's correspondence with Stuart Byron was an education in civil rights for the LGBTQ+ community; Byron had come out publicly in his first review in the *Village Voice* in 1971. As Demme confided to Byron in their letters, "Whether or not you realize it, our talks on everything from Civil Rights to my education to personal backgrounds, had a rather profound effect on me, I consider myself now, after my sojourn to New York, a more squared away individual than I have ever been, and I hold you responsible to a great degree."[4]

Working in the publicity department at United Artists had its perks. When François Truffaut was in New York promoting his Hitchcock-inspired thriller *The Bride Wore Black* (1968), Demme was assigned as his assistant, chauffeuring him to and from his hotel. Arriving at the front desk of Truffaut's hotel, Demme remembered, "It felt like God had landed, as I'm ushering up to the registration desk at the Algonquin Hotel, the guy behind the desk looked up and said, 'Oh, Monsieur Truffaut! Welcome! Senior Rossellini left this note for you.' I was going, 'A handwritten note from Roberto Rossellini?!'" Before Truffaut departed back to Europe, Demme brought his personal copy of *Hitchcock/Truffaut* for him to sign. The book, which Jonathan called "the film buff's bible," is based on a week of conversations between the two directors in 1962. Truffaut's inscription was surprisingly prescient: "I open to look at it, and it says, '*Pour Jon Demme avec mes amities and before your first film—François Truffaut.*' I said, 'This is awesome, but I'm not interested in directing.' He was like, 'Yes, you are.'"[5]

After his encounter with Truffaut, Demme had another unlikely fateful experience when he was assigned to chaperone Lucille Ball and her eighteen costars from Kennedy Airport into Manhattan as part of the promotional tour for *Yours, Mine and Ours* (1969). A predated, cinematic version of *The Brady Bunch* (ABC, 1969–1974), *Yours, Mine and Ours* is a family comedy in which a widower with ten kids (Henry Fonda) marries a widow (Lucille Ball) with eight children. One of the eldest members of the Beardsley clan, Greg, was played by Gary Goetzman, a fifteen-year-old child actor and aspiring lawyer from Van Nuys, California.[6] The brush between Goetzman and Demme backstage at the *Ed Sullivan Show*—during which Lucille Ball and the eighteen children sang, marched, and had a pillow fight in their pajamas to the film's theme song—would not be their last.

At the United Artists office, Demme would meet Evelyn Purcell, who would play a considerable role in the next decade of his life. Purcell, twenty-eight at the time, was born and raised in Australia. Her first movie job was at Cinesound Productions, which was once a major player in feature films and distribution in Australia but, by the fifties, had scaled back. "They did news, commercials, and the odd film," Purcell recalled. "I got the job where I did everything from continuity, to casting, to being a hand model in many commercials." When she moved to London in the early sixties, she landed at Harry Saltzman and Albert R. "Cubby" Broccoli's company, Eon Productions, as an assistant publicity director. At Eon, she worked on *Thunderball* (1965), *You Only Live Twice* (1967), and a family musical about flying cars, *Chitty Chitty Bang Bang* (1968): all adaptations of Ian Fleming novels.[7]

Purcell's work on these UA-distributed films next led to a yearlong position at their New York offices as the magazine contact for publicity. It was then that she met an eager Jonathan Demme. "Jonathan was a major film buff," Purcell said, "and kept a list of all the films he had ever seen. We were under a lot of pressure from the studio and the producers to get magazine covers and four-star reviews in the daily papers for every movie and the actors, whether they were worthy or not. Jonathan knew the terrain and was very supportive."[8] Soon after, Jonathan and Evelyn started dating, their love of film evolving into a decade-long partnership.

A Road Scholar (1968–1970)

Demme and Purcell would soon relocate to London, where Demme had secured a job as sales rep with HSFA Ltd., a small and short-lived company that sold advertising reels by various commercial directors. Arriving in the Belgravia neighborhood in the fall of 1968, Demme strolled up to 68 Ebury Street, was greeted by a cat roaming around the grounds, whom he'd call Leo, and knew he had found his new home. "He got there a little before me and found a lovely big old apartment just off Sloane Square," Purcell said. "This was to be the company apartment for the directors when they came to London to work. I joined him a month or so later, where we lived in the lap of luxury (with virtually no money) entertaining our friends."[9] One director who would become a lifelong friend to Jonathan and Evelyn was Joe Viola.

Viola had experience as a television commercial director for the ad agencies on Madison Avenue before moving to London, and he had worked for his older brother, Al, a commercial artist whose company had just merged with HSFA. Like Demme, Viola was a New Yorker. The youngest of six children from the Bronx, Viola had been a juvenile delinquent and had gotten into mischief that would rival the Artful Dodger. When an offer came to direct commercials in England, Viola answered the call and was picked up at the airport by an energetic American with a Beatles mop top and goatee. "Jonathan picked me up at the airport, and we're chattering away as if we'd known one another for years," Viola recalled. With the HSFA offices on Eccleston Street, it was a five-minute walk from Jonathan's apartment. After unpacking his bags, Viola was invited by Demme to look at some 16 mm film footage he had shot back in Miami.

Viola saw a familiar face on the celluloid: a young woman smiling and walking along the beaches of Miami named Kathryn Witt, a Floridian model and supporting actor in Bob Fosse's *Lenny* (1974) and *Star 80* (1983). "About six months earlier, when I had begun to direct, one of the first jobs I did was for Rayovac flashlight batteries. I shot it in Florida, and it was a gorgeous young lady walking around with a flashlight. You never know who's behind the flashlight, and it's very mysterioso. When she finally finds the light switch and turns it on, you see she's this beautiful young woman. Cut to six months later, London, top floor in the editing suite, and Jonathan starts running this material through the viewer." The evening ended with the two aspiring filmmakers having a late dinner at a nearby restaurant and sharing a bottle of wine.[10]

With his innate charm, Demme was a success at selling commercial reels around London. "I had my reel of work that Jonathan was peddling around town," Viola said. "We did big campaigns with Estee Lauder. It was a magical time, and Americans were in the fashion and advertising at that point, so everywhere we went, we were welcomed and had the crème of what was being offered."

Jonathan's United Artists comrade Larry Kaplan was also in London. "I would see them all the time," Kaplan remembered. "He was also writing for Fusion and got me involved a little bit; I didn't do much. I was doing unit work, and Jonathan needed a job."[11] Demme claimed in later interviews that he was "a stoned rock journalist" covering shows around London for some underground magazines.[12]

This may be how Demme got the UK psychedelic bands Kaleidoscope (not to be confused with the US Kaleidoscope led by David Lyndley) and Van der Graaf Generator on the soundtrack of *Eyewitness* (1970), directed by John Hough and produced by Paul Maslansky for Irving Allen's company. It would be his first production credit. "My idea was for Kaleidoscope to do the more romantic sequences in the movie," Demme said, "and Van der Graaf Generator were real freak-outs so they could do the suspenseful, terrifying schemes. Ironically, the fact is that Kaleidoscope wound up doing stuff far freakier for the suspense scenes."[13] As excited as Jonathan was to deal with the music for Allen's film about assassins targeting a family on the island of Malta, David Symonds, Kaleidoscope's manager, was dissatisfied negotiating with Allen over the use of the band's music. According to Symonds, "Irving Allen refused to release the copyright to us for release as a single."[14] *Eyewitness* director John Hough and fellow filmmaker Gary Sherman also tapped Demme to coproduce *Live 1970*, a live concert of Ginger Baker's Air Force filmed for German television.

A Road Scholar (1968–1970)

Next, Kaplan got Jonathan hired as a unit publicist on *Von Richthofen and Brown* (1971), a Roger Corman picture that was shooting in Ireland. "I was doing unit work, and Jonathan needed a job," Kaplan said, "and I didn't want to go to Ireland. I had just gotten back from Newcastle doing work for *Get Carter* (1971), and I didn't want to leave London, so I recommended him for the job on Corman's film."[15]

Accompanying Jonathan on his trip to Dún Laoghaire was Joe Viola, who was shooting a commercial for British television. "Jon and I would jump in my Mini," Viola said, "drive through England and Wales to the Holyhead ferry, and go across to Dún Laoghaire." It was at the hotel they were staying in that Jonathan first saw Roger Corman: he was starstruck. "Jon, having a background in film and having written so much promo material, he knew who Roger was," Viola said. "I didn't."[16]

Born in Detroit, Michigan, in 1926, Roger Corman grew up as the innovation of sound was coming into motion pictures: "The only jobs I could get in films was a messenger at Twentieth Century Fox, and I worked my way up from that to become a story analyst."[17] Starting at the low rung of the ladder at the studio, Corman was given the worst scripts that were circulating at Twentieth Century Fox. He understood how to increase the monetary return of making movies by using cost-effective ways of shooting on a low budget. "I would drive the truck to the location," Corman said, "and unload everything I could by myself, and I would save about an hour on the crew salary every morning."[18] His second film as producer, *The Fast and the Furious* (1954), was acquired by Samuel Z. Arkoff and Jim Nicholson, who had just started their own production company, American International Pictures, competing with the fare of diluted adolescent dreck like George B. Seitz's *Andy Hardy* series from MGM. "Times were changing," Corman said. "The major studios didn't really understand the audience was looking for a different type of film."[19]

Young newcomers like Jack Nicholson, Bruce Dern, and Peter Fonda made their acting debuts in Corman productions. *The Cry-Baby Killer* (1958), *A Bucket of Blood* (1959), and *The Little Shop of*

Horrors (1960) fueled the teenage angst that was already transmitted by Chuck Berry and Fats Domino on the radio. Corman expanded his autodidactic approach to filmmaking when he directed a series of movies based on the stories of Edgar Allen Poe. "We'd never miss a Poe movie," Demme said. "They were riveting and stylish and hip and funny. We couldn't wait for the next one. And, of course, with Roger, you didn't have to wait very long."[20] Lush, haunting, and evocative of Fellini's surrealistic oeuvre, Corman's movies stimulated the minds of aspiring filmmakers fresh from college and finding their footing in the film industry. Hofstra and UCLA graduate Francis Ford Coppola would direct his first film, *Dementia 13* (1963), for Corman after shooting parts of *The Terror* (1963) in Big Sur; NYU student instructor Martin Scorsese was picked by Corman to direct *Boxcar Bertha* (1972). New World Pictures was Corman's attempt to corral young, like-minded individuals to write, produce, and direct movies with the guarantee that they would get distributed.

"I had it in the back of my mind that Corman would be a good man to know if I had an idea for a movie," Demme said. "But he was the one who asked me if I had any ideas."[21] As production on *Von Richthofen and Brown* (1971) was coming to an end, Corman, noticing the ambitious energy gleaming from his unit publicist's smile, invited both Demme and Joe Viola to the hotel bar for drinks. "Roger was about as nonrelated as possible to his name and reputation," Viola said. "He had a slightly stern demeanor, quiet, and here were Jon and I running all over him: he was like our jungle gym, and he just put up with it. He said to us, 'Well, boys. Why don't you two make a movie for me?'" Viola saw Jonathan extend his arm to shake Roger's hand, taking the reins of the conversation by enthusiastically talking about biker films. Viola said, "I'm sitting there grinning and nodding my head, saying, 'I hope he knows what he's committing us to!'" It was settled: Jonathan would produce, and Joe would direct. In the meantime, they had to develop a screenplay that emulated the quintessential biker movies of the sixties.[22]

In preparation, they screened Corman's *The Wild Angels* (1966) in London. Demme turned to Viola and said the first thing that came to his head: "*Rashomon*." Viola replied, "Gesundheit." Demme and Viola drove back to Belgravia to pen a script about a brutal assault on a woman and varying accounts recalled by a biker gang. Where Akira Kurosawa's 1950 film about a rape and murder told from four perspectives took place in feudal Japan, the setting of *Savage Angels* would be transposed to the biker communes in the Southwest. When it came to writing the script, Jonathan and Joe would look to a four-legged friend for inspiration. "When we started to work early on in script, Leo was our muse," Viola said. "It was like a gag almost; when we were trying to figure out a line or how to structure a scene, we would say, 'Let's ask Leo.' Somehow, he was the magic talisman. In two minutes, we knew where we were going, and we were running ahead again."[23] Evelyn served as a script reader, suggesting ideas as the boys typed away. "We knocked out a treatment in about a week, and Evelyn was our resident muse," Viola said. "If the story looked off, we went back to the drawing board."

While still in England, in May 1970, Demme asked Evelyn Purcell to marry him. "We decided to go to the Chelsea Registry Office with just a few close friends as witnesses to the event," Purcell said. "Joe Viola had gone to the flower market early in the morning and decked out a taxi which was waiting for us outside to take us to lunch at Nemo's, the trendy Italian restaurant at the time."[24] Visiting from London was Jonathan's mother, who sat in awe as she heard about her son and Joe Viola's plans to make a movie. Viola remembered, "By the time Roger arrived, we had a very respectable treatment." Not long after, the newlyweds and Viola flew back to the United States and settled in Los Angeles.

4
A New World (1970–1973)

Arriving in Los Angeles in late 1970, Demme and Evelyn Purcell resided in the Beverly Glen neighborhood. Some of Demme's friends from London were also moving to California to pursue their respective artistic ventures. Dinner parties were Demme's specialty; it was a communal form of networking that would result in lifelong connections. Among the dinner guests would be Hercules Bellville, a cineaste of cultured stock dressed like an English dandy, whose enthusiasm for making movies led to working with Roman Polanski's production company, Caliban Films, while fulfilling his aspirations as a fledgling screenwriter and producer.[1]

Joe Viola and his wife lived nearby, which was convenient for Jonathan as he and Viola planned their biker film for New World Pictures. Initially, Demme and Viola set up shop in the back offices of Fat Bernie's Environmental Living at 17035 Ventura Boulevard, courtesy of Fat Bernie's proprietor, Gary Goetzman. Goetzman had left acting to become a waterbed and bean bag entrepreneur, promoting Fat Bernie's on local radio spots and in newspapers around Los Angeles. Demme and Viola had the earnest Goetzman, ambitious to get a foothold in film production, assist them on their film.[2]

Roger Corman had Demme and Viola write down five prospective titles for their *Rashomon*-inspired biker film and canvased outside Fairfax High School. According to Viola, "We would stop these kids and ask them which title they would rather see. We had to bring those sheets back to Roger. That's how we did it; it was marketing on the nickel. He knew how to do anything on the nickel."[3]

The title that got the most votes was the salacious *Angels Hard as They Come* (1971).

The paradoxical method of Corman looking for an audience for a film that was in preproduction foreshadowed the focus group strategy that the Hollywood studios would rely on decades later. "Roger taught me a life lesson I've passed on to others," Viola said. "You work backwards from your audience. Don't do a project that does not reflect the taste or the desire of the audience. The audience doesn't exist, you don't have a project; you just have a can full of film."[4]

Corman exploited his cadre of loyal filmmakers, stretching the pennies and shooting at a breakneck pace. "He knew how to do that," Purcell said, "having complete naive people there and get what he wanted."[5] Even Joe Viola's wife would wake up early to make sandwiches for the cast and crew as craft services were limited to Ralph's Supermarket. "He (Corman) gives you a chance to make a movie," Demme said. "And if he doesn't pay you much money, terrific. Who else was going to give you the chance to make the movie? And what are you worth anyway, at that stage of the game?"[6] Demme and Viola's selfless attitude and determination fueled them like the renegade bikers who covered the country's highways and headlines.

Assembling the production crew with a budget just under $100,000, Demme and Viola reached out to college students and aspiring artists, like Jack Fisk, to design the gothic-inspired sets for the film (a stepping stone in what would be Fisk's expansive career working with Terrence Malick, David Lynch, and Paul Thomas Anderson). Cinematographer Caleb Deschanel, later to become part of Francis Ford Coppola's American Zoetrope production company, shot additional photography for *Angels Hard as They Come*. As Evelyn Purcell noted, "For the people he hired, Roger started so many people in the business and he was prepared to do that. He was confident in that he knew what he wanted to make; he knew it wasn't going to make it with a lot of money, so he was smart to get these people around him."[7]

Viola and Demme would spend three weeks filming *Angels Hard as They Come*, shooting in between southern Los Angeles and Yuma, Arizona. The duo held a casting call at a Hollywood motel, specifically requesting actors who could drive a motorcycle. Scott Glenn, a former marine and journalist, drove his Honda motorcycle to the motel and read, clinching the lead. Determined to capture the realism of biker life in their movie, Demme and Viola hired members of the Hell's Angels and Gypsy Jokers, who were rival gangs. The film's social commentary was prescient, showing the decadence of the hippie generation clashing with the brutal territorial actions of the Hell's Angels—a toxic mix of indulgence and violence mirrored at the Rolling Stones' free concert at the Altamont racetrack in December 1969, where a gun-wielding Meredith Hunter was stabbed to death by the biker gang acting as the festival's security.

Released in July 1971, *Angels Hard as They Come* received little fanfare. *Variety* ran a scathing review noting, "Former United Artists publicity staffer Jonathan Demme and director Joe Viola have turned out a 90-minute offering that is without originality in any of its departments." The review concluded, "That the pic is only rated 'R' is another adverse light on the Code Rating situation."[8] The only positive review came from *Box Office Magazine*: "Starting off just like a dozen similar epics, the Jonathan Demme production soon becomes a fast-moving yarn and provides enough entertainment for regular patrons of such fare."[9]

Corman's next genre hop was a series of tongue-in-cheek nurse films. Corman had visited the Philippines in late 1970 and was impressed by the country's film production facilities. "Corman had a deal with a producer in the Philippines and offered Jonathan and Joe a deal to do a 'woman in jeopardy' story to be shot there," Evelyn Purcell said. "Jonathan asked me to help, and I became the associate producer."[10] Back in Los Angeles, Corman outlined his idea about nurses locked up by guerrilla soldiers to Demme and Viola. Originally titled *The Prescription Revolution*, Corman suggested renaming it *The Hot Box*, the script's slang for the cage in which the imprisoned quartet of buxom nurses is sprayed with a hose.

Flying to the Philippines could have been a film itself. Before takeoff, the stewardesses walked down the aisle with bags, collecting all the handguns from most of the passengers. "We stayed in this mosquito-infested hotel in Dumaguete City," Viola said. "We would walk to the only restaurant on our street and walk back. There were these rats running around the streets at night. One night, Jon picked up a stone, and I picked up a stone. We threw it at a rat twenty feet away, and one of us hit it. I was ebullient, and Jonathan was horrified. Poor Jon was almost sobbing at that point. I had to convince him that I hit the rat."[11]

Shooting *The Hot Box* would be an intense experience for him and Viola. "You have no idea how we upset the moral climate in the Philippines when we arrived with these four women into the jungle only to discover that we were at the mercy of the local Filipino army general," Viola recalled. "He took an instant liking to the ladies and insisted on visiting the sets. When the girls were not wearing any clothes, the sets were closed only to the crew, though the girls didn't mind at all, God bless them! Everything in the Philippines was so corrupt that no matter what our situation was, we could buy our way out of it."[12]

After *The Hot Box* wrapped, Viola and Demme penned the screenplay for another "women in jeopardy" film. *Black Mama, White Mama* (1973) was in part inspired by Stanley Kramer's 1958 film *The Defiant Ones*, about two prison escapees shackled together on the run. Demme and Viola's script told the story from a woman's point of view: Pam Grier, a veteran of several women-in-prison films, starred with Margaret Markov, who had been in *The Hot Box*. The film ended up being directed by Eddie Romero, Corman's man in the Philippines, but the premise of a white protagonist and a Black protagonist forming an unlikely bond would be paramount in the films Demme would direct later in his career.

Fly Me (1973) would be the last of the Filipino productions for New World Pictures. President Ferdinand Marcos had imposed martial law, and the Philippines was becoming a risky investment for American filmmakers until Marcos allowed Francis Ford Coppola to film his Vietnam War epic, *Apocalypse Now* (1979), there. The footage for *Fly Me* had been shot by director Cirio H. Santiago but was too grainy, and Corman decided to have Jonathan Demme and Curtis Hanson reshoot footage stateside, resulting in three days' worth of footage shot in the Yamashiro Gardens, Los Angeles.

Demme and Evelyn Purcell were eager to take the next step in their careers. "Jonathan was ready to direct, and I wanted to produce," Purcell said. "We approached Corman about the two of us making another film for him."

5

Girls, Guns, and *Shampoo* (1974–1976)

Demme and Purcell waited with bated breath for Corman to get their next movie off the ground. At the time, Demme was watching John Cromwell's 1950 prison film *Caged*, which had been based on the investigative article "Inside Women's Prison," written by Virginia Kellogg and published in *Collier's*. Stanley Kubrick's controversial 1971 film *A Clockwork Orange* and the California Supreme Court's decision in *People vs. Anderson*, which overturned the death penalty in the state's correctional facilities, put reportage on behavior control techniques in prisons on the front pages of California papers: "Certified criminals, however, are not the only target of today's lobotomists. Increasingly, they are focusing their irreversible procedures on the mildly disturbed, with women predominating among the targets and not a few children included as candidates for the operation."[1]

These influences came together in Demme's first directorial effort for Corman, *Caged Heat* (1974). In the film and the accompanying advertising campaign, Demme was adamant about emphasizing the social commentary on women liberating themselves from being targeted for lobotomies. Demme said, "It was more important to me because I felt we were making a very profound observation to point out that psychosurgery was going on in American prisons, and to emphasize that point, I really wanted to dramatize it in a strong way as possible."[2]

THERE'S NO GOING BACK

As producer, Evelyn reached out to Sam Gelfman, the former vice president of New York production for United Artists. Gelfman was working with Martin Bregman's production company, Artists Entertainment Complex, producing two features starring client Al Pacino, *Serpico* (1973) and *Dog Day Afternoon* (1975), directed by Sidney Lumet.[3] AEC not only wanted to work with Hollywood studios like Paramount and Warner Brothers but also to merge with New World Pictures. When Gelfman pitched *Caged Heat* to AEC, they agreed to finance the film's $150,000 budget.

In casting the revolutionary women who break out of prison, Demme sought out some of the leading ladies in sexploitation cinema. Erica Gavin, who had starred in Russ Meyer's *Vixen* (1968) and *Beyond the Valley of the Dolls* (1970), signed on to play Jacqueline Wilson, in Connersville Prison for her involvement in a violent drug deal in the film's prologue. Juanita Brown, a former sorority sister who got her acting break working alongside Pam Grier in Jack Hill's *Coffy* (1973), would play Maggie, the contentious inmate who wrestles with Jacqueline in the prison showers before they unite to break out of prison. Rounding out the prisoners were New World Pictures regulars Roberta Collins, from Jack Hill's *The Big Doll House* (1971), and Cheryl "Rainbeaux" Smith. Playing McQueen, the sexually repressed and wheelchair-bound prison warden, was horror film icon Barbara Steele. Her leading performance in Mario Bava's Italian horror film *Black Sunday* (1960) caught the attention of Roger Corman when he directed Steele opposite Vincent Price in *The Pit and the Pendulum* (1961).

Ensuring that the eye was stimulated, Demme brought on Tak Fujimoto as cinematographer. Fujimoto found his love for lighting at an early age when making decorations for the Buddhist Obon festival in west Los Angeles as a teenager.[4] After attending the London Film School, Fujimoto worked with fellow classmate Harley Cokeless on the documentary *Chicago Blues* (1970), as well as assisting Andrew Davis on Haskell Wexler's *Medium Cool* (1969), a film shot during the riots at the 1968 Democratic National Convention.[5] It was his work on Terrence Malick's directorial debut, *Badlands* (1973), that had made an impression on Demme, leading to a director/cinematographer relationship that would last for four decades. A man of few words, Fujimoto believed his work should serve the whole production: "When the audience goes into a darkened theater, they should experience the story, experience the emotion attached to the story. Any time the audience can slip out of that revery and say, 'Gee, that was a beautiful shot,' it sort of wrecks that bond the film has with an audience."[6]

Shortly before shooting commenced, Demme attended a party thrown by Hercules Belville, where he made a fortuitous connection with Bernardo Bertolucci and his girlfriend Clare Peploe. When the Italian filmmaker asked Jonathan if he was going to shoot long takes for his first movie, he froze: "I realized how terrifying that is to put your production day money on a long take, but it made me aspire to shoot long takes."[7] Demme revisited one of his favorite Bertolucci films, *The Conformist* (1970), when he was seeking inspiration on how to create a long, uninterrupted take.

The first day of production already had problems when some of the actors didn't show up on set. Demme, inspired by his meeting with Bertolucci and Peploe, composed a long tracking shot from right to left frame in the opening credit sequence of *Caged Heat*. The camera follows the female prisoners basking in the sun, smoking cigarettes, and walking around in hot pants and halter tops. It zooms in on Maggie (Juanita Brown) chatting with fellow inmates, then tracks from left frame to right before stopping on an inmate in mid-punchline of a joke about a man buttoning up his penis.

Assisting Evelyn's duties on set was Gary Goetzman. After Fat Bernie's waterbed service deflated, Goetzman kept busy working with Jonathan Demme. Not only would he play Sparky, the drug dealer who abandons Erica Gavin in the beginning of the movie, but he also eagerly worked behind the scenes. Gary's work on *Caged Heat* began a creative camaraderie with Demme that would last on and off for the next forty years.

Shooting around the San Fernando Valley and inside the Lincoln Heights Jail in east Los Angeles, Demme and the crew worked in substandard conditions. "The jail had been closed, so there was no electricity, no heat, and it was freezing cold," Erica Gavin recalled. It was especially difficult shooting the shower stall fight between her and Juanita Brown. "Talk about freezing! It was pouring rain outside, and the jail was like an icebox. Here I was, practically naked, in a cold, wet shower that took many hours to film."[8]

Tak Fujimoto pushed himself toward a fever shooting the same scene. "He's down there on his back in the shower with the water raining on him," Demme recalled to filmmaker Mark Cousins. "It's only when I leave that I notice I'm getting these incredibly dirty looks from the camera assistant. I asked, 'What's the matter?' He said, 'Tak has a 103-degree fever, and you had him in that shower. Do you know that?' I said, 'My God! He didn't say anything to me.'"[9]

Gavin was excited at the prospect of working with Demme, who presented his actresses in a manner that contrasted sharply with Russ Meyer's salacious canon of nudie cuties. "Russ was a T&A kind of guy when it came to directing his movies," Gavin said. "Whereas Jonathan didn't care about physical appearance as much as what was in your soul that he captured in *Caged Heat*."[10] Arguably the most intense scene in the film is when Jacqueline and Maggie, accused of starting a fatal riot in the prison, are punished through electroshock therapy. Erica Gavin's writhing and screaming as the apathetic Dr. Williams (Warren Miller) inserts earplugs and smokes his pipe is as desexualizing as when he pulls out the vaginal speculum on Jacqueline's arrival at Connorville. Gavin recalled channeling her grandmother, who had received shock treatment at Camarillo State Hospital. "It was an emotionally exhausting shoot that day," Gavin remembered. "Jonathan was extremely comforting and sympathetic to whatever you were going through at the time."[11]

The film's third act is an adrenaline-fueled ride, in which Jacqueline, Maggie, and Crazy Alice (Crystin Sinclaire) rob and carjack their way back to Connorville to save Belle and Pandora (Ella Reid). Gavin was impressed that Demme, an expat Los Angelino by way of New York, Miami, and London, captured the authenticity of the San Fernando Valley: "Jonathan felt at home behind the camera. It was a very relaxed family atmosphere."[12]

When McQueen, Pinter, and Dr. Williams are kidnapped by the gun-toting girls and ushered into the paddy wagon before being shot at by the police, the camera zooms in and freezes the frame on the ladies' getaway car, the audience left uncertain if they will live or die at the hands of the Connorville guards. The camera then pulls back to Crazy Alice as she shoots an officer, and his severed ear falls to the ground. The scene was in part inspired by the Marin County Courthouse shooting in 1970, when hostages were shot by members of the Black Panthers. Demme and Purcell's nod to the revolutionary militancy of the era is Erica Gavin's Patty Hearst–style beret.

For a revisionist prison genre film, it seemed fitting for Demme and Purcell to hire avant-garde composer/songwriter John Cale to compose the score to *Caged Heat*. Demme and Evelyn were fans of the Velvet Underground, Cale's first band, cofounded with Lou Reed. The twangy harmonica and steel guitar that open the film sound like a less upbeat version of "Adelaide" from Cale's *Vintage Violence* album. His trademark viola can be heard as Maggie and Jacqueline fight in the showers and again as Jacqueline is about to be subjected to electroshock therapy. "We went into a little screening room in Hollywood with John and his viola," Purcell recalled. "A piano was in the studio, and he improvised as the film played."[13]

Released in May 1974, *Caged Heat* was a critical and commercial hit. Kevin Thomas of the *Los Angeles Times* wrote, "With wit, style and unflagging verve, writer-director Jonathan Demme, a youthful and talented exploitation veteran, sends up the genre while still giving the mindless action fan his money's worth."[14] New World Pictures smartly released *Caged Heat* on double and triple bills with Blaxploitation classics like Melvin Van Peebles's *Sweet Sweetback's Baadasssss Song* (1971) and Gordon Parks's *Shaft* (1971). Six weeks into its release, the film would make back an estimated $750,000—five times the price of its budget. The poster itself proved to be a major draw. "Jonathan and I drove down Santa Monica Boulevard putting one of the posters on every telephone pole," Purcell said. "We thought it would be cool to go back and drive past them. When we did, there were only a few left!"[15]

THERE'S NO GOING BACK

In New York City, the film screened at the Elgin Theatre on Nineteenth Street and Eighth Avenue as part of its midnight movies series. Like the other films out of New World Pictures, *Caged Heat* sat pretty with the insomniac filmgoers smoking joints and sipping beer to Perry Henzell's *The Harder They Come* (1973) or John Waters's *Pink Flamingos* (1972). The film was even considered by some to be an aphrodisiac for couples. As noted in the *New York Times*, "'That was a rip-off,' says a young girl, standing under the Elgin's marquee after the film. 'Yeah, so did you have anything better to do?' replies a boy in blue suede earth shoes. She shrugs. 'Let's go to your place and see what's on the tube.'"[16]

With his directorial debut released, Demme was touted as the hot new kid in Roger Corman's stable. Hal Ashby, the freewheeling editor and director of *The Landlord* (1970), *Harold and Maude* (1971), and *The Last Detail* (1973), took note. After *Caged Heat*, Ashby invited Demme and Evelyn to a screening of a film he was editing at his house. The decor of Ashby's Laurel Canyon abode—psychedelic wallpaper and an eclectic record collection—was similar to the Demmes' apartment. "I go up to the screening room—a small screening room—and I'm sitting there, and someone sits down across the aisle from me," Demme said. "I look over, and it's Warren Beatty. We're watching *Shampoo* (1975), and it was an amazing experience! Then, he asked me what I thought of the film!"[17] Afterward, the two directors attended each other's screenings, and Demme became a regular at Ashby's Malibu home in the late 1970s.

Another director who resided in Laurel Canyon was Sam Fuller. Like Demme, Fuller started his career in the press, working his way from a copyboy to a crime journalist in his teens. While serving in the 1st Infantry Division during World War II, he found a Bell and Howell 16 mm camera and shot his first footage while liberating the Falkenau concentration camp. Fuller's work as a filmmaker caught Demme's attention when he saw *Shock Corridor* (1963) and *The Naked Kiss* (1964), films that inspired Demme when he was shooting

Caged Heat. After meeting Fuller and his wife, Christa, Demme would become friends with the couple over the next twenty years.

For Demme's next film, Corman assigned him to direct the next in his series of Great Depression shoot-'em-up "Mama" series for New World Pictures. *Crazy Mama* would be the third after *Bloody Mama* (1970), starring Shelley Winters as Ma Barker, and *Big Bad Mama* (1974), directed by Steve Carver. Demme was scouting locations in Montana for his next film, *Fighting Mad*, when Corman commissioned him to write a film based around the strip-mining industry. Clarke, an experimental filmmaker known for *The Connection* (1961), a gritty film about jazz musicians and heroin addiction, was set to direct *Crazy Mama*, but ten days before it went into production, she was out, disagreeing with Roger and Julie Corman over aesthetics and process. Demme was then told to forgo *Fighting Mad* and hop on to *Crazy Mama*.

Though Demme wasn't happy with the script, production ensued. One of the first actors he cast was Cloris Leachman. Leachman recalled that the script reminded her of the part she played in a CBS adaptation of Tennessee Williams's *The Migrants*, in which she starred opposite Corman disciple Ron Howard and Sissy Spacek. "When we had the first reading at Jonathan Demme's home," Leachman said in 1975, "I was impressed with the fact that my role was straight and rather sparse. We realized that the script was a marvelous skeleton and that it would be incumbent for us to flesh it out."[18] Leachman was fresh off her hilarious performance in Mel Brooks's *Young Frankenstein* (1974) and was confident working with a bright-eyed upstart like Demme, just as she had been when Peter Bogdanovich, another Roger Corman alumnus, directed her Oscar-winning performance in 1971's *The Last Picture Show*.

Crazy Mama is an offbeat folk hero tale of a fifties mother who seeks revenge on the corrupt bankers who murdered the family's patriarch and drove them off their land during the Great Depression. Mama (Ann Sothern), her daughter (Cloris Leachman), her granddaughter (Linda Pearl), and her granddaughter's boyfriend (Donny

Most) drive cross-country from California to their hometown of Jerusalem, Arkansas; the film is both a road picture and a social commentary. Their frantic act of retribution spoke to Demme more than the sex and violence: "This illustrates how when lower-income people disenfranchised by the realtors and landlords and put out on the streets can find themselves in desperate circumstances like this and be driven to a life of crime. They are basically decent people."[19] It was another Corman family affair; his brother Gene was the cofounder of New World Pictures; Cloris Leachman's son, Bryan, played the role of Snake; and Roger's wife, Julie, even though she was pregnant with her first child, helped shoot in Griffith Park.[20] The three-week shooting schedule was similar to the breakneck speed Demme and Joe Viola experienced making *Angels Hard as They Come* and sometimes meant casting within the crew. Even Demme's friend, screenwriter and director John Milius, made an on-screen appearance as the shotgun-wielding gunman who shoots Billy Bob (Stuart Whitman).

For the scene where Billy Bob is gunned down and buried under a tree not far from where Earl was gunned down at the beginning of the movie, Demme relied on Cloris Leachman to improvise the mourning scene. Demme said, "Cloris Leachman had the idea where they shout their souls into heaven. We tried to make it a lyrical moment."[21] Demme mustered pathos out of the scene with a reverse dolly shot of the family under the tree.

Crazy Mama opened in Los Angeles theaters on November 11, 1975. Kevin Thomas praised the leading women for their performances, concluding his *Los Angeles Times* review by saying that "there's really too much that's contrived, too much that's patently derivative to take the film as a whole seriously. What is worth taking seriously, however, is the vitality and talent of Jonathan Demme, who's past his due to graduate to worthier assignments."[22] The film did get a notice in *Variety* highlighting its "light" opening in eighteen LA theaters and earnings of $45,700 in its first week.[23]

The year 1975 ended on a high for Demme when he was singled out as one of the "Nine Directors Rising from the Trashes" with his

Girls, Guns, and *Shampoo* (1974–1976)

fellow Corman comrade George Armitage (who would later direct *Miami Blues* in 1990, produced by Demme). When asked about his favorite filmmakers, Demme cited Preston Sturges, Curtis Harrington, and his friend Hal Ashby.[24] The decent press and box office on *Crazy Mama* convinced Corman that Demme was ready to direct *Fighting Mad*. "At this time," Purcell said, "films about the 'little man' taking on the system were in vogue. *Billy Jack* (1971) had been a huge hit. So Jonathan came up with the idea for *Fighting Mad* and pitched it to Roger."[25]

Set in Arkansas, the film shows farmer Tom Hunter (Peter Fonda) as he tries to save his home from a strip-mining land baron, Crabtree (Philip Carey), who has the local sheriff (Harry Northup) in his back pocket. Evelyn Purcell would be Demme's producer and second-unit manager, while Tak Fujimoto was slated to be the cinematographer until the American Society of Cinematographers got wind of the situation. "He wasn't in the ASC yet," Demme said about Fujimoto, "so we snuck him to Arkansas in the hopes that Tak could do a lot of great shooting for us. Alas, he was caught and sent back to California."[26] Before Michael Watkins was brought in to replace him, Fujimoto managed to film Peter Fonda and his costar Gino Franco riding in the truck for the film's opening sequence.

Demme took to casting resident actors while listening to the local bands that filled the bars of the college town: "It was fantastic seeing people from the community that came out and a lot of people from the university."[27] Casting Gino Franco as Peter Fonda's son was bittersweet as Franco's own father, a Safeway employee from Springville, Arkansas, had been gunned down by armed robbers in 1971.[28] Peter Fonda, who had a splintered relationship with his father, Henry Fonda, found a kindred spirit in Franco. "Gino had no worries riding with me," Fonda said in 2002. "I was so thrilled that that young guy could trust me enough. I became his father figure; it worked pretty well."[29]

Three scenes were key in Demme's storytelling. In the scene before Tom's brother, Charlie (Scott Glenn), and his wife (Hal Ashby's then-girlfriend, Kathleen Miller) are attacked in their house by Crabtree's henchmen, there is an exterior view of the house shot from a canted angle. By Demme's admission, it was a nod to his friend. "Here's a Bernardo Bertolucci tilted composition," Demme said, "which he used in *The Conformist* a lot, which I found made the viewer uneasy, so we tilted the composition there."³⁰

Later, Demme makes the unconventional choice to cut from a robbery to a family party at Charlie's house. The revelry cuts the suspense of the violent break-in, with Tom sitting at the dinner table and the kids running around. It is also another example of Demme's reverence for the communal element of family gatherings that would echo in later films. Lastly, the actors look directly into the camera outside Crabtree's construction site after Tom's friend Hal (Ted Markland) is killed trying to confront Crabtree about his demolished house. The audience is in Peter Fonda's point of view as Harry Northup addresses him before the camera pans around the milling employees and then stops on Ted Markland's lifeless body. Demme would cite the scene as "one of our first uses of the into-the-lens POV shot."³¹

With the film in the can, Demme needed a musician to craft a score that would embody the rugged resilience of the South. He'd already cited John Prine's protest song "Paradise" in the prologue to the script as a possible opener.³² Peter Fonda suggested his friend Bruce Langhorne, the composer for his directorial efforts *The Hired Hand* (1971) and *Idaho Transfer* (1973). Langhorne was a musical prodigy who blew his fingers off during a cherry bomb incident as a child; his distinctive guitar strumming and tambourine playing caught the attention of the emerging Greenwich Village folk music scene of the early sixties. Bob Dylan immortalized him in song as the titular "Mr. Tambourine Man" after seeing him play a giant tambourine during a recording session for his album *Bringing It All Back Home*.³³

"This was one sort of time where Peter threw his weight around on the movie," Demme jokingly said. "He said, 'Of course, you'd love to have Bruce Langhorne score this movie, wouldn't you?' I did!"³⁴ Demme and Langhorne listened to Ennio Morricone's

Girls, Guns, and *Shampoo* (1974–1976)

scores for Sergio Leone's spaghetti westerns, seeking inspiration by bringing the elements of the western genre to Demme's tale of strip mining.

The film wrapped with a steak dinner at a Fayetteville restaurant. It was a bittersweet moment for Peter Fonda, Jonathan Demme, and Gino Franco. "He had such a great time, and on the last shot we finished," Demme remembered, "we said, 'Goodbye, Gino. It was great working with you.' He said, 'I've been dreading this.' He burst into tears, and it was the sweetest thing."[35] Fonda and Demme would meet again twenty years later when Fonda was cast in the leading role in 1997's *Ulee's Gold*, directed by Victor Nuñez with Demme as producer.

Released in April 1976, *Fighting Mad* coincided with the current wave of socioecological concern over corrupt forces pillaging natural resources. That same year saw the release of Barbara Kopple's Oscar-winning documentary, *Harlan County, U.S.A.* In Jeff Freedman's review for the *Hollywood Reporter*, he cited Demme's use of the camera to enrage the audience: "We sit behind a windshield about to be smashed, inside a house soon to be demolished, in the path of an oncoming coal truck." Regarding the ending, in which Tom goes fishing with his son after the departure of his lover (Lynn Lowry), Freeman concluded his review by stating, "Never has restitution seemed less sweet, retribution so empty."[36]

Now Jonathan Demme had completed his three-picture deal with Roger Corman. It was akin to a bird leaving its nest; Demme would be spreading his wings without Corman there to catch him from falling. Evelyn Purcell had projects she wanted to direct on her own. However, her working partnership and marriage with Jonathan would be tested when he caught the attention of the Hollywood studios. It wouldn't be long until Evelyn was kept out of the conversation.

6

Frequency Issues (1977–1979)

Demme and Roger Corman amicably parted ways in the wake of *Fighting Mad*'s release. Demme and Evelyn were visiting her parents in Australia for the holidays when he got a call that would change everything. Producer Freddie Fields wanted him to direct *Citizens Band*. Jonathan was set to direct his first studio-commissioned film. Initially, it was assumed that Evelyn would produce the film, but after hanging up on his call with Fields, Demme broke the news that he didn't want her on *Citizens Band*. "Freddie said that he knew I had been producing Jonathan's films," Evelyn said, "and that I could do that on *Citizens Band*. This [Demme's decision] was a bit of a shock and a big disappointment to me since one job had always led to the next, and as I understood it, we were working towards making bigger pictures together."[1]

The irony of Demme's decision to have his wife relegated to second-unit camerawork while he firmly planted himself in the director's chair coincided with his aspirations for Evelyn's future. Like his father before him, Demme wanted to keep his life at work separate from his life at home. "Jonathan explained to me," Evelyn said, "that he didn't want me to be both his producer and his wife."

"Why couldn't you just be Mrs. Demme?" Jonathan asked Evelyn. "You see how difficult it is to be a director."

Evelyn replied, "Jonathan, I've worked on films in London long before you. You knew that my ultimate ambition was to be a film producer."

As their plane landed at LAX, it was evident that Jonathan and Evelyn's relationship would never be the same. "At that time," Evelyn said, "for a woman to direct wasn't even a consideration. In retrospect, this was clearly the beginning of the end of the marriage."[2] Jonathan set his personal emotions aside as he focused on making *Citizens Band*. Although he did get support from Fields and Paramount's production executives, David V. Picker and production designer turned temporary production executive Richard Sylbert, the studio was undergoing a regime change that wouldn't hit Demme until after *Citizens Band* finished shooting.

Citizens Band is a character-driven ensemble piece. Spider (Paul Le Mat) is an earnest CB radio enthusiast policing the airwaves in his town of eccentric broadcasters; the Priest (Ed Begley Jr.) is a religious fanatic, the Red Baron (Harry Northup) a xenophobe, and Electra (Candy Clark) an audio-erotic siren; they all clog the airwaves with dispatches about off-road accidents. When a bigamist truck driver named Chrome Angel (Charles Napier) capsizes his sixteen-wheeler after hearing Electra's saucy broadcast, his wives from two separate marriages (Ann Wedgeworth and Marcia Rodd) are called out to see him while he's staying with his girlfriend, Hot Coffee (Alex Elias). It isn't until the wives share family photos on the bus that they realize they share the same husband. When Spider isn't deputizing the airwaves, he is taking care of his aging father, Papa Thermodyne (Roberts Blossom), and mending the complicated relationship with his brother, Blood (Bruce McGill). When Papa Thermodyne wanders off, the CB radio community leaves their houses to search for him.

As with his marital problems, Demme tuned out the industry news when he assembled his cast and crew. "I was a big Paul Le Mat fan," Demme said at Lincoln Center in 2012, "so the casting started with Paul." Le Mat, who had made a splash with critics and audiences after performances in George Lucas's *American Graffiti* (1973) and Floyd Mutrux's *Aloha, Bobby and Rose* (1975), was turned on by the offbeat characters in Brickman's screenplay when Jonathan offered him the role. Demme told Le Mat, "What I love about your acting is the unrehearsed stuff that you do in the moment. I think it's beyond rehearsal, your ability to get lost in the moment."[3]

Demme sought out Texas native Bruce McGill to play Blood after seeing him in a Shakespeare in the Park production of *Henry V*. When he came in to audition for his first film role, McGill took creative liberties, ad-libbing from the script he was given. "I had never auditioned for a film, and Jonathan was sitting in a chair," McGill recalled. "As soon as I finished the scene, he levitated up to where his feet were in the seat of the chair, and he was sitting on the back of the chair rail. It was sheer excitement. I said to myself, 'How did he do that? He must be a leprechaun!'"[4]

Charles Napier would play Chrome Angel. He had been shortlisted to play Pierce Crabtree in *Fighting Mad* but was not given the role. A former marine officer from Kentucky, the flat-topped, chiseled Napier started his career in bit parts on *Star Trek* (NBC, 1966–69) before appearing in Russ Meyer's *Cherry, Harry & Raquel!* (1969) and *Beyond the Valley of the Dolls* (1970); he would also appear in several Demme films in the coming years. Jonathan drove up from Los Angeles to Marysville, California, with Evelyn reluctantly accompanying him. "For me, it wasn't a great experience. I was with him because we were married," Evelyn said, "so I went on location." Paul Brickman was not happy to have his first script in the hands of a director who'd made exploitation films. He and Demme clashed on the set. "It wasn't a happy relationship between him and Brickman," Evelyn recalled. "The script had been submitted to twenty-two directors before they finally sent it to me," Demme said. "Paul Brickman was very clear in his disdain for me."[5]

The conflict began to show when Ann Wedgeworth approached Demme after filming the Chinese restaurant scene, in which she and Marcia Todd have a boozy lunch courtesy of Chrome Angel's credit cards. Jonathan was ecstatic with the performances, but Wedgeworth told him that Brickman was telling her how the lines should be read. Even Paul Le Mat mentioned in 2012 how Brickman would mill around the set. "He couldn't control himself with his ideas and was infringing on Jonathan's world," Le Mat said. Frustrated, Jonathan went to the film's production manager and former Republic studio head, Ben Chapman. "Ben, I don't know what to do!" Jonathan told him. "I'm really furious because Paul Brickman is now going to the actors saying he didn't like it." The seasoned Chapman told Demme to "throw his ass out of town. You give me the word, and he'll be on the next Greyhound out of here."[6]

For Demme, who prided himself on having energetic and communal experiences on his film sets, the prospect of firing someone left a bad taste in his mouth. "I couldn't believe I had done something so mean," Demme said. "But I understood that I was also being as professional and as grown-up as I had been so far on a movie set, and things went well after that. The good news was that Paul wasn't there. The bad news was that we would be getting these notes every day now. He would look at dailies and unleash these notes."[7]

Demme hired Jordan Cronenweth as cinematographer on *Citizens Band* after seeing his work lighting Frank Perry's adaptation of Joan Didion's *Play It as It Lays* (1972). "He was an artist," Demme said. "Such an artist that sometimes getting the day's work done wasn't as important as making the image as powerful and beautiful as it ought to be and could be. Jordie was setting up an outside shot at Blaine's farm. He'd say to the gaffer, 'Gary, put those Swedish filters in.' Then he would say, 'Put the French filters in.' At a certain point, Charlie said, 'Jesus Christ, Jordan! French, Swedish whatever it is! Make a choice. The sun's going to come up in five minutes!'"[8]

Citizens Band wrapped production in five weeks. Despite the internal clashes with Paul Brickman, Demme was sure he had a film that would appeal to the reported twenty million Americans in the midst of the thriving CB craze.[9] Freddie Fields hosted screenings for his high-profile clients and friends at his Beverly Hills mansion to rouse interest in his latest venture, but not all of them were enthusiastic. In some cases, he took their criticism to heart. One scene that irked veteran actor Tony Curtis was the emotional confrontation between Spider and Blood, ending with a fraternal hug. Days later, Jonathan went to see editor John Link II and noticed the cutting room floor cluttered with chunks of the film. "One night, I came into the cutting room," Demme said, "to find our editor, John Link, removing all the shots of Bruce McGill in the T-shirt and trying to find a way to present that scene without it because Tony Curtis had seen the film the night before and thought it was 'disgusting to see that guy's nipple.'"[10]

When McGill saw a finished print of *Citizens Band*, he was stunned by his scene being cut. It was a harsh lesson in the difference between movies and theater. "I was building to a climax like what I had done in the theater," McGill said. "I learned from that film that if they want, they could drop every fifth frame. So they cut the peak of my scene. I was shocked."[11]

These setbacks deflated energy during the sound mixing of *Citizens Band*. Freddie Fields hovered over Demme as he was fixated on synching the music of some local bands into the film. Freddie would say, "We'll use that second take," to which Jonathan would sarcastically reply, "You're the only one who gets his say, Freddie!"[12] His anger started to show. He needed a cigarette. The quarrel over the sound mixing led to Jonathan's being fired during postproduction of *Citizens Band*.

Demme's exile was brief thanks in part to Hercules Bellville. While visiting him at the Tropicana Motel, Demme expressed his frustration to his old friend. Within a few days, Fields got a call from Bellville's boss. "I didn't know about it," Demme told *DGA Quarterly Magazine* in 2015, "but Roman Polanski called Freddie and said, 'I hear you fired the young director that's making a movie for you. You better get him back, because directors won't want to work with you if you get that reputation.'" Fields called him back the next week to go over the mix. "I had to be very careful what I said," Demme remembered. "Freddie, bless his heart, is out on a massage table in front of the screen with teams of masseuses."[13]

In the spring of 1977, when the newly anointed Paramount production heads watched *Citizens Band*, one of them turned to Jonathan and said, "What have you people been smoking here?" The only studio executive who saw promise in Demme's vision of Americana was Barry Diller, after a preview screening at the La Reina Theatre in Sherman Oaks, California. Per Demme's recollections, "He loved it and said, 'No, we should release this picture. It's very good.'"[14]

Citizens Band opened in two hundred theaters in forty cities on May 18, 1977. One week later, *Star Wars*, George Lucas's ode to the science fiction radio programs of his youth, became a box office hit. With the success of *Star Wars*, Paramount pulled *Citizens Band* from theaters, as audiences preferred to be transported to a galaxy far, far away rather than riding shotgun in a Nomad through Yuba Valley. Thinking that a new title would attract audiences, Freddie Fields changed the film's name from *Citizens Band* to *Handle with Care*.

The American film critics had been warm to Demme since the release of *Caged Heat* three years earlier, and it was through the aegis of the New York Film Festival that *Citizens Band* played to rapturous reception on September 30, 1977. Weeks later, under its new title, *Handle with Care*, the film was released commercially at the Little Carnegie Theatre in Manhattan. Pauline Kael, America's foremost woman of film criticism, had first seen the film during the film festival and was shocked: the wedding sequence was cut to a freeze-frame of Paul Le Mat and Candy Clark kissing.

In an October 31 article in the *Village Voice* titled "Mangled with Care," Kael and Richard Roud, the programmer for the New York Film Festival, rallied around Demme's original cut with the wedding finale. When asked about cutting the ending out, Fields commented in the article, "He (Demme) had as much involvement (in the decision) as he was entitled to." Demme begrudgingly responded to Fields's comments. "I think he has the right to shorten the film," Demme said. "But it would make me happy if, perhaps based on feedback, Freddie changed his mind."[15]

After the article was published, Demme was reprimanded by the Paramount executives, who thought the former publicist-turned-filmmaker had a hand in placing the piece. However, Paramount's New York film distributor, Don Rugoff, told Demme, "I love this picture so much! What it needs is word of mouth. The fact that it's about CB radios is irrelevant." Rugoff was no stranger to seeking out international films like Costa-Gavras's *Z* (1969) or underground classics like Robert Downey Sr.'s *Putney Swope* (1969) to fill the theaters he owned in New York's Upper East Side. As Demme recalled in 2012, "He (Rugoff) showed the movie for free at the Waverly Theater [now the IFC Theater] for a week, and it was packed. Audiences clapped at the end of it. Then they started charging, and nobody came."[16]

The film did have a fan Jonathan couldn't shy away from meeting: President Jimmy Carter. After a White House screening of *Citizens Band*, President Carter turned to Demme and the audience, saying, "Now, that's America!" The thirty-ninth president of the United States' declaration that *Citizens Band* is a portrait of America isn't too much of a hyperbole. The climax of the film, in which CB radio fanatics leave their politics, marital issues, and anger at home to save the elderly Papa Thermodyne and Chrome's free-roaming cattle, offered a cinematic glimmer of hope in the communal efforts of citizens banding together.

Few of the seven hundred theaters that ran *Citizens Band* felt Carter's sentiment. After a screening at a theater outside of Denver, Colorado, Demme proudly remarked that the film only made $1.50 on opening day: "It was one child's admission. I believe that's a record. By the end of the week, the box office skyrocketed to $86, and the movie was yanked."[17] Even Paul Le Mat thought he could revive the film by redistributing it, but Paramount's fixation on CB radios shifted to disco when it rode the success of John Badham's *Saturday Night Fever* (1977).

Minus a role as a horny denim-clad victim devoured in William Sachs's *The Incredible Melting Man* (1977), nothing else was coming Demme's way in terms of film work. He and Evelyn attempted to write stories that would appeal to the studios. One treatment they wrote with Hercules Bellville in 1978 was an adaptation of Herman Melville's first novel, *Typee*. Its title, *The King of the Cannibal Islands*, was inspired by the 1858 Scottish ballad performed by the islanders in Melville's book.[18]

Frequency Issues (1977–1979)

Demme described the post–*Citizens Band* experience as if he had hit a wall. "Soon, I had difficulty paying my rent," he said. "But there's an emergency fund through the DGA Foundation that I love to make little contributions to whenever I can. That kept me going for probably three months until Peter Falk saw *Citizens Band* and invited me to do a *Columbo*, saving me."[19]

Although he wasn't the producer of NBC's hit primetime detective series, Peter Falk enjoyed working with enterprising filmmakers getting their foothold in Hollywood. Steven Spielberg directed the first episode ("Murder by the Book"), and Falk's friend and fellow actors John Cassavetes and Ben Gazzara also directed episodes about the charming, savant-like detective. Falk had a track record of successful and soon-to-be successful directors working on *Columbo*, and he trusted that Demme had the enthusiasm and work ethic needed to make a directorial contribution to the show's final season.

Meanwhile, by 1978, Demme's marriage to Purcell was coming apart at the seams. He had moved back to Manhattan when he met Sandy McLeod. McLeod was one of the few who saw *Citizens Band* at the Waverly Theatre. "When I saw the scene of the two women on the bus," McLeod said, "I said to myself, 'A woman had to have directed this film.'"[20] Jonathan Demme was immediately charmed by her when she entered his office inquiring about being a script supervisor on *Last Embrace*. Evelyn sat next to her husband, noting that the doe-eyed expression pointed toward McLeod reminded her of the way Demme had looked at her when she walked into the publicity offices at United Artists ten years before.

Born in Pontiac, Michigan, and raised in Arkansas, McLeod fled to New York City in 1968 after experiencing racism and conservative extremism. "During my freshman year in college, I had almost been lynched for going out with a Black student," McLeod said. "I was just getting into so much trouble." When she arrived in Manhattan, McLeod was determined not to go back to Arkansas. She searched the classified ads, finding a position at National Recording Studios operating the switchboard, and then worked her way up to editor in the National Recording Studios sound effects library. McLeod's obsession with film was piqued one night at the recording studio when she heard the music of the Rolling Stones. The Maysles Brothers and Charlotte Zwerin were mixing the sound on their documentary of the band's fateful 1969 concert at Altamont, *Gimme Shelter* (1970). "I stayed there that night and watched the mix from sound to picture and thought, 'Oh, I think I should get into the film business!'" McLeod said. "I never realized how involved the filmmaking process was in putting sound to image, enhancing the sound, finding that balance. They had all this rough footage, but they were really making something interesting out of it."[21]

From there, McLeod would work on a variety of films shot in New York, including as continuity assistant on Richard Attenborough's *Magic* (1978), featuring Anthony Hopkins as a ventriloquist at the mercy of his wooden puppet, and as script supervisor on Jerry Schatzberg's political drama *The Seduction of Joe Tynan* (1979), written by and starring Alan Alda. McLeod was determined to work behind the camera, learning how to load the magazines at the rental house and taking notes from the directors she worked with. She saw herself as someone who could be essential to Demme's filmmaking process, even if it was for a film that seemed flawed from the start.

Last Embrace began as an adaptation of Murray Teigh-Bloom's novel *The 13th Man* by David Shaber but evolved into a convoluted script. "There was an idea for a movie in the novel, that was all," Demme said to Carlos Clarens in 1980, "and David took it and virtually wrote an original screenplay from it. It seemed like a modern noir." Keeping the character names from the book, Demme and Shaber tried to parse out the screenplay but had a limited window of time if they wanted their first casting choice, Roy Scheider, as Hannan, the protagonist of the story. "We would have liked to work on the script for another month," Demme said, "but Roy Scheider was available, and UA thought it was a viable project."[22] Scheider was slated to play Joe Gideon in Bob Fosse's autobiographical *All That Jazz* (1979) in the fall of 1978, leaving him available to shoot *Last Embrace* in the summer.

Incidentally, Demme met Scheider's friend and associate producer on *All That Jazz*, Kenneth Utt, while they were watching production previews of *A Chorus Line* at the Public Theater. They just missed working together. "We had talked when he was doing *Last Embrace* with Roy Scheider," Utt said in 1990, "but the timing didn't work out."[23] A World War II air serviceman with aspirations of being an opera singer, Utt first appeared on stage singing for the US Armed Forces production of Moss Hart's *Winged Victory* on Broadway in 1944. Utt had moved from floor manager for CBS television programs into film production as assistant producer on Ulu Grosbard's *The Subject Was Roses* (1968) and John Schlesinger's *Midnight Cowboy* (1969). The seventies would be booming for Uttas as he worked alongside William Friedkin (*The Boys in the Band* [1970], *The French Connection* [1971]), Philip D'Antoni (*The Seven-Ups* [1973], *Moving On* [1974–76]), and Bob Fosse. Utt would play a substantial role in Demme's creative revival in the mid-eighties; however, in 1978, Demme was hovering under the radar.

It was during Sandy McLeod's first project with Demme as script supervisor that she inadvertently landed an acting role in the film. She had just had her hair done when "I went back to the set, and Roy Scheider, who had never looked at me twice, suddenly looked at me and said, 'I need you to play my wife in this movie.' Jonathan said, 'No way, I already cast that part.' After he and Roy had a sidebar conversation, Jonathan said to me, 'Roy is really determined to have you play this part.'"[24]

In one notable moment of the film, Hannan visits his boss, Eckart, at a nondescript clandestine office, requesting work in the wake of his wife's death. The shot begins with Scheider stepping out of the elevator, walking down the narrow hallway, and sitting in an office across from Christopher Walken. Demme and cinematographer Tak Fujimoto framed a subjective point-of-view shot as Walken talks directly to the camera, addressing Scheider about his paranoid delusion that someone tried to kill him after he was released from the Connecticut sanitarium.

There were also nods to Truffaut's *The Bride Wore Black* and Hitchcock's *Vertigo* (1958): one in a scene where Scheider chases after Dorothy's brother-in-law and commissioned assassin (Charles

Napier) in a bell tower and another in the lackluster ending at Niagara Falls in which Ellie Fabian (Janet Margolin) falls to her death. *Last Embrace* was a film that was lost in the denseness of the *Chinatown*-inspired screenplay. The reviews were mixed, though the critics did cite these references to Hitchcock as the few saving graces the film had to offer. Surprisingly, Demme told the *New York Times* on the film's May 1979 release, "There are no noticeable homages to anybody in this movie. I think they're dangerous. You're limiting the appeal of your film when you do that."[25]

Last Embrace left theaters with little notice, but the film's title inadvertently hinted where Jonathan Demme was at by that point in his life. His marriage to Evelyn Purcell came to an end. Their home and marriage weren't built for two directors with separate visions. "He thought he could lead his life and still have a relationship with me," Evelyn said, "and I wasn't interested in that. He stayed a lot at the Chateau Marmont."[26]

Though his dissatisfaction with the studio system was growing and he was homesick for New York City, Jonathan had his LA friends. Gary Goetzman and Joe Viola were always on call; and he took walks along Malibu Beach with Hal Ashby, sharing a joint with and seeking advice from the hippie sage of Hollywood. Bernardo Bertolucci and Clare Peploe, who had gotten married a year earlier, were also at the Chateau Marmont. Demme and Peploe struck up a romantic affair.

As the seventies came to an end, Jonathan spent his time at roller discos, going to the movies, or wandering around Central Park with Sandy McLeod, binoculars, and his bird guidebook.[27] He had started the decade as an earnest publicist and was now a budding filmmaker flying under the radar, eclipsed by box office behemoths engulfing Hollywood budgets. Demme felt like the wood thrushes that covered his childhood home, resiliently moving on foot before flying up to the next branch.

7

Easy Street (1979–1981)

In the wake of his divorce from Evelyn Purcell, Jonathan took up residence at the Navarro Hotel on Fifth Street and Sixth Avenue, just a mile north of the Carlyle Hotel, where Mike Nichols and Bo Goldman were developing a script, a stranger-than-fiction story ripped from newspaper headlines.[1] On April 5, 1976, Howards Hughes, the wealthy, eccentric film producer, playboy, and aviation enthusiast, died, leaving a will to sixteen benefactors. Beyond the Boy Scouts of America and the Church of Latter-Day Saints, Hughes left $156 million to a milkman and gas station owner from Utah named Melvin Dummar. A good Samaritan at heart, Dummar claimed to have found a wounded Hughes wandering through the Nevada desert in December 1967. He drove Hughes to the back entrance of the Desert Inn on the Las Vegas Strip, where he lived on the ninth floor. After Hughes's death, Dummar was in the national spotlight as his presence in the will led to cries of forgery. Dummar would claim that an unnamed well-dressed man left an envelope at his gas station containing a copy of Hughes's will, but he never saw a penny from the Hughes estate.

Thom Mount, a former New World Pictures employee who became the president in charge of production at Universal Pictures in 1977, recalls the origins of *Melvin and Howard*. "I was originally approached by Don Phillips," Mount recalls, "who came into my office with this newspaper article about this milkman who thinks Howard Hughes wrote him into his will. We did a lot of research about Melvin Dummar; we had detectives on it and researched it thoroughly. In the end, we thought, 'Okay, this guy may be lying, but if he's lying, he believes it. And if he believes it, then we have a story.' I approached Mike Nichols, someone I knew and wanted to make a movie with."[2]

Nichols bowed out of the project, and Mount was suddenly without a director. He reached out to his old friend from his days at New World Pictures, Jonathan Demme. "We talked through what *Melvin and Howard* could be, how it would feel, what was cool about it, and what wasn't. Jonathan reads the script. After some discussion over a couple of days, JD said, 'Yes.' That was great. Then we had to cast the thing." Universal initially wanted Gary Busey to play Melvin as he was coming off the success of his Oscar-nominated performance in *The Buddy Holly Story* (1978). However, Jonathan was set on Paul Le Mat and Roberts Blossom as the titular duo, given their cordial collaboration on *Citizens Band*. Thom Mount had a different idea and suggested Jason Robards to play Hughes.

As Mount explained, "Casting Jason Robards was our way, the company's way, to allow Paul Le Mat to take the part. In other words, to cast Blossom—a wonderful actor but relatively unknown from a marketing perspective—wouldn't be a draw compared to someone who was notable like Jason."[3] Jason Robards had an esteemed track record on stage and screen with notable performances in Sidney Lumet's film adaptation of Eugene O'Neill's *Long Day's Journey into Night* (1962), Sergio Leone's *Once Upon a Time in the West* (1968), and Sam Peckinpah's *The Ballad of Cable Hogue* (1970). From 1976 to 1978, Robards earned rave reviews and back-to-back Oscar wins for Best Supporting Actor in *All the President's Men* (1976) and *Julia* (1977). His midwestern baritone voice, warm smile, and steely gaze were the qualities Demme saw when they met at a bar in New York City. The first thing Demme said to Robards was "There's something very poetic about you."[4]

Lynda Dummar, Melvin's wife, would be played by Mary Steenburgen. "We liked Mary," Mount recalled. "She had greatness, and it was fully realized that she could do something extraordinary."[5] The Arkansas-born actress studied under Sanford "Sandy" Meisner at the Neighborhood Playhouse in the seventies while waitressing to pay rent, like so many other aspiring artists living in New York City. Steenburgen landed her first major role when Jack Nicholson cast her to play his love interest in the comedic western he was directing for Paramount, *Goin' South* (1978). Her sophomore performance in Nicholas Meyer's *Time after Time* (1979) for Warner Bros. garnered the attention of both Mount and Demme.

For the film's sanguine, folk-guitar-led score, Demme brought Bruce Langhorne on board. "I'd go over to Bruce's apartment," Demme remembers, "and he'd play music to the videotape."[6] It was the first time they worked together since *Fighting Mad*, yet despite the difference in tone and genre with *Melvin and Howard*, Langhorne's guitar-picking and sorrowful flute-filled leitmotifs are as enveloping as the smell of desert sagebrush after a passing rainstorm. More joy came for Jonathan in picking the source music from Phil Ochs ("My Kingdom for a Car"), the Rolling Stones ("[I Can't Get No] Satisfaction"), and Crazy Horse ("Gone Dead Train").

Jonathan tapped his trusted cinematographer Tak Fujimoto for the project. For the opening shot of the water hole, Demme wanted the camera to hold on the glistening water before Howard Hughes's motorcycle enters the frame; he took inspiration from Werner Herzog's *Aguirre, the Wrath of God* (1972). "I noticed that Herzog had a 20, 30, maybe 40 second shot of nothing but the river," Demme told *LA Weekly*, "and then a shot of nothing but a close-up of a portion of the river. I realized: of course, without the river there wouldn't have been this particular story. . . . So, I did the same with the water hole, and a little later, the highway Melvin is driving down during the credits."[7]

The shoot got under way in Las Vegas. From Jonathan's perspective, it looked promising. Paul Le Mat and Jason Robards had great chemistry; Demme recalled Paul's inability to hide his delight at working with Jason Robards. He was tickled with Jason's performance. In a scene on the road in Melvin's truck, Le Mat forces Robards to sing to avoid being kicked out, and the film takes a shift from a road movie to a nostalgic fixation on carefree existence. What starts off as soft humming leads to a quivering and tender version of Ray Henderson and Mort Dixon's "Bye Bye Blackbird" from Robards. The shot of Le Mat's astonished expression at Robards's airy timbre (generating a warmth in the audience as they hear a golden voice come from this mangy, blood-spattered millionaire) was the first of many such scenes Jonathan would recreate in his later films.

Mary Steenburgen, whose character was a stripper, wasn't used to appearing so scantily clad as she did for a third of a movie, let alone nude. When Melvin gets Lydia fired at the gentleman's club, where she is working as an exotic dancer, then presents her with divorce papers, she defiantly tears her clothes off and walks out of the strip club. After Jonathan yelled, "Cut!" Mary ran back to her trailer in tears. "I went out to congratulate her at her trailer," Demme recalled, "and she was crying. It was so difficult for her."[8]

Production was going smoothly until near the end of principal photography. Thom Mount got a concerned call from the set: Paul Le Mat didn't want to leave his hotel room. Jonathan got on the phone to Mount, telling him that Paul was talking to himself. "Acting is the most dangerous job I think anyone could have," Mount said. "It's physically and mentally taxing. You must go to places and be committed to the places you go in ways that are extraordinary, and by logic of that, commitment, safety, self-harm, and a thousand issues come to question. I asked myself, 'What's Paul worried about?'"[9]

Mount flew to Las Vegas to resolve the situation and ensure Paul was safe enough to finish the movie. Sandy McLeod was working as a production assistant on the shoot, and as she remembers, "Paul was essentially having a nervous breakdown when we were trying to finish the film."[10]

When Mount arrived, he and Demme went to Le Mat's hotel room and found him sitting on the edge of his bed studiously reading the Bible. Paul's wife, music and television producer Suzanne De Passe, was eventually called in and convinced him to go back to work.

Even with such hurdles to overcome on *Melvin and Howard*, Jonathan experienced a sense of reprieve in a movie that had a cohesive script and was captured through his eyes and a team of creators he assembled. Unlike with *Last Embrace*, in which both the script and film lacked substance, Jonathan had experienced creative freedom while keeping within the good graces of a major studio like Universal. Even though Evelyn Purcell and Demme had split, she contributed one of many memorable shots in *Melvin and Howard*. As head of second-unit photography, Evelyn captured the predawn footage of Melvin's truck driving off at the end of the film with Jason Robards singing his bouncy reprise of "Bye Bye Blackbird." As Demme said, "Evelyn did a great job shooting the drive-by scenes."[11]

Jonathan brought on Craig McKay to edit *Melvin and Howard*. McKay had won an Emmy for his work on the NBC miniseries *Holocaust* (1978) and was co-editing Warren Beatty's epic *Reds* (1981) with Dede Allen. Demme and McKay found a kinship at their initial meeting over lunch. "I loved his work," McKay said, "particularly *Citizens Band* and his perspective on American culture." However, McKay wasn't a fan of *Melvin and Howard* after being sent the script. "I wasn't impressed with it—I couldn't feel the narrative force in it," McKay recalled. But Demme found his honesty appealing. "It really impressed him what I honestly felt about the screenplay—I had some balls back then. What I did like about the story was this distortion of the American dream; [I told him] I think it's unique and nobody's representing it the way you do. At the end of the meal, he told me I had the job."[12]

"When there was something that he wanted to go over with me, we would go over it," McKay recalled. "When he felt it was working, he would let it play. It was a great working relationship that encouraged me to contribute everything I could to make it work. You have a voice in it. There was a lot of trust."

The real joy came to Demme when he and McKay decided which music to sync into the film. "Jonathan was heavy into music," McKay continued. "He was into seeing how the performances and story developed. We agreed on our axiom, which was never let the audience get ahead of the story, and we developed that in the arc of our relationship. Philosophically, we were both dead synched on that idea." From the camera pointing down at the highway traffic marks with the radio picking up samples of pop and country to Mary Steenburgen dancing to "(I Can't Get No) Satisfaction" by the Rolling Stones, the synergy of music and moving image was a common bond between the director and editor.

With the film completed, the only question left was how to distribute *Melvin and Howard*. Bob Wilkinson, Universal's head of distribution, asked Thom Mount and Demme into his office. Wilkinson said, per Jonathan's recollection, "Thom, it's a nice picture, and I'm going to tell you the same thing I told you when I read this script, 'You're pissing in the wind if you think anyone is going to see this thing.'"[13] Mount was unfazed by Wilkinson's reaction; he had heard worse from the tipsy distribution head. However, Mount did see that there would have to be a unique distribution strategy to give *Melvin and Howard* the audience it deserved.

Producer Don Phillips attended unenthusiastic test screenings and, along with producer Art Linson and Thom Mount, decided to release the film starting in the southern states, where, in Mount's words, "we believed the audiences would get a kick out of this colloquial character."

Melvin and Howard did play at the Venice Film Festival to a warm reception, but it received truly rapturous applause when it was screened at Alice Tully Hall at the opening of the 1980 New York Film Festival. In his coverage of the festival's opening night in the *New York Times*, Vincent Canby hailed Jonathan as "a lyrical filmmaker for whom there is purpose in style."[14] The word of mouth spread through critics across the country regarding this small gem of a film. However, positive film reviews are not always a strong indicator of box office success. "If you get unanimously good reviews," Mount explains, "then maybe you can see box office increase across the length of the film during its theatrical release when the reviews were being read in newspapers; that doesn't happen anymore. But in that era, people still read newspapers. They averaged 3 percent of the participation gross. Then the film disappears." The film only made $4.3 million at the box office, not breaking even with *Melvin and Howard*'s $7 million budget.[15]

Easy Street (1979–1981)

When the 1980 Academy Award nominations were announced, *Melvin and Howard* received three nominations, one for Bo Goldman's script, along with Best Supporting Actors for Steenburgen and Robards. Goldman and Steenburgen won in their respective categories, facing off with two major contenders at the Oscars that year: Martin Scorsese's boxing drama *Raging Bull*, nominated for eight awards, and Robert Redford's family drama *Ordinary People*, which earned him Best Director and Best Picture laurels. After Peter Ustinov read his name, Goldman went up to the podium, thanking Universal's president, Ned Tanen, "for his deep pockets, Jonathan Demme for his good eye" and also thanking Mike Nichols.[16] When Donald Sutherland and Diana Ross called her name, Mary Steenburgen held her Oscar with surprised joy. She dubbed Jack Nicholson her "patron saint" and thanked Jonathan Demme "for your vision, talent, and the plain, old fashion fun it was to work with you."[17]

While Demme was in Los Angeles during postproduction on *Melvin and Howard*, he had gone to the Whiskey A-Go-Go on the Sunset Strip to catch a band he'd been obsessing over. Based out of Haledon, New Jersey, the Feelies were a fixture of the evolving punk / new wave scene of the late seventies and early eighties, playing at venues like CBGBs and Maxwell's in Hoboken, where they were hometown heroes. After the show, Jonathan wrote to the band courtesy of the fan mail address marked on the back of their *Crazy Rhythms* LP.

Bill Million of the Feelies was watching the 1980 Oscar ceremony from his home in New Jersey when he got a call from his superfan. Demme arranged a screening of *Melvin and Howard* for the Feelies in New York and had them watch what was considered the pinnacle rock concert film at the time, Martin Scorsese's *The Last Waltz* (1978). Feelies guitarist/vocalist Glenn Mercer remembers that it "was pretty cool. We talked about that movie and what he hoped to do with a concert film to the Feelies."[18] Jonathan was mesmerized by the band's gritty, melodic sounds and envisioned a movie about them but with zombies. Not straying too far from Roger Corman's canon of supernatural pre–New World Picture films,

Demme wanted to combine the plot of George A. Romero's *The Night of the Living Dead* (1968) with a rock concert. The project's name was *The Night of the Living Feelies*. Demme couldn't get the studios to greenlight *The Night of the Living Feelies*, but he still saw a cinematic quality to the band that would remain in his mind, even during the turbulent early eighties.

Meanwhile, Jonathan and Sandy McLeod took in the hip and innovative shifts in downtown New York's worlds of theater, art, music, and cinema. They caught the Talking Heads performing in Central Park, shared tables at midtown restaurants with Susan Sarandon, and attended Broadway plays with Diane Keaton and Beth Henley. The disco grooves and halcyon headaches of Studio 54 were replaced by scratched records and pulsating treble at the Mudd Club. Edie Vonnegut remembers Jonathan taking her and Sandy to see Queen Latifah perform in Greenwich Village. "Jonathan had his finger on the musical pulse," Vonnegut said. "The music was so important to him, especially work that had a niche and wasn't popularized already."[19] Demme had connected with Vonnegut while corresponding with her father, Kurt Vonnegut, about adapting his 1961 short story "Who Am I This Time?" He wrote to Vonnegut, who lived a mile and a half away from the Navarro on 228 East Forty-Eighth Street, requesting his permission to adapt his story. Although he never met Jonathan, Vonnegut wrote back giving his blessing. The last time Vonnegut agreed to have his work adapted for film, it was for George Roy Hill and his 1972 rendering of the author's most celebrated, semi-autobiographical book, *Slaughterhouse-Five*.

Who Am I This Time? aired on PBS's *American Playhouse* on February 2, 1982. Howard Rosenberg of the *Los Angeles Times* would list the program in his thirty best made-for-television movies, citing that it was "Walken's character—a terror in front of the footlights but tongue-tied and painfully shy off stage—who gave the story its unusual edge."[20] However, the critic who was most pleased with Demme's production was Kurt Vonnegut.

Traveling cross-country to film festivals, Demme struck up a friendship with the Austin film critic who cofounded the *Austin*

Easy Street (1979–1981)

Chronicle, Louis Black, and hosted a series of screenings at New York's Collective for Living Cinema celebrating the works of the thriving independent filmmaking scene in Texas, which included Brian Hansen (*Speed of Light*), David Boone (*Everyman*), and Lorrie Oshatz (*Leonardo, Jr.*), among others. Demme would be a frequent guest of Austin over the next three decades. In 1985, Black cofounded the Austin Film Society with filmmakers Richard Linklater and Lee Daniel.

By 1982, Jonathan was a hot commodity to those who had seen *Melvin and Howard*; one such person was actress Goldie Hawn. After seeing the film, Hawn wanted to be involved in Demme's next project as the producer and leading actress. Warner Bros. was backing the project thanks to Hawn's box office draw in films like *Private Benjamin* (1980), but what seemed like a dream for Demme—making a big-budget studio picture—would turn out to be one of the most difficult films he would ever direct: *Swing Shift*.

8
Shift in the Breeze (1982–1983)

Swing Shift should have been a golden opportunity for Jonathan Demme. He saw it as a chance to retell the stories of his grandmother Edie's experiences working on fighter planes on the home front during World War II. It seemed as tailor-made for him as his camouflage pants and flat-top haircut. However, the script by Nancy Dowd had a troubled history, which would in part lead to a fragmented and confused finished film.

In 1975, producer Jerry Bick and Paramount's Richard Sylbert were looking for a project that would appeal to the second-wave feminist crowd. They thought they'd found it in a script by Nancy Dowd, a politically charged story about women on the home front while their men were fighting overseas. In the *Swing Shift* production notes, Bick said of the script, "I liked the story because it had in it that concealed message about women and their whole development. It seems clear that women loved the chance to work and be free economically. That their freedom was abruptly taken away at the end of World War II may not have immediately impinged upon them, but it marked the beginning of a social process that continued many years later."[1]

In 1976, before the project could get under way, Richard Sylbert left Paramount, and Michael Eisner stepped into his position as the studio's production executive. Dowd's script languished for years as she tried desperately to place it with another company. In

1978, Nancy Dowd, along with Waldo Salt and Robert C. Jones, won the Best Original Screenplay Oscar for Hal Ashby's Vietnam War drama, *Coming Home*. In 1981, Eisner and Dowd had what Demme characterized as "a falling out"[2] when Eisner put the project in turnaround. Dowd sued Beck, Eisner, and Paramount but ultimately lost, and the script went over to United Artists.[3]

Swing Shift finally went into production in 1983 with Ron Nyswaner's initial script and scenes rewritten by Robert Towne. Like *Coming Home*, *Swing Shift* takes a feminist perspective of women during wartime. The character of Kay Walsh, played by Hawn, is the wife of an enlisted navy seaman who works at MacBride Aircraft Company as a riveter along with her scrappy friend and neighbor, Hazel. On the work floor, she meets Lucky Lockhart, a jazz trumpeter rejected from military service. After passing on Lucky's numerous advances, Kay eventually has an affair with him. When Kay's husband returns home on shore leave, Lucky starts an affair with Hazel. As victory is declared by the Allied forces in 1945, the women leave MacBride Aircraft, having endured the hardships of sexism on the job and having formed cherished friendships with their fellow riveters.

Goldie Hawn was passionate about *Swing Shift*. In her 2005 memoir, she recalled pitching it to Columbia Pictures: "The head of production sighs. 'The problem we have here, Goldie, is that this is a period picture. As I'm sure you're aware period pictures are sometimes difficult and expensive to make, so I'm curious about why you think this one would work?'"[4]

In some ways, it was a rhetorical question; a series of big-budget period dramas were in production at the same time. For Paramount, Warren Beatty's *Reds* (1981) had a $32 million budget and would barely break even at the box office. At United Artists, Michael Cimino's *Heaven's Gate* (1981) initially had a $7 million budget that blew up to $44 million; it grossed only $3 million and would carry an infamous reputation as the film that upended the American New Wave. The only safe bet on period pieces at the time was Steven Spielberg's first installment of the Indiana Jones franchise, *Raiders of the Lost*

Ark (1981), which cost an estimated $18 million and earned $390 million for Paramount and Lucasfilms, George Lucas's production company.[5] However, the studio that didn't have much to lose in the early eighties was Warner Bros.

Goldie Hawn leveraged her success with *Private Benjamin* (1980), her first venture as executive producer, which earned her an Oscar nomination for Best Actress, to get Warner Bros. behind *Swing Shift*. Hawn had struck up a friendship with Richard Sylbert's then sister-in-law, Anthea Sylbert, dating back to 1974, when she designed the costumes for Hal Ashby's film *Shampoo*. Hawn recruited Anthea as her production partner, and their office, Hawn-Sylbert Productions, was located on Westwood Boulevard.

Fish-out-of-water movies were what the studios wanted from Goldie, yet she was determined to break away from the bubbly blonde persona she'd established in her go-go-boot-wearing days on *Rowan and Martin's Laugh-In* (NBC, 1968–1973). It was Sylbert who suggested, after the disappointing pitch to Columbia, that Hawn bring *Swing Shift* to Warner Bros. A few weeks later, as Hawn sat in her office watching *Melvin and Howard*, she realized she had found her director. Demme would bring a hip and articulate approach to depicting the important role women played during World War II; she saw it the minute he stepped into her office: "The first thing I see is his big colorful tie. Straight in from New York, this guy had tremendous style. He looks as if he has stepped out of a movie."[6]

There was an energetic spark from Jonathan that attracted her; they shared a common goal for how the film should be told. Still, Jonathan believed there needed to be rewrites and brought in Bo Goldman, fresh off his Oscar win for *Melvin and Howard*. Goldman wrote a draft for Demme, but it wasn't to be. "When Bo Goldman came on," Demme recalled to Michael Sragow, "the deal the studio and the producers were trying to work out with me didn't work out, so I wasn't directly involved in the writing of Bo's script. When I came on, Bo was no longer available."[7]

Demme brought on Ron Nyswaner to write the shooting script for the film. Ron worked on the script with Jonathan in his suite at the

Shift in the Breeze (1982–1983)

Chateau Marmont. "Working with Ron on *Swing Shift*," Demme said, "was a very pragmatic process of finding scenes from Bo's and Nancy Dowd's drafts that worked and then fitting them into an organic whole. Nancy's drafts were highly political, and the movie isn't."[8] By his own admission, Ron's experience turning Dowd's exposé into a salute to the Greatest Generation was a delight—even more so as he would be working with Demme. According to Nyswaner, "Jonathan believed in narrative storytelling and understood the importance of plot but really enjoyed exploring the quirks and inconsistencies of the characters. I wrote some pages," Ron remembers, "and once they've been distributed, I came up to Goldie and asked her what she thought. Goldie said, 'I think you're a brilliant, brilliant writer.' It was moving to me. It was an amazing time for this kid from coal-mining Pennsylvania to be making a film with Goldie, Christine Lahti, Ed Harris. Jonathan made all that happen."[9]

Goldie sat in on the auditions held at Jonathan's suite, not knowing it would be a life-changing experience for her. Kevin Costner seemed like a solid choice to play Lucky Lockhart before Kurt Russell walked into the room. With the rugged disposition of John Wayne and the meditative glare of Clint Eastwood, Russell had impressed critics with his performance as Elvis Presley in John Carpenter's 1979 made-for-television movie for ABC, *Elvis*. Russell had just finished working opposite Meryl Streep in Mike Nichols's film *Silkwood* (1983) before his fateful audition for *Swing Shift*.

Goldie was struck by Russell's charm. He reminded her they had worked together before on *The One and Only, Genuine, Original Family Band* (1968), a Disney production about a musical family with eleven children reminiscent of *Yours, Mine and Ours*. Ron noticed the instant chemistry between Kurt and Goldie. "I remember that one of them said, 'You know we have to dance in this movie? We should go out and dance!' I can imagine that was the beginning of the romance. It was genuine and sweet."[10]

Mary Steenburgen was initially slated to play Hazel but dropped out when she became pregnant with her second child. She suggested to Jonathan that her friend Christine Lahti take the role.

Lahti exuded a stoic presence and sharp wit reminiscent of Rosalind Russell, traits that brought her to the attention of Norman Jewison when he casted her opposite Al Pacino and their fellow acting teacher, Lee Strasberg, in . . . *And Justice for All* (1979). Fred Ward would play Kay's on-and-off boyfriend and dancehall owner, Biscuits Toohey. Ward had just finished filming what would become his breakout role as Gus Grissom in Philip Kaufman's *The Right Stuff* (1983). Rounding out the cast playing Kay's husband was Ed Harris (also in *The Right Stuff* playing John Glenn) and newcomer Holly Hunter, whom Demme came across via their mutual friend Beth Henley after he watched her onstage in Henley's play *Crimes of the Heart*.

Rehearsals began two weeks before the shoot. Demme was squirrely when it came to endless ruminations over the story. "Jonathan didn't like overanalyzing characters," Ron Nyswaner said. "Jonathan would do anything to avoid talking about the characters. When conversations came up about a scene, he would say, 'Did I tell you the song we were going to use that's going to play at the bar? Let me put that on!' He did it in his sweet and endearing way, so no one felt shoved aside or ignored."[11]

Choosing music during the preshoot preamble of *Swing Shift* evoked for Jonathan memories of his grandfather playing drums at Kelly's Bright Spot in Seaford, Long Island.[12] "This isn't just a movie—it's a musical!" Gary Goetzman said to Jonathan as they selected forty different songs for the film.[13] In between his projects with Demme, Goetzman was garnering a reputation in the music industry as a budding lyricist for Thelma Houston ("Never Gonna Be Another One") and Smokey Robinson ("Old Fashioned Love") while still acting; he appeared in Joel Schumacher's *The Incredible Shrinking Woman* (1981) and the Richard Pryor comedy *Bustin' Loose* (1981). With Bruce Langhorne as *Swing Shift*'s composer, Goetzman wrote the original songs for the film and made an on-screen cameo as a band leader.

Jonathan immersed himself in the fashion of the period, walking onto the first day of shooting like an extra in one of Martin Scorsese's films. "Ever since I saw *New York, New York* (1977)," Demme said, "I've worn baggy trousers, Hawaiian shirts, and clothing from the '40s. I felt that at last I'd found something that I didn't mind seeing myself in. It's just a coincidence that I'm directing a '40s movie, although I do kind of get into character when I direct a film."[14] Demme's sartorial mindset was as luminescent during production as the cigarettes he smoked during takes.

However, Jonathan needed more than vintage attire to weather the storm that was about to arrive when *Swing Shift* started production. Shooting was supposed to begin on February 28, 1982, with cinematographer Tak Fujimoto and the cast assembled on the Santa Monica Pier. Southern California was going through a rainy season, nearly destroying the set.[15] The opening skating rink sequence, in which Kay and her husband listen to President Roosevelt's historic radio address after the attack on Pearl Harbor, had to be pushed back for a month. "I remember him coming home from the first day of shooting," Sandy McLeod said, "telling me, 'That was the worst day I ever had on shooting a movie.'"[16] It was one thing for Jonathan to learn on the job, as he did nearly a decade before on *Caged Heat*, but in the eyes of the executives at Warner Bros., he was a newcomer making a bad impression in the first month of shooting.

The weather-induced hiccup in the schedule didn't deter the rest of the shoot. When the crew relocated to San Pedro to film the bungalow complex where Kay and Hazel live, the atmosphere was jovial. Goldie Hawn recounted in her memoir how Jonathan was supportive of having her mother play Ethel, the landlady, even when she was forgetting her lines. Ron Nyswaner recalled, "Jonathan would adjust on the set between takes, but I think when you look at his movies, what makes them so appealing is that it feels like it's happening in front of you as opposed to being staged in rehearsal. He wanted the freshest thing on film."[17]

One day after sitting in Kathy Blondell's makeup chair, Hawn became concerned about how her wig looked on screen. She asked Jonathan if she could sit in to view the dailies. Jonathan replied, "I would really prefer it if you didn't see the dailies, Goldie."[18] Hawn felt slighted, yet she claimed that before the film went into production, the heads at Warner Bros. requested she relinquish her role and executive producer fee to secure the film's $14 million budget. Hawn went back to the makeup chair as Blondell comforted her: "'Ah, well, you don't like to see the dailies anyway,' she reminds me. 'No, I know,' I told her sadly, 'but he doesn't know that.' While brushing my hair, Kathy says, 'Jonathan doesn't know you well enough yet.'"[19]

As the shooting progressed, so did Goldie's relationship with Kurt Russell. After a day's shoot, Hawn and Russell would ride off on his motorcycle. Occasionally, Goldie would bring her children along to the set. Although Hawn was still married (like her character in *Swing Shift*), her and Russell's affair became the centerpiece of discussion as the crew waited for their leading actors to arrive for hair and makeup. "Sadly, Goldie was notoriously late every day to the set," associate producer Charles Mulvehill recalled. "She wouldn't make the call time, so you were constantly adjusting around that, making the shoot more difficult, adding more pressure on Jonathan and the production."[20]

Jonathan remained calm, even with the shooting schedule and expectations from Warner Bros. looming over him. "He had a pretty positive attitude and tried to not let it get to him," Mulvehill said. "But the pressure got to everybody. It was a big period picture that was difficult to shoot in LA, and you had to agree to a budget that had some validity. Compound that from the pressures of the star not showing up on time; it was rugged. However, Jonathan dealt with it." The pressure was evident on the film's production call sheet dated May 19, 1983, where under the cast's schedule, it reads, "NOTE BENE!!! VEHICLES WILL ROLL PROMPTLY—STRAGGLERS WILL HAVE A LONG WALK TO SET!!!"[21]

Principal photography on *Swing Shift* wrapped in June 1983. A snapshot was taken of Goldie kissing Jonathan, and pleasantries were shared by all. It seemed like a sigh of relief for Demme until Hawn and Warner Bros. viewed the work print for *Swing Shift*. Turning to Kurt Russell as the credits rolled, Hawn told him, "My character has no conscience!"[22] Hawn's reaction to seeing herself on the screen contrasts with her quote in Stephen Farber's on-set coverage

Shift in the Breeze (1982–1983)

on the making of *Swing Shift* for the *New York Times*: "The movie has sexuality. The character I play is a woman breaking loose from her Iowa upbringing, discovering her own sensuality and lust."[23]

When Jonathan was called into a meeting the next day with Warner Bros. studio heads, Goldie Hawn sat next to him, telling an anxiety-fueled Demme that she was going to have to emphasize her role as producer on the film, leading to reshoots.[24] Editor Craig McKay was also in the meeting. "Goldie asked, 'How come there's not a close-up of me here or there?'" McKay said. "I really got pissed off because they were ganging up on Jonathan; I was a protective editor. I turned to her and said, 'Goldie, it's an awfully big screen there.' I turned to Jonathan, and he was in shock; his jaw was wide open. They wanted to bring other people to do reshoots, and they didn't like the movie either."[25]

Jonathan's initial cut of *Swing Shift*, shaped by his intention to make the film a salute to women, clashed disastrously with the vision of the star of the studio. McKay recalled, "Warner Bros. systematically undermined Jonathan and got rid of him. One day, I got a call in the cutting room saying, 'I'm leaving the picture. You're on your own.' I said, 'No, I'm not. I'm leaving the picture too. I can't deal with how they're chopping it up and star-fucking it to death.'"

Demme had another ally who supported his initial cut—writer, director, and comedienne Elaine May. After watching Jonathan's cut, she went to lunch with him, Hawn, and Anthea Sylbert. "This was a great moment," Demme said. "Elaine May, who I never met before, God bless her, came walking into the room and said, 'Are you Jonathan? What a wonderful movie; it's fabulous! Are you guys out of your mind?'" As Hawn and Sylbert explained the importance of focusing the movie on the blossoming romance between Kay and Lucky, like the romantic comedy couples of the World War II era, Elaine replied, per Jonathan's recollections, "Well, all these ideas sound great for some movie, but they go completely against the ecology of this movie as it now exists, and you'll never pull it off."[26]

Jonathan may have had his collaborators and Elaine May supporting his version of *Swing Shift*, but he was still David to the Goliath that was Warner Bros. Sandy McLeod recalled Jonathan was told he was losing control of the film over dinner with Goldie and the studio executives. "I remember being at the dinner when it was brought up that Robert Towne was going to do rewrites," Sandy said. "I was so shocked, I put my cigarette out in someone else's mashed potatoes. Robert wanted the job and needed it, so he took Goldie's side and wanted to fulfill her wishes."[27]

"How Robert Towne could participate in this always amazed me," Demme said. Jonathan's heartfelt salute to his grandparents eventually ended up as a sugarcoated mess that would wreak havoc on his nerves. Hailed for his work as the script doctor on *The Godfather* (1972) and *Marathon Man* (1976), and as the stogie-chomping scribe behind what is considered the greatest film noir screenplay, *Chinatown* (1974), Robert Towne was treading water in the early eighties. "I never forgave him for that," Demme said. "It was appalling what he did."[28]

Towne turned Demme's *Swing Shift* into a lackluster romantic comedy. In a meeting with Warner Bros. executives Robert Daly and Terry Semel, Demme recalled, "There was a moment that they looked up at the scenes which had to be shot next week and just said, 'Jonathan, these scenes are terrible. What are we going to do?' I said, 'What are we going to do?! We shouldn't be doing this at all!'"[29]

Jonathan had never had a film taken away from him like that, so it was painful for him. After going through the Writers Guild of America's arbitration process, Nancy Dowd had her name removed from the film. Ron Nyswaner didn't get credit for his shooting script, and the writing credit would be given to Rob Morton, a pseudonym indicating that no one wanted their name associated with the studio-approved alterations of the movie.

The studio-released version omitted Bruce Langhorne's original score and Gary Goetzman's songs, leaving behind a musical trying to find its beat to a nonexistent rhythm. In one scene of the studio version, a montage of Kay writing a letter to her husband, riveting a plane, and fixing a toaster is intercut with exterior and interior shots of the MacBride Airplane Factory, all to the accompaniment of an upbeat number, "Big Bucks." This contrasted drastically with

Demme's version, in which there was no montage. Rather, in a subtler and more evocative scene, the camera holds on Hawn as she contemplates what to write to her husband overseas, and when she finishes, she leans forlornly against the kitchen wall.

Additionally, one of Jonathan's favorite scenes from the film was cut from the studio version. A convoy of Japanese Americans is shown being driven to the internment camps as Kay and Hazel walk to the factory for work, while the male factory workers shout out, "Damn Japs! Go back to where you came from!" Demme told Stephen Farber, "It's really just an aside in the movie, but it's a chance to show the humiliation of the Japanese, which is something a lot of people have forgotten."[30] Sadly, the executives at Warner Bros. didn't want this brief social commentary on one of America's flawed actions during wartime.

As pointed out in Steve Vineberg's 1991 article "*Swing Shift*—A Tale of Hollywood," Demme's focus on the characters who make up the workforce is sharply reduced in the studio cut. "The actresses who play Kay and Hazel's co-workers" Vineberg writes, "have wonderfully expressive faces and bodies, but Demme's cut gives us specific details about them at the beginning so we can keep track of them through the picture."[31] For example, after her husband dies overseas, Holly Hunter gives a speech honoring him at the MacBride Airplane Factory as Kay and Lucky sneak off to kiss. Additionally, footage of Stephen Tobolowsky pursuing Susan Peretz during the workers' jamboree is also omitted from the studio version.

The emotional connection the audience is supposed to feel with Hawn as she falls in love with Lucky is cut in an awkward manner. In the studio cut, Lucky goes to Kay's bungalow. The exterior shots show her slightly nervous as Lucky invites himself in. The next scene is an interior shot of the kitchen, with Kay drying her hair and chatting with Lucky as if they were already a couple. The scene ends with Lucky cooking her dinner, and they passionately kiss before adjourning to the bedroom, where they briefly quarrel the morning after.

Another example from Demme's cut is a scene where Kay is lightly grilled by Lucky about how happy she is with her marriage.

She goes over to the gramophone to put on a record, with Lucky behind, caressing her. She breaks down as she thinks about her marriage to Jack, but Lucky continues to console her, and she gives in to her lustful desires. The scene then cuts to a dimly lit bedroom as Kay puts a blanket over Lucky's nude backside, anxious that someone was watching them from outside. Vineberg points out, "Hawn has heartbreaking scenes in Demme's cut that remind you how gifted an actress she really is—especially the ones with Ed Harris during Jack's disastrous leave, where you see Kay's misery at having to make him so unhappy and her sad understanding that she can't continue to lie to him. And even when the scenes Demme shot are lifted whole into the version Hawn approved, they don't mean the same thing; you lose the significance, the weight of some of her best moments."[32]

The ending to the studio cut, equally out of sync, has Kay and Hazel patch up their friendship after a drunken fight over Lucky, and they hug in freeze-frame as Carly Simon's theme song swells through the end credits. Demme's ending, where the two women have beers on the beach in the warmth of the San Pedro sun, has more pathos and authenticity. This was thanks to his focus on a relationship that blossomed over the course of World War II, not between men and women, resulting in the Baby Boom generation, but between women and women, which contributed to the beginning of the second-wave feminist movement.

"*Swing Shift*, in its original form, wasn't a great picture," Jonathan said, "but it was a good picture—a good, solid picture with a feminist theme that revealed the fact that women on the homefront in World War II saved the day. It had no possibility of being a romantic comedy about Goldie and Kurt."[33] Despite Demme's intention to make *Swing Shift* a film that would be a successful social commentary on women in the workplace, it was undermined by the studio executives' attempt to play it safe by making the film a predictable, yet disheveled, romantic comedy. Ten years later, when he came across a copy of *Swing Shift* in a Philadelphia video store, Demme wrote a note and attached it to the videocassette box. The note read "don't check this out!"[34]

9
Juggling Act (1983–1984)

In a fateful turn of events, in August 1982, Gary Goetzman had a ticket to see the Talking Heads at the Greek Theatre in Los Angeles that he couldn't use and gave to Demme, but the idea of working with the band had sparked earlier. Goetzman's brother had been booking bands at California State University, Northridge, and Demme pitched the idea of filming the show. The band balked at the idea of playing a low-paying college gig for a film that would air on television.

Still, the Talking Heads had been Demme fans since they saw *Melvin and Howard* during their 1980 European tour, and Demme and David Byrne hit it off after meeting backstage at the Greek Theatre show. Demme knew how he wanted to film the Talking Heads. Rather than cutting away to interviews with the band members or having them followed around by a camera crew like the Rolling Stones (*Gimme Shelter*) and the Band (*The Last Waltz*), Jonathan wanted to simply film them on stage: "The quality of the Heads' show was so great that I thought that by just taking an uncomplicated, straight-forward approach to it, a pretty thrilling movie probably could be made."[1] Gary Goetzman, who was still moonlighting as a record producer, went to Warner Bros. Records asking for $1.2 million to finance the film.[2]

Demme was still editing *Swing Shift* and was in a sticky situation with Warner Bros. It was Joe Viola who came to the rescue, as he recalls from a phone conversation with Demme: "'Joe, man! They're giving me such problems.' Jonathan was telling me how they wouldn't let him leave the cutting room. 'I can't get out of here, and I have this concert to shoot. You're a DGA member; could you work as an AD on this film? I must avoid the credit situation or I'm in deep shit!' Being a DGA director member, no permission was required for me to be the temporary director on the set in JD's absence."³

Two days before cameras started rolling at the Pantages Theatre, Viola got word back from the Directors Guild of America that he would be able to shoot the film. "That day, we went over his script and notes at my place," Viola said. "The next day, we went to the Pantages and started laying out the film with the crew, Jordan and I with the main camera and spotting with the other two cameras and marking rehearsals with the band on stage." Under the watchful eyes of the producers at Warner Bros., Jonathan would correspond with Viola by phone from the editing rooms in Burbank. Viola said, "I was like his mechanical arm. Jon was omnipresent except when the producers showed up in the cutting room at Warner Bros., he would have to end the call. Then he would have to call back as if he were talking to Sandy."

Demme enlisted Sandy McLeod's help, and she went on tour with the band in his place. She took notes and mapped out shots, though she is credited as a visual consultant. "Jonathan and I split up during *Swing Shift*," Sandy recalls, "and he convinced me to work on *Stop Making Sense*. He left the film with me; I went on the road with the Talking Heads, designing the shots while he was shooting *Swing Shift*."⁴

Demme caught up with Sandy during the band's concert in Texas and noted the special collaborative efforts taking place behind the scenes. His trusted colleagues—Sandy and his former *Citizens Band* cinematographer, Jordan Cronenweth—played crucial roles. "Once we started shooting," Demme said, "so many wonderful things happened that we never could have dreamt up or planned. About 50 percent of the movie is stuff that was preplanned, and then the other 50 percent are wonderful happenings that just occurred while it was happening."⁵

Jonathan was still enmeshed in reshooting *Swing Shift*, complicating matters considerably. On the day of the first Pantages show, he was in Burbank to film reshoots, then had to drive to Los Angeles to film the Talking Heads. When Jonathan arrived on the set of *Swing Shift*, he encountered a director's worst nightmare—his name upside down on the slate, a symbol that he wasn't in charge of the movie anymore. "My days consisted of driving up to the lot 'directing,'" Jonathan said with distain, "which translates as 'Action!', 'Cut!', 'Goldie, was that okay for you?'"[6]

That first night of shooting did not go well. Initially, Jonathan wanted to film the audience and incorporate their reactions to the Talking Heads throughout the film: "What's a concert without its audience?" Jonathan posed the rhetorical question in 2007. "But we found out that we had to put light on the audience to photograph them properly. The more light we would put on them, they became inhibited; and the more inhibited they were, the more insecure the band was. I wound up being responsible for the worst Talking Heads performance in the history of the band's career."[7] Subsequently, the band played at breakneck speed compared to the moderate, yet punctuated, funk that defined their sound

For Sandy, it was devastating seeing the first night's concert descend into bedlam. "There were some lighting effects we couldn't get during the day," McLeod said, "so I would shoot during the day with Jordy Cronenweth while Jonathan was shooting *Swing Shift*, and we would shoot the concert at night. It was a very tough moment for me. I remember watching the dailies with David, and he turned to me and said, 'This sucks! We hired Jonahan, and he's barely around!'"[8]

The next day, Jonathan awoke to more anxiety-ridden nausea. "No more audience shots," he told himself. He was relieved the second night after seeing the work Sandy, Jordan, and the crew managed to pull off. There was no longer a conflict between the audience and the band. "It was great for him to come at night to those concerts," Sandy remembers, "because it was a great show, very uplifting. I remember him telling me how much he loved the footage I captured."

The morning of the last show, Jonathan was in a state of exhaustion and depression. "I found myself sitting in my bathtub crying," Demme said, "I just couldn't take it anymore."[9] The Talking Heads ended the show with "Crosseyed and Painless" as handheld cameras captured the audience dancing in the aisles. "The movie believes that there's nothing more interesting going on in this room than these musicians making their music and it's entirely for the movie viewer," Demme said. "There's not going to be any moment where you are reminded that other people got to see this live and that must've ultimately been the best way of all to see it. This is strictly for the movie. It's only in the last moments of the final encore that we felt relaxed enough to cut to the audience. Specifically, to Jordan and myself rocking out."[10] A child hoisted above a parent's shoulder is grooving with a stuffed unicorn while Jonathan, his depression subsided, is rocking his head back and forth with Jordan Cronenweth behind the camera.

Demme's friend Hal Ashby was editing *Let's Spend the Night Together* (1983), his concert film of the Rolling Stones during their 1981 stadium tour of America. Jonathan recalled visiting Ashby in New York after the shooting of *Lookin' to Get Out* (1982). Touring with the Rolling Stones had eased some of Ashby's pain after Lorimar's rejection of *Lookin' to Get Out*; the studio had recut the film and it flopped. Demme visited Hal, Pablo Ferro, and assistant editor Lisa Day in Ashby's editing suite in Malibu Colony and observed his radical ingenuity. As Demme described, "It was pre-computerized editing, Hal had devised this system himself because they had filmed three performances with twelve cameras each, so they have thirty-six angles on every song. Hal created a system where he had these three thirty-six quarter-inch decks brought into a room with thirty-six little projectors aimed at one wall—all the other walls were these projectors. He had it synched up so that every deck had one of the cameras with all these wires everywhere, and you would hit a button and suddenly all thirty-six angles were up on the wall." Through his noblesse oblige, Ashby let Demme use the editing facilities for free. "He didn't charge us anything—he was a godsend!"[11]

Next was to decide on a title for the film, which had stymied the production team. Jonathan, in a later interview with Deirdre O'Donoghue on KCRW, explained, "We were really stuck for an idea as to what to call the movie, and we didn't want to get too clever. We couldn't think of any good ideas, so everybody started writing their favorite lines from the various songs on a list in the cutting room, and that's the one that everybody kind of gravitated to, so we went with it. We thought that the good thing about it was that it really captured the spirit of the movie, which was, you know, kind of 'come in, relax, stop making sense, enjoy yourself.'"[12]

On April 13, 1984, *Swing Shift* opened in theaters to a reception from film critics that ranged from bland to mixed. David Denby of *New York Magazine* praised the detail-oriented focus of Demme's interpretation of the early forties but noted that "even these touches, satisfying as they are, do little but complete the movie's harmonious tone. *Swing Shift* isn't boring, but nothing in it startles, nothing explodes."[13] Despite Gene Siskel praising Christine Lahti's performance, he noted that "too often, we want more from this movie. More of a reason for her (Goldie Hawn) taking up Kurt Russell. More of a reaction from her husband when he eventually learns of their affair. At times, *Swing Shift* almost seems afraid of its subject." Roger Ebert retorted, emphasizing the concluding freeze-frame shot of Hawn and Lahti embracing each other as "the discovery of what goes on in this movie, not your desire that the husband play another one of these spurned and jilted scenes or that the lover explains something about why he's so desirable."[14]

Swing Shift earned a dismal $2.2 million at the box office. The film would ultimately gross $6.6 million worldwide, failing to make a return on the $15 million budget. Demme recalled how his friend, composer Bruce Langhorne, reacted when he saw the film: "They threw out Bruce's entire score. That's when Bruce said, 'You know what, I'm going to move to Hawaii, learn how to grow macadamia nuts, and learn how to use a welders torch.' And that's what he did!"[15]

What could have been a career-ending misfire for Jonathan Demme was ameliorated eleven days later when *Stop Making Sense* played in select theaters on April 24, 1984, before opening nationwide in November. In her glowing review in the *New Yorker*, Pauline Kael praised Jonathan Demme's simplistic approach in capturing the Talking Heads without subjecting them to the fast-paced editing style prevalent in music videos at the time. Roger Ebert exclaimed, "There are times that this looks like an aerobics class. Enormous energy, enormous goodwill, a lot of joy and power in the music! The lighting and shadows are coordinated so well with the music this becomes not just a musical film, but the record of a real theatrical event."[16]

Jonathan was obsessed with making sure each movie theater would give the film a sonic energy as palpable as what he had felt while filming *Stop Making Sense*. He traveled to theaters, giving managers and projectionists instructions on how loud the film should be played—"a pep talk," in Demme's parlance. After tears rolled down his face during a screening at San Francisco's Castro Theatre, Demme wanted all the theaters to replicate that energy. As he told a Bay Area journalist, "I'm telling them to play our film a little louder than their normal level and how vital it is all their speakers are working."[17]

Stop Making Sense set a creative watermark compared to previous concert films in that Demme's primary focus is on the band as performers. As soon as Pablo Ferro's title design appears on the screen, the camera follows David Byrne's feet as he walks onto the stage, putting down a beatbox and pressing the play button on the tape deck. The camera moves up as Byrne taps his foot to the backbeat of "Psycho Killer" before strumming the opening A-minor chord. His head contorts to the beat, and his body shimmies and staggers around the stage like Fred Astaire's movements in the "I Left My Hat in Haiti" sequence from Stanley Donen's 1951 film, *Royal Wedding*.[18]

As the concert progresses, so does the presence of the band as the members come out one by one: Tina Weymouth playing bass, with Lynn Mabry adding backing vocals to "Heaven"; Chris Frantz jumping onto the stage in his aquamarine polo shirt, grabbing the CB-radio-styled speaker to match up with the tempo before breaking into "Thank You for Sending Me an Angel"; Jerry Harrison playing rhythm guitar on "Found a Job"; backup singers Lynn Mabry and Ednah Holt entering stage left while Steve Scales and Alex Weir add percussion and guitars to "Slippery People"; and Bernie Worrell of the band Parliament-Funkadelic positioning himself at the keyboards during "Burning Down the House." "Jonathan treated all the musicians as if they were characters or actors in an ensemble piece," Byrne said. "You got to know them as people. You got to see the inter-reactions between the musicians and how each one, as a person, was having a good time."[19] The inclusion of all the musicians in the film was a task Demme pulled off thanks to studying each performance as cameras rolled.

The pace and energy of the concert was lit with futuristic sheen by Jordan Cronenweth, who, after working with Demme on *Citizens Band*, gained acclaim as Ridley Scott's cinematographer on *Blade Runner* (1982) and shot a Joni Mitchell concert. The musical and optical marriage is exemplified when David Byrne and Jerry Harrison take a break near the end of the concert while Chris Frantz and Tina Weymouth perform as the Tom-Tom Club with their dancehall ode to underground hip-hop, "Genius of Love."

As the band returns to the stage, David Byrne's boxy, silhouetted frame—made possible by his giant suit—envelops the screen like a creature from Corman's canon of fifties horror films as he struts to the opening measures of "Girlfriend Is Better." The presence of the camera operators is evident when Byrne points the microphone at one of them, giving the illusion that he's pointing it at the filmgoing audience. While Frantz and Weymouth were rocking out on stage during "Genius of Love," Demme noticed David Byrne snacking before getting into his iconic giant suit. He joked, "Byrne would go backstage and gorge himself in order to be able to fit into the big suit, then come back and immediately have to shed that weight again."[20]

The joy Jonathan felt filming the Talking Heads really shines during the band's funky cover of Al Green's "Take Me to the River." Although he's not present in the frame, Demme recalled how his screaming made it on to the audio track. "While we were at the mix," he said, "there was a moment where David went out and I got into the booth and did that scream and laid it in as a joke. He came back in, and when we reviewed the reel, nobody noticed anything."[21]

Although the band would no longer tour after 1983 and formally dissolved in 1991, the Talking Heads would gradually build their worldwide fanbase through *Stop Making Sense*. When the movie toured the film festival circuit, Demme and the band would host screenings: "I'll never forget the time Bertolucci came to a screening of *Stop Making Sense* in Florence, Italy." Jonathan and the Talking Heads were in attendance, and from Jonathan's memories, Bernardo was stunned by the audience forming conga lines and dancing in the aisles. Bertolucci told Demme, "I want to see the audience for one of my films dancing like that to the screen except with no music." Demme responded, "Many of us do already."[22]

Jonathan ended 1984 in somewhat of a creative crisis. Despite the acclaim for *Stop Making Sense*, Demme was still recognized as the director of *Swing Shift*. When he returned to New York City, he was left with few possibilities in working with the film studios. Initially, he and Mark Peploe (Clare's brother and Bertolucci's brother-in-law) collaborated on an adaptation of Dashiell Hammett's *Red Harvest* that didn't come to fruition. Before his death from alcoholism in 1984, Truman Capote was in contact with Demme about filming his story *Handcarved Coffins*, but that had the same fate as *Red Harvest*. Demme considered helming a project from John Milius, *Extreme Prejudice*, which he described as "a semi-futuristic account of a Green Beret acting within the boundaries of the United States, which is a semipolitical fantasy thriller." However, the project was terminated. In his interview with Hal Hinson for the *Washington Post*, Demme said, "I'd like to do something tough; something gripping and mean for a change. I'm wide open."[23]

Nothing with theatrical merit was coming in Jonathan's direction. Instead, Jonathan hosted dinner parties and immersed himself in his expanding book collection. When he picked up a copy of Hayden Herrera's biography on Frida Kahlo, Demme told *Vanity Fair*, "Her life was every bit as amazing as her extraordinary paintings and therefore induces top-notch dream material while sleeping."[24] One night, he told Sandy, "Maybe I should give up filmmaking and open up a bookstore."[25] In the autumn of 1984, the couple took a vacation in the Caribbean, where they stumbled on a hair salon called Clinica Estetico.[26] The name stuck with Demme, even after he flew back to the States to revive his career, working on his terms.

10

Something New (1985–1986)

Jonathan may have had critical buzz from the press after *Stop Making Sense*, but he needed the right studio behind him to make his next film without any interference. Demme found his answer through Orion Pictures and one of its founders, Mike Medavoy. "Orion was like a Camelot," Demme said in 2016. "It was like, 'Come filmmakers, show us the script you want to do; we're financiers, we're not movie makers; we'll give you the money and then we'll try our hardest to release it well.'"[1]

Medavoy had known Jonathan since the mid-seventies when he was Hal Ashby's agent. "They were super sweet," Medavoy remembers. "They both had that in common, that sweetness. Hal probably was a little bit into smoking weed, but Jonathan was clear-eyed and clean."[2] Under the watchful eyes of its chairman and president, Arthur Krim and Eric Pleskow, respectively, United Artists was a haven for directors to broaden their cinematic horizons, from Hal Ashby (*Bound for Glory*, *Coming Home*) to Milos Forman (*One Flew Over the Cuckoo's Nest*). After Medavoy and his crew left United Artists in 1978, they formed Orion Pictures and released acclaimed films like Forman's *Amadeus* (1984) and Woody Allen's *The Purple Rose of Cairo* (1985). Mike Medavoy gave Jonathan a shot by backing *Something Wild*. "You can't be in a room with Jonathan and not get excited," Medavoy explains, "because he's got this excitement and this vision."[3]

THERE'S NO GOING BACK

It was executive producer Ed Saxon who came across a script that seemed tailor-made for Demme, *Something Wild*, by E. Max Frye. Jonathan connected with Frye's script, a diasporic exercise in reviving his Corman-style approach to filmmaking. Frye attended the same film school as Martin Scorsese, Oliver Stone, and Spike Lee. Unlike his distinguished NYU alumni who would spend years trying to get their careers off the ground, Frye was one of the few who had set plans after graduation when he flew to Los Angeles. He brought copies of his screenplay along with him to pass around to anyone who had a foot in the door at any film studio in town: "One day, I got a call out of the blue from an agent who had read my screenplay and wanted to represent me. He asked me, 'Who would you like to see direct your script?' I said, 'Martin Scorsese or Jonathan Demme.'"[4]

"*Something Wild* became a chance to kind of start all over again," Demme said. "I felt that in many ways it was my first film. I love road movies, I love crime-story movies, and I guess, in a way, *Something Wild* is an amalgam of those genres, but again, all mixed in a totally original, endlessly surprising way."[5] When recalling the casting process for *Something Wild*, Jonathan said, "It was two-thirds fun and one-third challenging." The actress who came to Jonathan's mind when he read the script was Melanie Griffith, whom he had seen in Brian De Palma's 1984 film *Body Double*. The role of Charlie Driggs was deserving of an actor with comedic timing and charm. Jonathan was good friends with Kevin Kline and saw him as the comedically neurotic yin to Melanie Griffith's uninhibited and vivacious yang. However, Orion had in mind Jeff Daniels, who'd become an industry favorite after his performances in Milos Forman's *Ragtime* (1981), James L. Brooks's *Terms of Endearment* (1983), and Woody Allen's *The Purple Rose of Cairo* (1985).[6] Daniels could project Charlie's neurotic yuppieness with affable grace and a dash of deviance; he was the perfect fit for Charlie.

"One of the things that intrigued me about Charlie," Demme said, "is that he's going to be on the road, but what's he like with strangers? What's he like with people who [he will] have momentary encounters with? . . . I wound up putting an emphasis on showing how effortlessly Charlie is nice with everybody. It was implicit in Max's script, but it wasn't explicit."[7]

With most of the cast assembled, the role of Ray Sinclair, Lulu's estranged criminal husband, was still up in the air. Although casting directors Risa Bramon and Billy Hopkins scoured photos and audition tapes, nothing stood out. At one point, John Doe, bass player for the LA punk rock band X, auditioned, yet Demme didn't see him as Ray. Melanie Griffith suggested Ray Liotta, one of her friends from an acting class taught by her then-husband Steven Bauer. At first, Bramon and Hopkins passed on Liotta's audition, but when a staged reading was held, Jonathan knew he'd found his Ray Sinclair. As Frye recalls, "We were doing casting at a dumpy motel on Hollywood Boulevard and Sunset, and Ray shows up and it was sparks all over the place. It was immediate that he was right for the part. Once he got into the mix with Melanie and Jeff, we knew we had a movie. All the credit goes to Melanie for bringing Ray in, but it was clear that everyone thought 'This is the guy!'"[8]

Jonathan needed the assistance of his script supervisor and on-and-off girlfriend, Sandy McLeod, to scout locations. The two drove from New York City down the Eastern seaboard to Tallahassee, Florida. While in Tallahassee, they met artists Jim Roche and Alexa Kleinbard. Their and Demme's love of folk art carried over into the film's production.

Shooting began on March 22, 1986.[9] One of the early scenes shot was of Roche, credited as the Motel Philosopher, giving Charlie a hangover remedy after a night of whiskey-fueled passion with Lulu. Initially, Roche was to just hand Jeff the Pepto-Bismol cocktail. Before the cameras rolled, he went up to Jonathan and said, "If this guy came up to me and asked for an Alka-Seltzer, I would wanna give him some advice. Could I say something to him?"[10] Jonathan was not a stranger to improvisation, and Roche delivered one of the film's most memorable lines in the first take: "Remember, it's better to be a live dog than a dead lion. I've felt the same way before."

Unaware of Roche's dialogue before the cameras rolled, Jeff reacted with a surprised chuckle before Jim walked out of the frame.

After Jonathan said cut, Jeff ran up to him and asked, "Where did you find these people? This is amazing what's going on!"[11] Jonathan would remember Jeff's off-camera reaction as "one of the greatest compliments a director can get from an actor." During dailies, Demme would sit with producer Kenny Utt, who, along with Ed Saxon and Ron Bozman, made up the director's production team; they would watch to see if he would wink and nod with approval for the day's shoot.[12] Jonathan's mother, Dodie, was on set having a say, suggesting that he leave in the scene where Jeff Daniels convinces Melanie Griffith to drink the hangover cure concocted by Jim Roche.[13] Meanwhile, Jonathan's brother, Peter, plied his carpentry skills working on the set, another Demme family affair.

According to Sandy McLeod, Melanie Griffith was not only delivering a memorable performance but also soldiering through the shoot during a personal and emotional whirlwind. "Melanie was still seeing Don Johnson but still married to Steven Bauer. She had a difficult time managing to remember what she did in the previous take," McLeod remembers. "You just didn't know what you were going to get."[14] Despite her cocaine addiction at the time, Griffith was flawless in Jonathan's eyes.

On this film, Demme indulged in rehearsals for the first time rather than planning out his shots. "I was always afraid of the idea, 'What if the actors get it just right on a rehearsal and you're not filming? Wouldn't that be awful?'" Demme said. "So, Tak Fujimoto and I got into this idea of we're going to rehearse on film. Let's get the actors on the set, let's find out how they want to move around, then Tak can light it, and then the actors can get their makeup and costumes on, and we can start rehearsing on film, which I love."[15]

The Sawano Country Club served as the gymnasium for Lulu's high school reunion dance. For music, Jonathan called in one of his favorite bands, the Feelies, to liven up the set and the movie. *The Night of the Living Feelies* was a distant memory, and the band was performing regularly at Maxwell's in New Jersey. Guitarist Bill Million got a call from Jonathan that the band could be back in the movies—not as the Feelies but as the Willies. "He reached out to us and wanted to know if we wanted to play this high school reunion band," Million said. "Then he sent us a list of the hit songs from 1976. He wanted us to go over the song list and see what we were interested in playing."[16]

The Feelies were initially set to play a surf-rock version of the theme from *Rocky* (1976) as Lulu and Charlie enter the bicentennial-designed dance hall, but before the band got to the country club, the song had to be changed when Sylvester Stallone refused to give permission for the use of the iconic theme.[17] Instead, the band broke into Neil Diamond's "I'm a Believer," a 1966 hit for the Monkees and a signature song from the Feelies' days playing at CBGB's. The only hit song from 1976 they ended up playing was David Bowie's "Fame."

In the scene, the camera starts off on Brenda Sauter on bass during the song's introduction, then pans across the stage over Bill Million and Glenn Mercer playing a funky rhythm on guitars; it stops on Dave Weckerman on backup vocals and maracas, wearing a bright yellow shirt with a drawing of a hunchback with a walking stick, which Demme nicknamed "Jorobado." Weckerman remembers,

> Jonathan gave me that shirt, which has the logo to this production company, and I told him, "Jonathan, I didn't wear this in the last scene." He said, "You're in a local band. You guys took a break, it's hot, you unbuttoned your dress shirt, and you're wearing a T-shirt." Before doing so, he took me aside and told me the significance of the design. He told me that down in the islands, it's misfortune to pass the hunchback with the walking stick without giving them some sort of currency. He kind of spooked me when he said, "If you don't wear the shirt, the curse of the hunchback will be upon thee."[18]

Cursed or not, the image Demme initially found on a medicine bottle would become synonymous with his production company after Religioso Primitiva: Clinica Estetico (translated as Esthetic Clinic).

Another scene that captures the film's sonic and visual energy is when Ray leaves Audry in the car for an impromptu beer run at a convenience store, with the Motels' "Total Control" playing on the radio. In the store, the clerk wears a sleeveless shirt emblazoned with the Talking Heads' *Little Creatures* album cover art, and Charlie waves at the CCTV camera and monitor like Peter Sellers in *Being There* (1979). As the clerk rummages under the counter for a pack of Marlboros, Ray pulls out a gun and shoots the monitor, knocks out the clerk, and steals the money from the register. Charlie tries to revive the clerk while scolding Ray for his actions before being thrown over the counter. The camera slows down as Ray grabs his cigarettes in midair and runs out of the store dragging Charlie with him. The scene ends from the perspective of the CCTV camera capturing Ray knocking Charlie in the nose with his shoulder as "Total Control" continues to pulsate through the soundtrack during this violent dance. Lulu and Charlie are manhandled into the car as Ray drives off. The beat of the Motels continues as Ray regales Charlie with stories of robbing other convenience stores. The camera then pans over from Ray to Charlie, who is writhing in pain and shock from being knocked square in the face.

Initially, the climactic scene of the knife fight between Ray and Charlie was never going to happen. As Max Frye recalls, "Originally, they (Orion) didn't want Ray to die. I ended up rewriting that fight scene a dozen ways. Finally, I said, 'Jonathan, he has to die. The whole movie leads up to that.' I'll never forget that moment of Jonathan looking at me and saying, 'You know? You're right.' And that was it; the fight was dialed back to where Ray throws himself at Charlie, and it's almost inadvertent that he fell on the knife."[19]

During the shooting of the bathroom brawl on Long Island, the crew was getting soaked with water. Rain gear was draped over the cameras. According to camera operator Tony Janelli, "We had to shoot in our bathing suits."[20] Wearing flipflops, assistant cameraman Vinnie Gerardo screamed when the knife fell on his foot. While Jonathan was watching the scene from monitors in the hall, he heard a shout. "In that obsessive director's moment," Demme recalled,

"I went, 'Keep it quiet in there!' and I hear this voice go, 'Fuck you! I just got stabbed with the knife!'"[21]

In the final scene, the camera films a reunited Lulu and Charlie driving out of frame in the station wagon, then turns toward Sister Carol East as she serenades the audience with a reggae-infused version of "Wild Thing." Sister Carol wasn't privy to the world of filmmaking until she arrived on the set for her scene. "At first, I thought he was shooting a documentary," East recalled. However, Jonathan's presence behind the camera dissolved any concerns for her. "There's something about our spirits that connected so much that it felt like we knew each other in a previous life," East said. "We had a special bond that he nor I could explain. There was an angelic, spiritual thing about him telling people what to do with a smile, with that assurance."[22] With Bob Marley's keyboardist, Glen Adams, playing on the track, Sister Carol East's version of "Wild Thing" was the vibrant performance that rounded out *Something Wild*.

Something Wild turns the trope of the road movie on its head. Demme and Frye take the audience out of the claustrophobic and manic energy of New York City on an existential, yet sinister, road trip through suburban America. For Lulu and Charlie, the celebratory promise of the bicentennial becomes the melancholy reality of two diverging roads: the Fifth Avenue security of yuppiedom or a life of crime and excitement. Demme's identification with the character Charlie can be read as autobiographical. It was hard for Jonathan not to see the connection between him and Charlie: two affable, inquisitive, and good-natured men attracted to those living on the edges of deviancy.

Pauline Kael classified *Something Wild* as "a party movie with both a light and dark side."[23] The musical vibrancy of the film didn't shy away from Demme's interpretation of Frye's screwball love story. In his review for the *Chicago Tribune*, Dave Kehr noted Demme's ascent from the shaky grounds of his first Hitchcockian attempt in *Last Embrace*, noting that he managed to outdo Hitchcock in *Something Wild*: "He (Demme) has brought off something Hitchcock tried only once (in the 1969 film *Topaz*), and then, not successfully. He has made a non-linear thriller, in which the descent from order to chaos is made, not just in content, but in form."²⁴

Reflecting on his experience with *Something Wild* in a 2022 email, Jeff Daniels wrote, "Jonathan's enthusiasm for filmmaking was palpable. There was no such thing as a bad idea. 'Try it,' he'd say and go back behind the camera. Didn't matter if he had ten grand or a hundred million, he loved making movies. I can only remember him with a smile on his face."²⁵

Despite the warm embrace of the critics, *Something Wild* wasn't a box office success. Released in almost a thousand theaters on November 7, 1986, the film placed seventh at the box office. Peter Faiman's film *Crocodile Dundee* was riding high on its seventh week at number one. Still, *Something Wild* eventually grossed $8.3 million, which made up for the film's $7 million budget.²⁶

Back in New York City, Demme gathered a cadre of actors, artists, and performers that he would soon collaborate with. In one instance, Demme was in a cab after his car broke down in Manhattan, and while stuck in traffic, the cab driver played a tape of her own compositions. Demme was captivated, and the driver, Q Lazzarus, would appear on the soundtracks of his next three films.²⁷ He collaborated with choreographer Tisha Brown, directing a performance of her piece "Accumulation with Talking Plus Water Motor" on the short-lived PBS series *Alive from Off Center*. Another episode in the series featured artist/actor Spalding Gray in a piece called "A Personal History of the American Theatre."

Hailed by David Letterman as "the WASP Woody Allen," Gray was one of the founding members of the NYC-based theater company the Wooster Group before dipping his toes into the film world.²⁸ The performance space the group occupied on 33 Wooster Street in SoHo would be the stage for Gray's monologue performance piece *Swimming to Cambodia*.

Gray's foray into films came in supporting roles. His voice can be heard at the other end of Sandy McLeod's receiver as the perverted caller in *Variety* (1983). However, it was his role as the US consul in *The Killing Fields*, Roland Joffé's 1984 epic about the ordeal of Cambodian journalist Dith Pran during the reign of Pol Pot after America's withdrawal from Vietnam in 1975, that became the basis for Gray's one-man show *Swimming to Cambodia*. With topics ranging from his complex relationship with his first wife, *Variety* producer Renée Shafransky, to monologues about cocaine-sniffing CIA agents and Bangkok massage parlors, Gray's show became the talk of New York City's performance art contingency, ushering in a wave of artists inspired by his candid, intense, and self-effacing monologues—from Eric Bogosian (*Talk Radio*) to Sandra Bernhard (*Without You, I'm Nothing, with You, I'm Not Much Better*).

Demme frequently attended shows staged by the Wooster Group and the Public Theatre. "I took Jonathan to see Spalding," Sandy recalls, "and we had this relationship with Cinecom, and they were willing to put up the money for *Swimming to Cambodia*." As with *Stop Making Sense*, McLeod would be integral to the process of capturing Gray's show on film. As Sandy remembers, "It was trying to figure out what elements could support the narrative and not be too overwhelming. I was trying to figure out how to do the lighting design more than camera design. It was a painless, three-day shoot."[29] Emulating the light pattern of the fan blades circulating above Martin Sheen's hotel room in *Apocalypse Now* (1979), McLeod's lighting savvy adds pathos to Gray's dialogue on America's involvement in Vietnam and is complemented by lime green and red lights illuminating the stage for Gray's digressions on Bangkok's red-light district.

Swimming to Cambodia was a critical arthouse hit when it was released in 1987 yet was not the financial juggernaut that *Stop Making Sense* had become since its release three years earlier. That didn't stop Jonathan from continuing his journey to create. His energetic nature for creativity fixated on something he wanted more than adulation as a filmmaker; he wanted to be a father. Back in New York, he sensed his relationship with Sandy was unraveling when he told her of his aspirations to be a father.[30] However, it was another love in Jonathan's life that emboldened his decision to toe the line between filmmaking and fatherhood: Haiti.

11

Second Chances (1987–1989)

Returning to New York City after promoting *Something Wild*, Jonathan Demme stopped by Sandy McLeod's SoHo loft; he was amazed by the Haitian decor that adorned her living room. "There was a garage in front of my loft," Sandy said. "Jacqueline Fils-Aimé opened this Haitian painting shop. I said to Jonathan, 'You have to check this shop. The woman who runs it is very nice.'"[1]

In the eighties, New York City was a haven for the thousands who fled Haiti during the reign of François (Papa Doc) Duvalier, who was elected president on a reformist platform before declaring himself president for life in 1964. Haiti had gained independence from colonial rule in 1804, and the country sustained its economy by growing sugarcane and rice. Under Duvalier's authoritarian rulership and violent intimidation carried out by the Tonton Macoutes, Haiti became the antithesis of what Duvalier had promised. When Papa Doc died in 1971, his son Jean-Claude "Baby Doc" Duvalier perpetuated his father's rhetoric and rulership. In May 1984, a pregnant woman was beaten by police at a protest rally in Gonaives, leading to a period of civil unrest, bloodshed, and cries for democratic reform known as the anti-Duvalier movement. As the civil unrest intensified in February 1986, Baby Doc exiled himself to France, leaving Haiti under the rulership of the National Governing Council and Army Commander Henri Namphy.

Second Chances (1987–1989)

Jonathan remembered his first encounter with someone asking to be his friend when he arrived in Port-au-Prince. "Someone who I just met asked me, 'We're friends, right?'" Demme recalled. "And I was thinking to myself, 'I'm an American, I don't even know you. We may eventually become friends.' He said, 'Well, why can't we start as friends?' I couldn't not justify this basic American thing of 'no friends yet, maybe over time.' When you meet Haitian people and you're faced with this instant generosity. I learned so much about myself being there."[2]

For Jonathan, being in Haiti a year before the country held its first democratic election was an enlightening experience. "I'm not saying that I'm a good person," Demme said, "but it made me so better a person; I learned so much about America from going to Haiti. This exceptional idea of democracy, the passion with which everybody I met was anticipating that and working towards that. As an American I thought, 'Wow! These people love the idea of democracy' and the first little, tiny taste they had to turn this whole country on. So, I went home, got a friend who's a filmmaker and we went back and did a documentary down there."[3]

Haiti: Dreams of Democracy was shot by Demme, Sandy McLeod, and South African filmmaker Jo Menell at the peak of the country's anti-Duvalier movement. Beyond the sociocultural impact Haiti had on Jonathan, it made him realize that something was missing in his life. That realization came when Jonathan spent some time walking around Port-Au-Prince, seeing children laughing and dancing on the beach.

Demme's relationship with McLeod ended midway through the shoot. "That's when I broke up with Jonathan," McLeod said. "He left me down there with Jo."[4] As McLeod and Menell finished filming additional footage, Jonathan flew back to New York to edit the film.

Haiti: Dreams of Democracy is an engaging and empowering look at the democratic impact of the post-Duvalier movement. Demme's politics are in the hands of the Haitians talking directly into the camera while waiting in line to cast their ballots and schoolchildren talking about what they would do if they became president of Haiti. It was in Haiti that Jonathan met radio personality Jean Dominique. Taken by his energy behind the microphone at Radio Haiti, Demme would become firm friends with Dominique for the next thirteen years.

In contrast with the inspiring images that Demme and crew captured on camera, a month before the film was released most Haitians had boycotted their own elections due to the corruption evident under Namphy's rule. Despite the pleas for peace and unity made by the newly elected president, Leslie Manigat, his victory underscored the violent actions on November 29, 1987, when the Macoutes attacked voters, killing fifteen people at a polling station in Port-au-Prince.[5] Haiti would be in Jonathan's periphery for the next twenty-nine years.

Martin Scorsese and Demme had offices in the Brill Building. Beyond sharing projects in their editing rooms, they also shared their views on the atrocities in South Africa, leading to the formation of Filmmakers United against Apartheid.[6] They would call on their friends Bernardo Bertolucci and Paul Newman to be involved, with the goal of withholding American films from South Africa until President Frederik Willem de Klerk ended the ban on the African National Congress and released Nelson Mandela.

Flying back from Haiti with his growing art collection, Demme indulged in his other passion: the theater. Like his collection of Masonic prints, Demme's circle of friends started to grow. After standing in for Ron Vawter in a production of *Brace Up*, Paul Lazar had become a mainstay of the Wooster Group. He and his wife, choreographer and cofounder of the Big Dance Theatre, Annie-B Parson, immediately had a friend in Demme when they met in 1986. "We knew each other when we were dating our wives-to-be," Lazar said. "Joanne and Annie were roommates, and Joanne took Jonathan to a play I was in that my wife codirected and choreographed. Afterwards, the four of us became lifelong friends."[7]

A Syracuse graduate, artist Joanne Howard designed sets for the Big Dance Theatre, touring with the troupe in Europe after their successful run at the Brooklyn Academy of Music. It was Tony Fitzpatrick, who designed the poster art for *Something Wild*, who introduced Joanne to Jonathan.[8] Unlike in his past romances, Jonathan was involved with someone outside of the film industry; it was refreshing for him to be with someone who wasn't working on his movies. Howard's artwork would find a home at Demme's Clinica Estetico office, framed along with the Haitian canvases and Marcus Garvey posters that covered the walls.

Not long after their courtship, Jonathan and Joanne married in the summer of 1987. In January 1988, they welcomed their first child into the world, Ramona. For Demme, the joy of fatherhood was more of a thrill than being behind the camera. As he told Fred Schruers of *Rolling Stone* magazine, "I had probably thought, without a lot of remorse or anything, I'd miss the boat—and wasn't that interesting, one of those people who never will have a kid. And then suddenly this comes into my life. You get a great thrill out of making a picture, but . . ." Schruers noted how Demme "sweeps a hand and does one of his big-eyed takes to show his contentment."[9]

Jonathan's marriage to Joanne seemed like providence when he was attached to direct *Married to the Mob*. From a screenplay by Barry Strugatz and Mark Burns, the film focuses on Angela DeMarco, the widow of Long Island hitman Frank "the Cucumber" DeMarco. Before her husband was killed by his boss and father figure, Tony "the Tiger" Russo, Angela was living in depression, uncertain if the police or undertaker would be at her front door. Frank's death and Tony's unwanted advances signal a chance for Angela and her son to start over, living in a decrepit apartment on the Lower East Side. Little does she know that she is under surveillance by FBI Agent Mike Downey, with whom she falls in love when their paths cross as he's bugging her apartment. Angela finds solace working as an assistant at Hello, Gorgeous!, a beauty salon run by a Jamaican woman who befriends her. In Jonathan's eyes, the script had themes he'd been looking for since his days at New World Pictures: women finding independence from phony masculine men and a Black woman saving a white woman from a perilous existence.

Additionally, Demme's childhood connections to Long Island and Miami made his eyes widen with delight when reading the script.

For Strugatz and Burns, it was a dream come true having Demme direct their screenplay. "Before all this happened, we went out to LA to pitch five different low-budget films shot like AIP, Corman films," Burns recalled. "We knew his body of work since *Caged Heat*, so it was legendary for us."[10] By March 1986, the duo visited Demme's office, conducting the first in a series of rewrites of the script.

Matthew Modine would play Downey. Having delivered acclaimed performances in Harold Becker's *Vision Quest* (1985), Stanley Kubrick's *Full Metal Jacket* (1987), and Alan J. Pakula's *Orphans* (1987), Modine had a quality that Demme saw as reminiscent of Jimmy Stewart. "I met Jonathan at a Chinese restaurant on Sunset Boulevard," Modine said. "I know it was during the preproduction period of his film. At that time, he had already cast his principal actors, and we met at the restaurant because he was trying to talk me into playing the role of the FBI agent. I already had passed on the role a couple of times. He thought if we met, I might change my mind. Obviously, it's very flattering when a director of Demme's stature, character and ability wants you for their film."[11]

Initially, Jessica Lange was approached to play Angela DeMarco before her pregnancy took her out of the running. However, Mike Medavoy saw Michelle Pfeiffer as the mob wife who strikes out on her own. "If I feel strongly about something," Medavoy said, "I will try to convince others. That being said, I'm not going to tell a director who to cast in a movie and find out that he's upset about it, and he can't work with the actor. I'm not the guy saying, 'Action!' and 'Cut.' You can't convince someone to direct an actor they don't want."[12]

Michelle Pfeiffer began her career as a beauty pageant queen from Orange County, California, before she landed roles in *Grease 2* (Patricia Birch, 1982) and *Scarface* (Brian De Palma, 1983). She had just finished shooting *The Witches of Eastwick* (George Miller, 1987) in Massachusetts opposite Cher, Susan Sarandon, and Jack Nicholson, but Pfeiffer had yet to find a role where she played an independent woman. Demme and Pfeiffer had briefly met on the set of John

Second Chances (1987–1989)

Landis's *Into the Night* back in 1984, and he revisited her films when casting *Married to the Mob*. "She's been excellent in everything she's done and none of it has begun to test the waters," Demme said. "I think she's amazing and can hold her own against anybody."[13]

Initially apprehensive about being a lead in a romantic comedy, Pfeiffer credited Demme for his ceaseless encouragement. "I loved Angela. I was so excited for Jonathan to take a chance on me playing this Long Island housewife with the accent," Pfeiffer said. "Why would he think I could do that?"[14] Jonathan enlisted his nephew Ted, an aspiring filmmaker who would cocreate the music video program *Yo! MTV Raps* (MTV, 1988–1995), to drive the actress around Long Island while Pfeiffer tape-recorded conversations with his friends throwing out slang in their Long Island accents.[15]

Demme saw something unique in casting Pfeiffer and Modine in a comedy. As with Melanie Griffith and Jeff Daniels, a screwball romance between an upstanding citizen and a woman with a wild past seemed like the perfect combination for an entertaining movie. Tony "the Tiger" Russo was a character that demanded an actor who possessed charm and humor and could be immersed into the role: Dean Stockwell had all those qualities.

Despite memorable performances in Wim Wenders's *Paris, Texas* (1984) and David Lynch's *Blue Velvet* (1986), Stockwell got his real estate license and wanted to settle down in New Mexico with his family.[16] Mike Medavoy convinced him to read the script by focusing on the humor of the story. Stockwell couldn't stop laughing and started to develop the gangster's seductive and charming timbre. During the shoot, Stockwell reportedly stayed in character even when he was smoking Cuban cigars.

Rounding out the cast was Paul Lazar as Tony's muscle, Tommy, and Mercedes Ruehl, a mainstay at the New York Public Theatre, as the animated and paranoid Connie Russo, the jealous wife who suspects Tony has been unfaithful to her. Although she had a brief, yet unforgettable, role in *Something Wild*, Sister Carol East played Dottie, the owner of Hello, Gorgeous!, who hires Angela before the two become best friends.

THERE'S NO GOING BACK

Jonathan assembled his cadre of creative friends: Tak Fujimoto as cinematographer; Ed Saxon, Ron Bozman, and Kenneth Utt as producers. Another key figure in Jonathan's career would be *Married to the Mob*'s production designer, Kristi Zea. Starting off as a commercial stylist before working as a costume designer for Alan Parker (*Fame, Shoot the Moon*) and James L. Brooks's 1983 Oscar-winning film, *Terms of Endearment*, Zea had a keen eye for making sets come alive, which was evident when she entered Jonathan's office with a series of books by Amy Arbus and William Eggleston. "There was a furniture store on Grand Street," Zea said, "and inside the store were floors of furniture that were all these very eccentric lacquered-styled furniture, which I used like crazy in both *Married to the Mob* and *Goodfellas*. That store catered to a lot of the people that *Married to the Mob* had in it; whether it was the Long Island look or the Italian look, it just blended into this crazy aesthetic that we came up with in the film that also included the hair by Alan D'Angerio and Colleen Atwood's costumes. Everything to do with Michelle Pfeiffer's look just embellished what we were also doing physically."[17]

When the audience is first introduced to Angela DeMarco, Charles Napier is perming her hair in a Long Island hair salon. Pfeiffer's trademark gold locks are tucked under a raven bouffant wig designed by Alan D'Angerio. Numb to the gaudy and extravagant lifestyle of her fellow mob-wife friends, Angela finds comfort in raising her son despite the inevitable fear of violence or incarceration. Her pleas for a divorce from Frank are met with gaslighting ("Go upstairs, take a Valium, and lie down") while he has a lethal assignation with a waitress who happens to be Tony's mistress.

Although the film is a campy precursor to Martin Scorsese's 1990 crime saga *Goodfellas*, Demme's acute eye for detail was present. Bill Todman Jr. sensed this verisimilitude when he made his first visit to the set of the supermarket where Mercedes Ruehl angrily breaks a package of eggs in front of Michelle Pfeiffer. "I looked at Kenny Utt," recalls Todman Jr., "and said, 'Wow, this film is being done on a budget, but this entire store is filled with extras!' Because everyone is all in costume, dressed to the nines. Kenny turned to me and said, 'Okay, we're shooting in this aisle, but the rest of the store are all the people who live in this town.'"[18]

The collective excitement was felt on Suffolk Street, where Zea's design turned a public school gymnasium into the Caribbean club for Mike and Angela's date. Demme hired the eleven-piece samba band Pe De Boi as the club's band. As the music's tempo progressed, the cast and crew started to dance while Demme and Tak Fujimoto circled the camera around Pfeiffer and Modine. In between setups, laughs were shared with Michelle Pfeiffer while Matthew Modine asked Carol about reggae music. "Jonathan held that glue to make everyone on the set feel like family," Sister Carol East said.[19]

Beyond the set crew feeling like a family affair, Demme sought creative counsel from his wife, Joanne, when he was deciding to shoot the scene where Angela invites Mike back to her apartment. Initially, the scene would end with them having sex after a tear-ridden Angela is consoled by Mike after Connie barges in on them, assuming she was fooling around with Tony. When Modine and Pfeiffer read the scene, they felt that the sex should be cut so that, as they are about to be intimate the next morning, Downey's partner would again interrupt them, reminding him that he was investigating her.

"I brought this up to Demme a couple days before we filmed the scene," Modine said, "and Demme disagreed—strongly. Demme felt they should make love that night. Period. I believe I lobbied my idea with Michelle, but she didn't want to take sides. So I pushed on with Demme, and it wasn't until the very day we set up to film the scene that he came around to seeing it my way. Demme said he had talked to his wife about the scene, and she agreed that I would have been taking advantage of Angela at a moment when she was so vulnerable and emotionally broken. So it's really Ms. Demme I'm grateful for."[20]

Angela agrees to cooperate with the FBI when she seduces Tony in his office. He buys her a plane ticket to accompany him to a mob summit in Miami, while Mike acts as the eyes for the FBI's sting operation. In the original screenplay, Angela, Tony, and Mike have a chase sequence through the Florida Everglades with tigers running around. For budgetary concerns and safety, the climactic fight was shot in the same room where Hubert Humphrey had awaited the results of the 1968 presidential election. Demme needed, in Kenneth Utt's words, "a second set of eyes," if not for the set designs, then for staging the scene. "In desperation over lunch one day," said Kristi Zea, "I created this little whiteboard model of this space, and I basically told him how it should be shot going from the point where Tony's wife shows up, and what ensues thereafter had to be choreographed. To do that, I basically had to tell Jonathan how it should be shot."[21]

A psychotic and emotionally stunned Connie Russo tracks Tony to his honeymoon suite wielding a handgun and firing off rounds as Tony tries to calm her down. His pleas for clemency fall on deaf ears as she aims the gun at Tony's pants. Before she pulls the trigger, the camera holds a tight shot on Angela winding up her fist to knock out Connie, a visual nod to the beginning of Samuel Fuller's *The Naked Kiss* (1964). Before he runs out the door with his wounded cronies, Tony is greeted by the FBI as Mike tells him he's under arrest.

Married to the Mob ends with Sister Carol East smiling at the camera after Angela accepts Mike's apology for lying to her about being an undercover agent. However, Demme and editor Craig McKay felt the footage that didn't make it into the movie should be shown during the ending credit sequence. "I was talking with Kenny Utt," McKay said, "and he was pissed off at me saying, 'I could've saved myself two-and-a-half million dollars!' Somehow, that got mixed up with Kenny's feelings and Jonathan's feelings. It was kind of like it was in the air, and Jonathan probably pushed it. I created an end section with all the outtakes of the movie."[22]

The outtakes of Dodie Demme playing the grieving mother throwing herself onto Frank's coffin and Dean Stockwell and Nancy Travis in the Roman-themed motel room with the words *Veni, Veni, Veni* (I came, I came, I came) etched above the waterbed made their way into the credits. One outtake nearly broke Michelle Pfeiffer's neck: a scene when she and Modine dance on the steps of a New York courthouse. She leans back onto the stair rail, falling headfirst until Modine catches her before her head meets with the pavement.

In a freeze-frame, the end credits reveal Jorobado, the Clinica Estetico mascot, along with the motto of the Mozambique Liberation Front, *A Luta Continua*. "It was an encoded message to the black people of South Africa that were going to segregated cinemas," Demme explained. "We put it on there, because that was our way of protesting against segregated cinemas." First spotted in *Something Wild*, the motto would appear in the credits of Demme's films up until *Philadelphia*, when the Mozambique Liberation Front and the right-wing Mozambican National Resistance signed a peace accord in October 1992.[23]

Fresh from his Oscar win for co-scoring *The Last Emperor* (1987), David Byrne composed the funky synth-xylophone-sax score for *Married to the Mob*. As he told *Rolling Stone* about Demme, "He delivers everything with a large dose of sugar. Then he slips in whatever criticism or whatever might be more unpleasant. His enthusiasm is contagious. I'm by nature less outwardly enthusiastic, and it's nice to catch a little bit of that from Jonathan."[24] Subsequently, Demme tipped his hat to Bertolucci with his homage to *The Spider Stratagem* (1970) and *The Conformist* (1970) with the red-lit canted tracking shot of Dean Stockwell ascending the staircase to the motel.

As with most of his films, Demme would rely on Gary Goetzman to supervise the music for the soundtrack. His musical alter ego, Guido Paonessa, makes an appearance behind the piano of the medieval restaurant, serenading Tony. Additionally, Goetzman's jingle for Burger World restaurant can be heard on the radio in Angela's house and sung by Tony and Tommy before they are assassinated by Chris Isaak. Besides Isaak, whose song is featured in the end credits, Demme's love affair with the New York punk / new wave scene carried over to casting David Johansen, lead singer of the New York Dolls, as the priest conducting Frank's funeral service and when he directed Debbie Harry's music video for "Liar, Liar."

THERE'S NO GOING BACK

Released to theaters nationwide on August 19, 1988, *Married to the Mob* made just over $5 million in its first week at the box office and would eventually gross $21.4 million during its six-week run—not bad for a film budgeted at $10 million. In her review of *Married to the Mob* for the *Washington Post*, Rita Kempley cited Michelle Pfeiffer's performance as "the pivotal role of the movie and perhaps of her career. . . . Shedding her WASP identity completely, Pfeiffer becomes the Italian princess, right down to the Long Island accent. Angela is an updated suburban moll, a gum-popper with press-on nails and lots of sweaters appliqued with feathers. She looks like a caricature, but there's anguish under all that mascara."[25] Roger Ebert compared the film to *Something Wild* but wrote that "Demme enacts his own theme about second chances by bringing a less threatening attitude to bear on the same basic story. The results are very good—far better and funnier than most of what is being made these days."[26] Ebert might have been referring to the slasher film *A Nightmare on Elm Street 4: The Dream Master* (Renny Harlin, 1988), as it was the top placeholder during *Married to the Mob*'s theatrical run.

Demme's fixation with Haiti was evident in the soundtrack to *Married to the Mob*. On a further listen to the music piping from the Hello, Gorgeous! salon near the ending of *Married to the Mob*, one can hear the music of Les Freres Parents, the blind musical brothers featured in *Haiti: Dreams of Democracy*. During the postproduction period of *Married to the Mob*, Jonathan traveled back down to Haiti, researching the importation of American pigs coinciding with the expansion of US business on the island since Duvalier's ouster. He would read Russell Banks's *Continental Drift*, determined to turn his story about Haitian migrants living in Florida into an epic.

Demme took a step further in his musical romance with Haiti by producing the compilation album *KONBIT: Burning Rhythms of Haiti* when Les Freres Parents visited the Clinica Estetico offices. "Clarke, Alan, and their exceptional sister Claire visited our office in New York to discuss the possibility of making a video for one of the great new songs they have written," Demme wrote in the album's liner notes. "The idea of making an album like KONBIT came to life during that meeting along with an agreement to figure out a way to get a Freres Parents video."[27]

In early April 1988, while researching the pig trade and shooting the Neville Brothers and Freres Parents' video for their song "My Blood," Demme was close to the splintered divide left by General Namphy's egregious use of military force and the inevitable coup in Haiti. "We were supposed to return to the states the following morning," Demme wrote, "but on Sunday night munitions units of the fractured Haitian army initiated a full tilt coup attempt against the beleaguered military leadership and turned the country upside down once again." Jonathan spent the next two days in Haiti patiently waiting to fly home as the violence intensified. "By Wednesday," Demme said, "the situation had calmed to the extent that the airport reopened. We Americans were free to leave the frightening situation behind ... a situation of perpetual fear, insecurity and profound struggle that defines the ongoing lifestyle of the overwhelming majority of Haitian people who remain trapped in the turmoil of their own tortured homeland."[28]

Recording at Sea-Saint Studios in New Orleans, Jonathan was mesmerized by the cultural melting pot of the Crescent City and his friendship with the Neville Brothers, which would play a significant role later in his career. "The next thing I know," Demme said, "I was in New Orleans with the Neville Brothers helping make a video for another of their great songs, 'Sister Rosa.' Cyril Neville, as important a lay scholar on historical and contemporary matters of race as exists today in America, got very excited about the potential of the KONBIT project. Cyril's brothers Charles, Aaron and Art shared Cyril's enthusiasm as did A&M Records, the Neville's recording label."[29] Although the album didn't raise as much money as USA for Africa or Band Aid, *KONBIT* did gain solid reviews and became a personal favorite of fellow New Yorker Lou Reed, who called it the best album of 1989.[30]

With *Married to the Mob* out in theaters, Demme revived his aspiring horror music movie, *The Night of the Living Feelies*, when he contacted the band to shoot the music video for their single

"Away" from their third album, *Only Life*. In quirky, Corman-esque fashion, the Feelies perform to a sold-out audience of mutated zombies at Maxwell's in Hoboken, New Jersey. Operating the camera would be Demme's creative confidant for the next twenty-seven years, Declan Quinn.

After his return from New Orleans, Jonathan, Joanne, and their infant daughter, Ramona, left the intensity of Manhattan for the peaceful ruggedness of Nyack. For Joanne, it was a pleasant area for raising the family and delving into her artwork not far from the home of Edward Hopper. Jonathan was struck by Rockland County's Haitian population, its revered school system, and the artistic vibrancy Nyack had to offer his family. However, the peace and joy of Jonathan's newfound fatherhood would be interrupted by the screaming of farm animals—not the Haitian pigs, but lambs.

12
Dinner with Friends (1990–1992)

The eighties ended on an optimistic note for Jonathan Demme, both personally and professionally: he was a devoted husband and father, and he and Joanne settled in Nyack on the Hudson River. Joanne would look after Ramona and paint in her studio, while Jonathan would spend his days driving to and from the Clinica Estetico offices in Times Square. His partnership with Orion Pictures gave Demme the opportunity to not only direct but also produce films that fit his aesthetic of entertaining, feminist-based stories. However, Demme was restless; he still wanted to make a film that would be a runaway success. As he told a reporter for *People* magazine, "I'm still waiting for my *Terms of Endearment*."[1]

The Silence of the Lambs, by Thomas Harris, was developed as a six-year project for the Associated Press crime reporter. The novel focuses on Clarice Starling, an FBI cadet picked by her mentor, Special Agent Jack Crawford, to find serial killer Buffalo Bill. The plan is to seek advice from another serial murderer, the renowned psychiatrist Hannibal "the Cannibal" Lecter. The book had originally been optioned by Dino De Laurentiis to adapt with Gene Hackman starring.[2] Hackman had dropped out of the project, Orion picked up the option, and Mike Medavoy sought out Demme to direct. Playwright Ted Tally had been working on the script when it was still with De Laurentiis; Orion kept him on to complete it.

When Demme read Ted Tally's script, he envisioned *The Silence of the Lambs* as not just a suspense film. In fact, he was intrigued by the feminist theme underlying the story. "Ever since my days working with Roger Corman, and perhaps before that, I've been a sucker for a woman's picture," Demme said. "A film with a woman protagonist at the forefront. A woman in jeopardy. A woman on a mission. These are themes that have tremendous appeal to me as a moviegoer, and, as a director."[3]

Another experience that stuck with Demme was when he took his daughter along birdwatching. With astute curiosity, Ramona noticed a lifeless bird along the Tappan Zee River. Demme told children's author Maurice Sendak the anecdote at a party, to which he replied, "Adults just don't give children credit for their ability to look at and accept almost anything, especially the great mysteries of life. They're always ready to question them and to begin the amazing process of trying to learn something about them over the course of a lifetime."[4] Revisiting Tally's script for *The Silence of the Lambs*, Demme sensed that the connection to Clarice Starling was hitting close to home.

After their successful collaboration on *Married to the Mob*, Demme wanted Michelle Pfeiffer to play Clarice Starling; Pfeiffer read the script and was horrified by the violence. So was Meg Ryan. But Jodie Foster was game after reading the book, even before it landed at Orion. Foster had grown tired of playing victims, like her role as a prostitute in Martin Scorsese's *Taxi Driver* (1976) and her most recent Oscar-winning performance as the rape victim in Jonathan Kaplan's *The Accused* (1988). Demme wasn't so sure she was right for the role, but she was determined and flew from Los Angeles to New York City to meet with him in person.

"She said, 'Listen, I know that you're seeing other people,'" Demme recalled, "'and I just wanted to have the opportunity to tell you that I love this book so much, and I love this part so much.'" Foster told Demme that Harris's book was unusual as the main character was a young woman: "'Clarice is faced with the overwhelming obstacle of all these asshole men; they may be brilliant assholes, but everywhere she turns, she's faced with this."[5]

Demme had his eyes set on Laura Dern. Her arresting presence, steely-blue eyes, and intensity caught Demme when he saw her in David Lynch's *Blue Velvet* (1986). "She was just it! I knew from the moment that Laura came in," Demme said. He was captivated by Dern, who balanced the vulnerability and determination of Harris's protagonist. "Then, the folks at Orion they were like, 'Jonathan, we're really worried about that in the context of Jodie Foster, who won an Oscar, who everybody loves, and she's desperate to do this. Please meet Jodie one more time.'"[6] Jonathan thought back to his initial meeting with Foster and their shared enthusiasm over the feminist critique Tally captured in the script. They had also agreed that Hannibal Lecter should be played by a European actor, one who wouldn't overshadow the story with an immersive, Stanislavsky-inspired performance. Demme was moved by Foster's determination, and when he saw her walking down the hall to his office for this second meeting, he realized Foster was his Clarice Starling. He dubbed the film a Strong Heart Production after Foster's earnestness in landing the role.

Humanity, intelligence, and horror were the characteristics Demme saw in Hannibal Lecter when he read the book; Demme believed the actor who would embody these conflicting traits of Hannibal Lecter was Anthony Hopkins. "I felt convinced that Anthony Hopkins would be the best Dr. Lecter imaginable," Demme recalled, "especially coming from his performance as the kindly doctor in David Lynch's *The Elephant Man* (1980). In addition to having to radiate tremendous brilliance, and Hopkins certainly does that—you take one look at his face and see this is someone of superior intelligence—he should also radiate tremendous humanity."[7] The Welsh-born actor studied under the tutelage of Laurence Olivier when he attended the Royal Academy of Dramatic Arts before making his on-screen debut opposite Peter O'Toole and Katharine Hepburn in *A Lion in Winter* (1968), executive produced by Demme's former Avco / Embassy Pictures boss, Joseph Levine.

THERE'S NO GOING BACK

Demme originally had his sights on Trey Wilson for the role of FBI Agent Jack Crawford. Sadly, Wilson died of a cerebral hemorrhage before production, and Demme called in Scott Glenn, whom he had worked with on *Fighting Mad*. Several actors with props showed up at the casting office delivering hammy performances in auditions for the role of Buffalo Bill. Then Ted Levine, a tall midwestern actor, came in, shocking Demme the same way Ray Liotta had during casting for *Something Wild*. "I was like everybody in the room," Brooke Smith recalled. "Before going in to read, Ted was Ted: charming, supportive. When he was in the room, I couldn't describe it. My initial thought was, 'If everybody acted like this, I would be out of a job!' It was like he became Buffalo Bill. Afterwards when the cast said thank you, he became himself again. He had a ball with it."[8]

Brooke Smith, who would play the kidnapped daughter of Tennessee senator Ruth Martin, got some advice from friend and fellow actor, Vincent D'Onofrio, when she was told she would have to put on weight for her performance. "He had just done *Full Metal Jacket* and had to gain eighty pounds," Smith said. "Vincent told me, 'It costs money. You need them to pay for your food.'" Orion gave Smith a credit card to pay for her meals. "I always joke about how Orion went under because they had to pay for my food." She laughed. "While shooting on location, I would take Ted out to dinner every night."[9]

With the cast assembled, Demme took them to the FBI Training Academy in Quantico, Virginia, where they received a crash course in the Behavioral Science Unit from FBI Agent John Douglas. Scott Glenn was reduced to tears when looking at the accompanying crime scene photos while Douglas played him an audio recording of a woman being murdered. "It took months during the preproduction process to get over being appalled at the subject matter," Demme said. "By the time it came to film it, I was happily desensitized, to the degree that I could go out and just do it with great gusto and abandon."[10]

Dinner with Friends (1990–1992)

On November 15, 1989, cameras rolled on the first day of shooting *The Silence of the Lambs*.[11] Initially, the opening sequence was going to feature a SWAT team quelling a terrorist attack before one of the FBI instructors looks into the camera, saying, "This is just a drill." However, it was decided at the last minute that having Jodie Foster run the academy's obstacle course would be an exemplary introduction to Clarice Starling. The scene also featured actual signage posted throughout the course by the academy on the Northern Red Oaks: "Hurt, agony, pain—love it!"

After the first two weeks of shooting, the crew flew to Pittsburgh. The city was the perfect replica for Maryland, Ohio, Tennessee, and Illinois. Rick McMasters, the proprietor of the Grand Concourse restaurant and a member of the Pittsburgh Film Board, had shared an understanding with Demme ever since he scouted the area for *Something Wild*: if the crew was in town scouting locations, he would host lunch at his restaurant. When word came to McMasters that Demme loved oysters, he had the chef make up a table-sized platter of thirteen different varieties of oysters. Though hamburgers were his preferred meal on the go, Demme tended toward food as exotic as his tastes in clothes and music.[12]

Production designer Kristi Zea was just coming off work on *Goodfellas*, one of Martin Scorsese's most explicitly violent films. However, she was shocked after reading the script for *The Silence of the Lambs*. She called Demme: "I don't know if I can do this, Jonathan. This book gave me the creeps! What if someone commits copycat crimes based on this story?"[13] Jonathan convinced Zea that they were making a feminist film, not a horror movie, and she signed on as production designer and head of second-unit photography.

Designing Lecter's cell was of the utmost importance to Demme. In Harris's book, Lecter is in a caged cell sheathed by a mesh curtain displaying his pernicious silhouette. Ever since *Caged Heat*, Demme had had an aversion to the claustrophobic and critically impinging aspects of shooting people through rows of bars. "He wanted the camera to be able to move around without any obstacles between the camera and the person. That was a real challenge because we had different kinds of wire, bars of all sizes and shapes, and hardware cloth," Zea explained, "Ultimately, that concept was nixed. We could take away the back wall of Lecter's cell in order to have camera positions. These were things we could do on a soundstage and not in a prison."[14]

In setting up the scene in which Clarice first encounters Lecter, Jonathan told Zea, "I want people to know there's something between them, but I want it to be seamless and not keep us from understanding the proximity that you can have between a prisoner and Clarice." The two of them reread the second chapter of the book. "They would've created some form of barrier," Zea said, "that would have been impossible for him to reach out and get to somebody. I started thinking of all these liquor stores and taxi drivers that had this shield between the driver and the passenger. We tried that out, and Jonathan loved it."[15] When the sound man, Christopher Newman, asked Zea and Demme how Clarice and Hannibal would hear each other, they drilled holes at the top of the plexiglass.

They scouted the 1910 Victorian house used for exterior shots of Gumb's home an hour south of Pittsburgh in the town of Perryopolis. Gumb's house is a hoarder's paradise with sewing equipment, fried food containers, and moths flying throughout the room. Kristi Zea had viewed Frank Scherschel's photos of Ed Gein's house for *Life Magazine* and noticed its striking resemblance to Norman Bates's house overlooking the Bates Motel. The photos of the Plainfield, Wisconsin, home in which Gein's victims' body parts were uncovered by police in November 1957 were of special interest to Zea when she designed Buffalo Bill's house: "I instantly picked up on a photo of the kitchen. It was just being the most unbelievably filthy, hoarders-styled kitchen, which is replicated in Jamie Gumb's kitchen. You see a couple of angles of it, but we took that idea from Ed Gein's biography."[16]

Hopkins and Foster barely saw each other until the cameras rolled. The noise of the Makita drill drowned out the actors waving hello before taking their places. It took fifteen minutes to lock

Hopkins in his cell in between setups. When cameras rolled, Foster was not directly looking at the lens as she reacted to Lecter's scathing tongue-lashing. After Lecter slams the iron slot containing Starling's questionnaire, the camera turns to the left, shifting Foster's gaze into a point-of-view shot. Bela Lugosi, the Romanian actor who horrified audiences with his titular performance in *Dracula* (1931), entered Hopkins's subconscious as he slithered his tongue at the camera, recalling how he ate a census taker's liver with fava beans and chianti.

After Catherine Martin is captured by Buffalo Bill à la Ted Bundy's ploy of luring women into his van, she is imprisoned in a twenty-foot hole reminiscent of Gary Heidnik's basement. A reverse Steadicam shot reveals the nude killer sitting at his sewing machine, the sound drowning out Catherine's screams, along with flying moths and Colin Newman's alternative/industrial-rock song "Alone" blaring in the cavernous basement. Similar to the dynamic of *Married to the Mob*, Zea worked in direct collaboration with Tak Fujimoto and Demme. "Jonathan was always asking me how I thought scenes should be shot," Zea said. "That was part of his working style. He would lean heavily on me and Tak to come up with the necessary visual interpretation of the scene. If he didn't like it, he could change it. He would say to us repeatedly, 'Okay, this is great. How would you do this? How do we shoot this?'"[17]

One of the more unusual challenges was wrangling the moths to fly around Buffalo Bill's cavernous space. "We would put a tiny monofilament around one of the moths and then attach it to the light so it would swing around the light in a specific way," Zea said. "We were bringing these tiny heaters in, and they weren't doing anything. The paint was freezing. Everything was a headache. As soon as those moths and actors came in, boy, did we get bigger heaters!"[18]

To get to the state of claustrophobic terror the character Catherine Martin must feel in the pit as she is desperately crying for help, Brooke Smith shut herself into her parents' closet for hours. "I couldn't pretend the crew wasn't there," Smith said, "so I went into some deep psychological mindfuck game of 'These people aren't helping me. They're exploiting me.'" In one of many hair-raising scenes, Buffalo Bill, perched over the edge of the pit, orders Catherine to put a bottle of body lotion in a basket after moisturizing herself in front of him. The camera points up the blood-stained walls of the well to where she spots Frederica Bimmel's fingernail embedded in the cement and screams in shock. "At the time, I was very insecure and young remembering feeling that things couldn't have been good enough," Smith said. "But Jonathan was like, 'We definitely got it! I'm not going to move on until we got it!' It would make me go as far as I could and trusted him that we must've gotten it and moved on."[19]

Before Lecter is transferred to Memphis to deliver the identity of Catherine's kidnapper to Senator Martin, he divulges clues to Clarice about the Buffalo Bill case but only if she reveals to him her closely guarded childhood traumas. Demme recalled how he and Fujimoto mastered the subjective camera shots. "Tak was very concerned about when Jodie told her story as she's transported back to the past losing all visual references for where she actually is," Demme said.

> As the camera pushes in on her, it goes so tight you can't see much anymore. In addition to that, he dropped out all the fill lighting in the room and that was one of those things where Tak would come over to me every ten minutes or so and say, "Do you think we should drop out all the light and go surreal or keep it the way it is and trust the push in?" and I go, "Gosh, I'm not sure Tak!" He'd say, "Okay" and walk away and probably asked me two or three more times, then finally just went ahead and did it.[20]

With music representing action as a storytelling device, Demme employs Johann Sebastian Bach's "The Goldberg Variations" to play on Lecter's tape recorder as his last violent actions ensue. "The music lulls the audience into a sense of relaxation before the surprise emerges," editor Craig McKay said. "I did that with Howard Shore (who scored the film). When the 'Variations' reaches the tonic, I cut it so Howard could come in with that hard introduction. It was a combination of cutting the music and Howard scoring to that moment."²¹ Demme considered the process of filming Lecter's violent escape a fun day on set. Even Hopkins felt the easygoing vibe when he imitated Sylvester Stallone's Rocky Balboa in takes left on the cutting room floor with Demme's cackling laughter heard out of frame.²²

As the police and SWAT team enter the courthouse searching for Lecter, they see Charles Napier's bloody, disemboweled body draped and hoisted by tricolor banners with the silhouette of an eagle, not only a nod to Francis Bacon's 1954 painting "Figure with Meat" but also a reminder of the symbolic association between psychopathy and America's history built on violence. "In the cage in Memphis," Zea said, "we had a whole rock 'n' roll scaffolding system put up over the cage in a deliberate way because the notion would be that Lecter had no privacy whatsoever."²³ The overpowering backlights surrounding the hanging body give a visual aesthetic akin to a rock concert, but the reverse zoom on Napier's body synched with Howard Shore's booming E-minor chord is as horrific as Norman Bates stabbing Marion Crane in the shower to the sound of Bernard Herrmann's E-natural strings in Alfred Hitchcock's *Psycho* (1960).

The lead-up to the raid on Gumb's house is a prime example of how Craig McKay's parallel editing magnified the suspense: it cuts from Catherine Martin screaming for help as the doorbell rings to when Clarice ends up on the killer's doorstep. "Some directors will shoot straight through the action, and when you cut it later," McKay explained, "you need to break up the action so that you can play with the other characters. Sometimes, they don't stop; they just go right through it. Very often, you have to split an action up so you can extend it. In that particular sequence, we shot it that way. Things weren't broken up so much; they were shot linearly. When I looked at the dailies in, I said to myself 'This scene needs to be parallel cut.'" During the third day of editing the sequence, McKay was frustrated over the scene not being completely spliced to perfection until he saw some film hanging by the editing machine: "I looked across the room at my trim bin and saw a shot hanging. I looked over at the shot, and that's what I needed—when Crawford comes in, and the camera zoom on him."²⁴

Clarice's point of view is unflinching when she sees the torn map of America with arrows indicating the location of Gumb's victims and is greeted by the chilling sounds of The Fall's "Hip Priest" blaring from the basement. When Clarice opens the doors revealing Gumb's unfinished skin suit and the presence of a decayed corpse in the bathtub, the shock was felt on the set when the mayor of Pittsburgh made an impromptu visit. "She shows up in the small area where Mrs. Lippman is buried in the tub and lets out a pure scream of horror," Zea said. "Everybody laughed! We even had 'Gumb the Game.' Art Director Tim Galvin created this board game in the style of Chutes and Ladders going down into the briny depths of the basement."[25]

Shot in the abandoned GM factory, the scene has Clarice drawing her gun at Gumb, starting an intense showdown that would take over twenty hours to shoot. "Punch-drunk" is how Jodie Foster described the day's work.[26] "Put your hands on your hips!" she says into the camera before she laughs off her gaffe. The sequence in which Clarice saves Catherine Martin after gunning down Gumb recalls Demme's New World Pictures roots and his desire to tell stories about women saving other women. The last day of the Pittsburgh shoot concluded as the sun rose over the Youghiogheny River. The band that was expected to play for the wrap party was sleeping in their van.[27]

The final scenes were shot on the Bimini Islands in the Bahamas. From a payphone, a tan Lecter in a Panama hat and white suit congratulates Starling on solving the case and graduating from the academy, then walks off trailing Dr. Chilton on vacation like Joseph Cotten in Hitchcock's *Shadow of a Doubt* (1943). Like Hitchcock, Demme and his wife made cameos as a couple on vacation nearly bumping into Hannibal. Beyond his salute to Hitchcock, Demme's ending in Bimini was a fitting tribute to his father, who started his publicity career writing about the Cat Cays Islands fifty years earlier. As far as Demme and the crew were concerned, the film was done, and they spent the next several days basking in the glow of the island sun before flying back to America. Shortly after, Jonathan and Joanne had their second child, Brooklyn Demme.

Dinner with Friends (1990–1992)

When Jonathan was sitting with Craig McKay in the editing room sifting through the footage, Demme told his trusted editor to always keep the audience guessing. Little did Demme know that his first blockbuster film would be a divining rod into the cultural split between homosexual and heterosexual America. After a screening in San Francisco, it was reported in the *Los Angeles Times* that two women refused to leave the movie theater until they were escorted to their car. Beyond the screams of shock came violent threats hurled from the audience at the screen when Clarice chases after Jamie Gumb: "Kill the faggot!" Before writing her review of the film for *Outweek* magazine, Monica Dorenkamp entered a theater and saw "HOMOPHOBIC SHIT" scrawled in magic marker across the film's poster.[28]

The controversy surrounding the film began at Vito Russo's funeral service in December 1990, when playwright/activist Larry Kramer went from honoring the author of *The Celluloid Closet* and cofounder of the Gay and Lesbian Alliance against Defamation (GLAAD) to an angry diatribe about the film before its nationwide release. Eventually, there were reported walkouts by critics. Even Pauline Kael, a self-proclaimed fan of Demme's movies since *Citizens Band*, lambasted the film, saying, "It's pulp material treated as art, and I think that's a bit of a fraud."[29]

Amy Taubin was one of many leading female film critics who took to Demme's defense, saying that America's reaction to the film was emblematic of the country's attitude toward the gay community. "In the context of American Culture, where homosexuality is viewed as a disease and is a mental illness," Taubin said, "it's extremely easy to say, 'this is an example of a mentally ill person who has certain affinities in terms of the way that he's depicted to a gay man.' I never read him as a gay character in any sense, but that's where the controversy comes in. Since feminists felt that this was their first film that they could feel strongly about in terms of a Hollywood film, feminists have been outraged by that attack."[30]

The Silence of the Lambs opened in theaters nationwide on February 14, 1991, and became a critical and commercial hit, earning over $1.4 million in its first weekend and topping the box office for five consecutive weeks.³¹ In her review for the *Los Angeles Times*, Sheila Benson decried the assumptions that caused Demme to be pegged for only making quirky comedies. "So much for pigeonholing," Benson wrote. "Demme's vision of *The Silence of the Lambs*, Thomas Harris' truly terrifying novel, is stunning."³² Vincent Canby of the *New York Times* hailed the film as "a knockout," citing that "Mr. Demme is a director of both humor and subtlety. The gruesome details are vivid without being exploited. He also handles the big set pieces with skill."³³

As *The Silence of the Lambs* played to packed cineplexes across America, Demme was in Germany, his grandfather's native country, to accept the Silver Bear Best Director award at the Berlin Film Festival. The European press started asking Demme questions about America's obsession with serial killers. In May, during a Q&A session at a career retrospective at the Music Box Theatre in Chicago, an audience member told Demme that he was unimpressed with his reverence for Clarice Starling, calling the film "very Hollywood" regarding Lecter having superhuman abilities. Demme's response was, "You mustn't make me responsible for America glorifying serial killers."³⁴

The furor surrounding *The Silence of the Lambs* amplified on July 22, 1991, when Jeffrey Dahmer was arrested after attempting to murder Tracy Edwards. Edwards led Milwaukee police to Dahmer's North Twenty-Fifth Street apartment, where they found dismembered body parts in his freezer. Dahmer, who targeted young men for sex before killing and eating them, became part of the growing tabloid sensationalism of US crime in the early nineties. Gregg Kilday, senior writer for *Entertainment Weekly*, noted that "Jeffrey Dahmer kept *The Silence of the Lambs* in the news."³⁵

The commercial success of *The Silence of the Lambs* carried over into awards season, a time usually reserved for films released near the end of the year. *The Silence of the Lambs* was brought up by critics in the same breath as Oliver Stone's polarizing retelling of the Kennedy assassination in *JFK* (1991), which was also accused of peddling antigay sentiments. Outside the New York Film Critics dinner, where Demme was to receive his award for Best Director, GLAAD activists handed out pamphlets highlighting the few mainstream movies that depicted heroic gay characters. Anthony Heald, who played Dr. Chilton in the film, recalled Jonathan at the podium. "Jonathan was introduced," Heald said in 2001, "and he said, 'I don't know if any of you were aware of these leaflets that were passed out. I think that was extremely gracefully done, and I think we should all read these and pay very close attention to the message because Hollywood has been guilty.'"[36]

13

Angels Crowding Heaven (1992–1995)

The year 1992 saw the release of a highly personal documentary project, *Cousin Bobby*, a portrait of Demme's father's cousin, the firebrand Episcopalian minister Reverend Bobby Castle. The film had been in production off and on since before *The Silence of the Lambs* began filming. Tesauro, a Spanish production company, had approached Demme to make a documentary. He thought immediately of his cousin, in part due to the warming relationship between Jonathan and his father, Robert. As Demme started his own family, the two began to mend fences, and memories of the reverend came flooding back over family photos.

The reverend had been activated by the inner-city violence and lethal narcotics overwhelming Harlem at the time, and his convictions boiled over in sermons and marches Bobby held on 126th Street. Inspired by New Jersey Black Panther leader Isaiah Rowley, Castle acknowledged the revelatory paradigm shift in his beliefs about community and service when he marched in solidarity with the civil rights movement and opposed the Vietnam War. Rowley was assassinated in 1972 in what Bobby claimed was a vendetta. "As an American," Demme told Amy Taubin of the *Village Voice*, "I share Bob's feelings and I marvel at his devotion, but I'm not an activist and I hate sounding as if I thought I was. I'm a taxpayer who hates the way my government is behaving."[1] He elaborated, "I was interested in Rowley's story. And as a filmmaker, I was thrilled

Angels Crowding Heaven (1992–1995)

that the film starts out as a portrait of one man and in the last third becomes a portrait of another American."²

Filming over time and between other projects, Demme worked with cinematographers Ernest Dickerson, Bennett Miller, Matty Rich, and Victoria Leacock. The portrait captured not only Cousin Bobby serving his parish at St. Mary's Church in Harlem but also the warming renewal of the broken family's ties. The cameras rolled on the reunion of Jonathan, his father, and Bobby as they leafed through family albums, with Demme looking at the camera and saying, "Isn't this a great moment?"

Demme also wanted to present the issues that were still apparent long after the civil rights movement—namely, institutionalized racism—with a montage of riot footage from the sixties cued up to KRS-One's "Blackman in Effect." *Cousin Bobby* premiered at the 1992 Cannes Film Festival, one month after the LA riots spurred on by the acquittal of four LAPD officers who brutally assaulted Rodney King.

In the meantime, even with the success of *The Silence of the Lambs*, Demme couldn't shake the controversy surrounding that film. What was initially intended to be a positive feminist narrative had become a target of ridicule by the gay community. When limousines pulled up to the Dorothy Chandler Pavilion on Monday, March 30, 1992, police were in riot gear preparing for the throng of gay activists protesting the Academy Awards after *The Silence of the Lambs* received seven nominations, including Best Picture. The twenty-four-foot Oscar statues situated by the red carpet were surrounded by the gay rights groups UpFront and Queer Nation as activists slapped "Fag" stickers on Oscar's thighs.³

The protests outside didn't deter the Academy voters from declaring *The Silence of the Lambs* the Best Picture of 1991. It was a near sweep: Best Actor for Anthony Hopkins, Best Actress for Jodie Foster, Best Adapted Screenplay for Ted Tally, and Best Director for Jonathan Demme. Not since Milos Forman's *One Flew Over the Cuckoo's Nest* (1975) and Frank Capra's *It Happened One Night* (1934) had a film won what film-critic pollsters considered "the big five." After Kevin Costner called his name from the podium, Demme kissed Joanne and anxiously walked up to give his acceptance speech, an AIDS ribbon adorning his tuxedo. "In the context of my movie-loving life," Demme began, "this is very unanticipated."[4]

Before thanking his parents, Demme paid tribute to the emerging filmmakers who had, in his words, "really breathed tremendously important new life into our whole cinematic landscape," such as John Singleton (*Boyz N the Hood*), Matty Rich (*Straight Out of Brooklyn*), Ernest Dickerson (*Juice*), and Jodie Foster (*Little Man Tate*). Demme also paid tribute to Hal Ashby, who would remain an inspiration; Ashby had died of pancreatic cancer in December 1988. A week after Ashby's death, Demme had received a package from Grif Griffis, Ashby's partner. "In the box was the vest that Hal directed in," Demme said. "So I actually wear this whenever I'm working."[5] Demme would honor both Hal's spirit and those affected by the HIV/AIDS crisis in his next film, *Philadelphia*.

When the phone rang at Ron Nyswaner's home in Woodstock, New York, Jonathan was on the other end. "Hey, Ron," Demme said, "I love you, and I miss you! I want to talk to you about something. My friend Juan has just been diagnosed with AIDS. I'm freaking out. The only thing I know how to do about something is make a movie. Will you make a movie with me about AIDS?"[6] Ron knew the ordeal of seeing loved ones lost to the epidemic; his eighteen-year-old nephew, Kevin, a hemophiliac, died of AIDS in June 1992. By then, an estimated 33,590 Americans had died of the disease.[7]

Hollywood films handled the AIDS crisis as if it were a plot twist to a horror film. Critics assumed the position that David Cronenberg's *The Fly* (1986) and Adrian Lyne's *Fatal Attraction* (1987) were metaphors for the HIV/AIDS pandemic as the films were pegged as erotic thrillers: erotic for the choreographed sex on screen, and thrilling because of the fear that a character is encountering someone who might be infected.

Demme and Nyswaner developed stories surrounding HIV/AIDS, including a drug-smuggling story that would have preceded

Angels Crowding Heaven (1992–1995)

Jean Marc Vallée's *The Dallas Buyers Club* (2013). "Jonathan was interested in these stories involving people smuggling in medicine across the Mexican border," Nyswaner recalled. "Then we got back to the issue of civil rights, and at some point, Jonathan and I realized that the point to make this movie was to make the biggest, most commercially successful movie you could because that movie would reach the people that actually need to hear its message."[8] They decided to focus on the bigotry and stigma the gay community endured during the HIV/AIDS crisis.

Philadelphia began its circuitous journey in 1987 when Twentieth Century Fox bought the rights to an unpublished novel, *At Risk* by Alice Hoffman. Demme was attached to the project in 1988 and brought in Ron Nyswaner to work with him on the script, originally with Mike Medavoy and Marc Platt at Orion, but as Orion went into bankruptcy, they jumped ship to TriStar.[9] Medavoy and Platt wanted *Philadelphia* to be their top priority on learning that other films about AIDS were in development. It was Marc Platt who suggested to Demme and Nyswaner that the script diverge from Hoffman's novel and focus on the lawyer defending Andrew Beckett, putting his character into the foreground. According to Nyswaner, "Marc said, 'There are ten movies in development in Hollywood right now about AIDS. All of them have heterosexual main characters; that is immoral. We're going to make the movie about AIDS that needs to be made with a gay male character. You know the lawyer that he works with? What if you brought him forward so he wasn't a supporting character, it was actually their relationship that becomes the center of the movie?' That was such a great idea. Every movie has to have a central relationship."[10]

Demme and Nyswaner developed the script in the Love Shack, Jonathan's unofficial name for a guest cottage not far from his house in Nyack. Before putting pen to paper, Jonathan asked Ron, "I'm Joe, you're Andrew. Tell me what I should know about being gay."

"We had some arguments," Nyswaner said. "Jonathan would say provocative things that a heterosexual might feel but would be too embarrassed to say. For example, we argued about gay people adopting children. He wasn't opposed to it; he was exploring that issue coming from the point of view of the character. We would wrestle with those issues and develop the script together, and it was fantastic."[11]

The role of Andrew Beckett demanded a leading actor with commercial and critical acclaim. Daniel Day-Lewis's name was brought up, as was F. Murray Abraham's. With the script sent out to the top agencies in Hollywood, Demme received a phone call from Tom Hanks's agent, who was, in Demme's words, "instructed by my client to call you to let you know that he read this script and thinks it's excellent. For what it's worth, he wants to throw his hat in to play Andrew Beckett. I'm further instructed that when it comes to a salary, price will be no object."[12] In the early nineties, Tom Hanks was one of Hollywood's most sought-after leading men. Needless to say, Hanks got the role.

"One of the things I talked about with Jonathan," Hanks said in a 1993 interview for *Esquire* magazine, "is that we were not dealing with people's understanding of AIDS from the first days. My character has not been to three memorial services for friends of his who have died: he's been to three hundred. What happens is not a shock."[13] To immerse himself in the role of Andrew Beckett, Hanks read the works of Paul Monette and would undergo a diet regimen, eating only fourteen hundred calories a day throughout production.

Fresh off his controversial and revered portrayal of Malcolm X in Spike Lee's titular 1992 epic, Denzel Washington signed on to play Joe Miller, the personal injury lawyer who wrestles with his own homophobia while taking on Andrew Beckett's case. Coincidentally, he and Tom Hanks sat next to each other at the Academy Awards when Jonathan won his Oscar for *The Silence of the Lambs*. "We were actually cracking jokes about Jonathan going on forever about his speech," Washington said in 1993.

The next day, I got on a plane on my way to North Carolina, and I happened to run into Gary Goetzman, who was

Angels Crowding Heaven (1992–1995)

Jonathan's producer. There was another film that Gary wanted me to do which I didn't do, so we were talking, and he brought up this film—at the time it was called "Probable Cause"—and he was talking about Jonathan, and I said, "Well, I think he's a great director and I would love to work with him." He said, "Well, let me talk to him and I'll see if he's interested, and he'll send you the script." That's how it started.[14]

Miguel Alvarez, Andrew's lover, would be played by Antonio Banderas, who had yet to be embraced by American audiences. He was a star in his native Spain, appearing in Pedro Almodóvar's films in the mid- to late eighties (*Tie Me Up! Tie Me Down!*). Demme and Nyswaner saw Banderas read with Hanks during the audition; the duo got on swimmingly.

Demme brought back his *Melvin and Howard* collective to play key roles in *Philadelphia*. Jason Robards played Charles Wheeler, Andrew's employer, who terminated his trusted protégé on the revelation that he had AIDS; Robert Ridgely was Walter Kenton, the senior partner who notices a lesion on Andrew's forehead moments after he is promoted to senior associate; and Mary Steenburgen played Belinda Conine, the stone-clad corporate defense lawyer representing Wyant, Wheeler, Hellerman, Tetlow, and Brown.

Ron Vawter, the lauded stage actor and member of the Wooster Group, signed on to play Bob Sideman, the senior partner who admits that he suspected Andrew had AIDS before he was fired on the false grounds of work-related incompetence. A former Green Beret and aspiring Franciscan priest who was devoting his life to acting, Vawter knew the subject matter of *Philadelphia* all too well; he was living with AIDS, and he and his partner, Greg Mehrten, endured the bigotry that was prevalent toward same-sex couples during the peak of the AIDS crisis. "Very early on in the pandemic," Mehrten recalled, "Ron had this episode where he came to my apartment. He came home earlier than usual, went to bed, and seemed incoherent. I foolishly called 911 and immediately got swept up into a homophobic, bureaucratic nightmare. When they took him to the hospital, they would not let me see him. They said, 'Since you're not an immediate member of his family, you can't visit him.'"[15]

As always, Demme brought on his friends and mentors to be in the film. He cast cousin Bobby Castle in the role of Andrew's father; executive producer Gary Goetzman made an appearance as Guido Paonessa singing Frank Sinatra's "All the Way"; and Roger Corman took the stand while Steve Scales, Harry Northup, and Kenneth Utt filled the jury bench, along with Jonathan's mother, Dodie. Kathryn Witt, the woman who starred in Demme's first short movie back in Miami, gave an impassioned performance as a woman who contracted AIDS from a blood transfusion. Even some of the staff and patients featured in a Demme-produced documentary, *One Foot on a Banana Peel, the Other in the Grave: Secrets from the Dolly Madison Room*, played small roles in *Philadelphia*.

In October 1992, two weeks before production started on *Philadelphia*, Vawter and Mehrten attended the unveiling of the AIDS Quilt on the National Mall in Washington, DC. Soon after, Vawter was admitted to George Washington University Hospital. Demme was also at the unveiling and visited Ron in the hospital, uncertain if he would be healthy enough to get through the shooting schedule. Despite his illness, Vawter was determined to be in the film, and when Ed Saxon and Kenneth Utt visited him days later, he was out of his hospital bed preparing for the shoot. "We later learned that Jonathan personally financed his insurance, which still amazes me," Mehrten said. "Ron went to the set and came back to the suite. He had almost all his meals in his room; there was always someone there, either me or our cadre of friends, to make sure he had clean clothes."[16]

For Andrew and Miguel's apartment, Kristi Zea ensured that the layout of the loft would not fall prey to campy decor or kitsch. As Zea recalled, "Jonathan said, 'I don't want to scare anybody away. I don't want anyone to look at that couple and think, *Oh, they're so out there!*' I even had a toreador's outfit on a stand. That managed to stay in, but it was definitely a challenge because of Jonathan's desire

Angels Crowding Heaven (1992–1995)

to make it as friendly an environment as possible because the point he wanted to make was, 'This could be in your life just as it was in their lives.'"[17] For the party sequence, notable gay activists like Quentin Crisp (dressed as Oscar Wilde) and Greg Mehrten (dressed as Vincent Van Gogh) reveled with the cadre of actors and Jonathan's close friends. In traditional Demme fashion, a series of musicians performed live during the shoot, including Q Lazzarus, who delivers a soulful version of the Talking Heads' "Heaven" as Joe and Andrew dance with their significant others.

Although Joe is presented in the trial as an advocate for Andrew, his prejudice toward homosexuality is explicit outside the courtroom; it is seen as he confides in his wife about his ignorance about same-sex relationships and as he interacts with his legal colleagues at the bar. It isn't until he declines an offer to grab a drink with a gay law student (Andre B. Blake) at a pharmacy that he physically acts out his frustration, grabbing him by the shirt collar and saying, "That is exactly the kind of bullshit that makes people hate your faggoty little ass!" Even as Andrew and Joe's camaraderie expands to compassion toward the end of the film, Washington acknowledged that Miller is not a changed man. In an interview with *Esquire*, Washington said, "(Joe's) not going to be the grand marshal of any gay-pride parade. We didn't want a rah-rah, everything-is-wonderful ending because that ain't the way it is."[18]

One of the most controversial, and emotional, scenes in the film is when Andrew plays Maria Callas for Joe as they prepare for Andrew's testimony in court. Initially, the scene was not well received by the studio. Nyswaner said, "We had a stack of faxes. There were colleagues who thought Andrew's interest in opera was a stereotype. People suggested the two guys talk about baseball or the lyrics to a pop song—perhaps Madonna could do a cover of something for us. Jonathan read the faxes to me one day. We were blindsided, but the response was so strongly negative that we took it seriously. I remember him asking, 'Ron, do you like this scene?' I said, 'Jonathan, I love this scene.' He took the faxes and said, 'Well, fuck them!' and threw the faxes in the trash."[19]

It took five takes to shoot the scene with Garrett Brown operating his patented Steadicam. The red light piercing down on Andrew as he tells Joe the story of *Andrea Chénier* is reminiscent of Orpheus singing out to the spirit of his beloved, yet slain, Eurydice in Camus's *Black Orpheus*. The reaction shots of Joe tearfully listening to Andrew and the music represent the heterosexual audience watching the film swayed by Andrew accepting his fate with poetic dignity rather than self-pity. "We were a wreck," Kristi Zea said. "We were sobbing in the end. I think that's the most remarkable scene in any film. It resonated so much with all of us, whether we had people we lost to this disease or not; it had such an incredible translation of some music affecting someone in such a way. That's Tom all the way."[20]

When Andrew takes the stand to give his testimony, the camera holds on both the stand and jurors before it zooms in on him expressing his appreciation for the law and his initial ambitions to be a lawyer before it cuts away to reaction shots of Charles Wheeler stoically hearing his former protégé talk highly of him. Like in the probate trial sequence in *Melvin and Howard*, Demme and Fujimoto use the courtroom to full advantage, capturing the realism of shots positioned from the spectators' benches as well as the subjective camera shots of Joe asking Andrew questions directly into the camera. When Belinda Conine cross-examines Andrew, the camera is canted, showing Andrew's distorted point of view and emphasizing the emotional pressure of revealing his sexual exploits to the court and the effect his illness is having on his testimony. Nyswaner remembered how Mary struggled with playing a character anathematic to her own personality.

"She asked me, 'Certainly, she's on the other side, right?'" Nyswaner remembers. "I said, 'No, because we have an adversarial courtroom system where each side deserves the best representation possible. As a corporate defender, you probably get plenty of people filing fake lawsuits or false claims. They don't always do the wrong thing, and it doesn't matter.' But Mary was uncomfortable, and she ad-libbed a line that made it into the finished film."[21] After Andrew is unable to see any lesions in the mirror Belinda is holding, she goes back to her table, saying under her breath, "I hate this case." Later, when Joe asks Andrew if he had any lesions resembling those that were on his face before his termination, Andrew responds, "On my torso." Demme is deliberately sentimental in having Andrew reveal his torso to the court as Howard Shore's heroic score heightens the communal emotions shared by the court and the film's audience.

Jonathan wanted to capture Andrew's emotional state before he faints in the courtroom. When Charles Wheeler takes the stand, Andrew believes the witness is laughing at him. As Andrew falls to the floor and the camera circles 360 degrees from the ceiling, Wheeler's sliver of humanity is exposed when he calls out for a doctor. "When we were shooting the juror reactions," Demme said, "I had to cut to them and find fresh ways to see them. Wouldn't there be a moment when you're hung up with the jury?" In shooting Jason Robards from the witness stand, Demme wanted the effect to be as chilling as Lecter roasting Clarice Starling. "The grips built up a special chair with a crane," Demme said, "and we dollied on him even as we craned him forward."[22]

Demme's camera tracks from Ron Vawter on the stand to Andrew's abandoned chair as he admits that he knew Andrew had AIDS. By that point, Vawter couldn't fit into his clothes as he had lost a large amount of weight, yet Demme knew that he played a key role in ending the trial. "I was just taken with how much Jonathan trusted Ron," Greg Mehrten said. "Most directors wouldn't have gone out of their way, but Jonathan wasn't like most directors."[23]

Philadelphia is bookended by the music of Bruce Springsteen and Neil Young. Initially, Demme wanted a rock anthem like Young's 1970 song "Southern Man." Pablo and Allen Ferro did an edit of the opening sequence with the song and sent it to Young, asking for something similar. The first version of the song "Philadelphia" Young sent was a gentle ballad that Demme thought was "too pretty" for the dark story of injustice. He asked Young to tweak it, and he delivered the soft piano-based ode to family and love that plays during the film's final scene of Andrew's memorial service. Inspired by Derek Jarman's *Blue* (1993),[24] his last film before dying of AIDS, Demme had the camera zoom in on a television set playing home movies of a young Andrew with his brothers, sisters, and parents.

Demme gave Springsteen a similar request for the film's opening credits, for a rock ballad to back a montage of daily life in Philadelphia: "The same exact dialogue [as with Young] goes on—'So we still need to kick ass at the beginning.' Then, one day, this tape shows up. Again, it was not the guitar anthem I had appealed for. Springsteen, like Neil Young, trusted the idea of the movie much more than I was trusting it."[25] From Craig McKay's perspective, Springsteen spent two months writing "The Streets of Philadelphia." "What we didn't know was that Bruce was frozen," McKay said. "He couldn't write anything; he had writer's block all through that. We played it, and we thought it was fantastic."[26]

On November 13, 1993, one month before its release in theaters nationwide, *Philadelphia* was screened at the White House. For Demme, it was a litmus test in terms of how a mainstream film about the stigma of a global epidemic could sway politicians. During the party sequence as Andrew and Miguel dance in their naval costumes, President Bill Clinton left the room. Though he had advocated for gay members of the military during his presidential campaign and initiated "Don't Ask, Don't Tell" during his first term in office, he was unable to watch. "When Antonio and Tom dance together," Demme said, "Clinton just gets up and said, 'I have to go to the bathroom.' He just didn't want to see that part."[27] Clinton's bathroom break foreshadowed the ho-hum attitude the critics took toward *Philadelphia*.

In his mixed review of *Philadelphia* under the heading "'Tis Not a Jolly Season," David Ansen of *Newsweek* wrote, "You can feel the pressure on the filmmakers to design a film that will speak to the widest possible audience, to reach people who may not know anyone who's died of AIDS. But the film pays a price for it. Heartfelt and stylishly made as *Philadelphia* is, it has, almost by definition, the feel of a movie made from the outside in."[28] Janet Maslin praised *Philadelphia* in her *New York Times* review, stating that the film "succeeds in being forceful, impassioned and moving, sometimes even rising to the full range of emotion that its subject warrants. But too often, even at its most assertive, it works in safely predictable ways."[29] However, the most ardent criticism of *Philadelphia* came from Larry Kramer when the *Chicago Reader* published his January 1994 review titled "Philadelphia Sorry."

Lambasting the film from cast to director, Kramer wrote that "*Philadelphia* doesn't have anything to do with the AIDS I know. Or the gay world I know. It doesn't bear any truthful resemblance to the life, world, and universe I live in. And every person I know lives in. And every gay or PWA (person with AIDS) the film's director, Jonathan Demme, and its screenwriter, Ron Nyswaner, know lives in."[30] Kramer's unwarranted attacks on Demme and Nyswaner did little to keep the public from seeing the film, which grossed nearly $77.5 million at the box office before earning over $206 million worldwide.[31] "From where we came from," Greg Mehrten said, "we always thought of Larry Kramer as the Establishment—too conservative. We were living in a very noncommercial existence as artists before this commercialized ideology came in; it really bends people out of shape. That's why I admired Jonathan because even though he was working in a commercial vein, he didn't seem like he was."[32]

The controversy mounted around the film and TriStar was tangled in a publicized lawsuit that was eventually settled. Prior to Demme and Nyswaner's involvement on *Philadelphia*, producer Scott Rudin had interviewed the family of Geoffrey Bowers, a lawyer who died of AIDS after suing the law firm Baker and MacKenzie on the grounds of discrimination. Rudin made a verbal agreement of compensation with the Bower family before leaving the project when it was still at Orion Pictures.[33] When the film was released, the Bowers claimed that Andrew Beckett was modeled after Geoffrey, further complicating Demme's initial conceit of honoring his friend Juan Botas, an artist and family friend who was documented in *One Foot on a Banana Peel, the Other in the Grave: Secrets from the Dolly Madison Room*.

Tragedy struck Demme and the staff at Clinica Estetico on January 19, 1994, five days after *Philadelphia* topped the US box office, when Kenneth Utt died from bone and colon cancer. The month before, he had celebrated his fiftieth wedding anniversary with his wife, Angie, and was developing a children's movie, *Baubles*, with his daughter and assistant, Robin Fajardo, with Ted Demme slated to direct. At Utt's funeral at the Unitarian Church of All Souls in Manhattan, Jonathan held back tears as he stood at the podium saying goodbye to his friend and mentor. He said, "I just feel that the world is a scarier, more dangerous place without Kenny."[34]

In spite of the onslaught of pressure, Demme was excitedly unapologetic for the film and how he had strived to reach a mainstream audience. As he told *Rolling Stone*, "I didn't have some better vision—some deeper, more complicated version—of this movie that we turned away from. We set out to make a movie dealing with AIDS discrimination, and there it is. And I've got to tell you: When I sit in a theater, and Denzel says, 'Let's talk about it, our fear, our hatred, our loathing of homosexuals,' I'm like 'What? An American movie saying that? Holy shit! I love that.'"[35]

Philadelphia earned five Academy Award nominations, winning Best Song in a Motion Picture for Bruce Springsteen's "The Streets of Philadelphia" and Best Actor in a Leading Role for Tom Hanks. When his name was called by Emma Thompson at the Dorothy Chandler Pavilion on March 21, 1994, Hanks delivered an emotional speech acknowledging the cast, crew, and Jonathan Demme, "who seems to have these [referring to the Oscar] attached to his limbs for every actor that works with him of late." Hanks would end his speech acknowledging the dilemma of being an actor addressing the present issues of justice and equality, stating that "the streets of heaven are too crowded with angels. We know their names. They number a thousand for each one of the red ribbons that we wear here tonight."[36] Ron Vawter was one of those angels who passed away on April 16, 1994.

Ten days later, Jonathan's father died in Miami.[37] It was bittersweet as they had just reunited at a benefit screening of *Philadelphia* at the Inter-Continental Hotel three months earlier.[38] Despite the tension and separation Robert had put his family through during Demme's childhood, it was Bob who introduced Jonathan to Joseph

Angels Crowding Heaven (1992–1995)

Levine when he was working at the Fontainebleau Hotel, setting him on his Candide-like path through publicity toward filmmaking. His presence in *Cousin Bobby* sifting through old photos of himself and Jonathan presents a loving resolve in an otherwise strained relationship.

With *Philadelphia* behind him, Demme went back to his activist work, this time against the detainment of 250 HIV-positive Haitians at Guantanamo Bay. After President Bill Clinton refused to release the refugees, nationwide protests broke out. Hunger strikes were held on the college campuses of Harvard and Yale. Blocking traffic along Fifth Avenue, Demme was arrested along with Rev. Jesse Jackson, Susan Sarandon, and forty others outside the US State Department's passport office.[39] This arrest was one of a few that Demme shared alongside his cousin Bobby.[40]

In the wake of *Philadelphia*'s commercial success and controversy, Jonathan sequestered in Nyack to be closer to his family while welcoming their third child, Jos Demme, in 1995. His mother, Dodie, passed away on November 20, 1995, at the age of eighty-one. Before her death, Dodie played a juror in *Philadelphia* adorned in white, no different than Henry Fonda's moralistic Juror #8 in Sidney Lumet's *12 Angry Men* (1957). A champion of her son's accomplishments who nurtured his thirst for film, Dodie was buried at Rockville Cemetery three miles from Jonathan's childhood home. The inscription on her grave reads "Mother-Artist-Friend."[41]

14

Subways, Galleries, and Storefronts (1996–1997)

Meanwhile in Nyack, scripts had piled up in Demme's home office, and he wanted to expand his horizons. Over the next couple of years, he would work with his *Philadelphia* collaborators as producer on *Devil in a Blue Dress*, starring Denzel Washington and directed by Carl Franklin, then Tom Hanks's *That Thing You Do!* "I was back with Jonathan Demme in New York," Hanks said in 1996. "He said, 'You know, if you want to do something bodacious right now, you should go off and direct this movie.'"[1] The picture landed at 20th Century Fox with Demme, Ed Saxon, and Gary Goetzman as executive producers. Goetzman had his work cut out for him cowriting some of the songs that appeared in the film and promoting the Wonders, a fictitious garage band from Erie, Pennsylvania. In many ways, it was a nostalgia trip for Goetzman back to the days when he managed teen rock bands in the San Fernando Valley.

The film became a box office hit in October 1996, and the soundtrack featuring the titular song written by Adam Schlesinger from the band Fountains of Wayne peaked at 41 and stayed on the Billboard charts for fifteen weeks.[2] Goetzman and Hanks would form a production company named after the Wonders' record label, Playtone Productions. Demme had a cameo in the film playing a director of a campy surf movie the Wonders appear in. He directed a Bruce Springsteen music video and the short *The Complex Sessions* for Neil Young. The latter is a highly regarded hidden gem in Demme's filmography, a live performance of four songs from Young's *Sleeps with Angels* album, which many consider Young's best live release.

Demme was not one to forget his artistic mentors during his success streak in the mid-nineties—if not getting Roger Corman to appear in *The Silence of the Lambs* and *Philadelphia*, then attempting to get Samuel Fuller back behind the camera. Demme and Martin Scorsese both wanted to coproduce Fuller's film *The Chair vs. Ruth Snyder* about Ruth Snyder, the 1927 high-profile murderess who became the source of inspiration for James M. Cain's novel *The Postman Always Rings Twice*.

The Fullers visited Demme's Nyack cottage for a barbecue lunch. As they ate hamburgers and Samuel Fuller ecstatically chatted with Jonathan over the prospect of making another movie after the studios had turned their backs on him following *White Dog* (1982), Brooklyn Demme caught everyone's eyes. "Little Brooke is sitting there watching Sam, and with the smoke wafting and ash falling from his cigar," Christa Fuller recalled. "Brooklyn picks up a wine cork from the table and starts imitating Sam, pretending to smoke a cigar. We laughed so much!"[3] The prospect of Samuel Fuller directing another studio picture was short-lived; he passed away on October 30, 1997.

If one were to mark where television and cinema aligned before the competitive world of streaming platforms, it would be when Barry Diller headed Paramount in the mid-seventies after leaving his post at ABC and before Jonathan Demme made his television directorial debut with *Columbo*. Yet the cinematic and televisual scopes were still distant from one another until filmmakers like Steven Spielberg and Francis Ford Coppola ventured to the small screen, with HBO acting as a safe haven from the standards and practices regulations of network television. Demme was friendly with Colin Callender, the president of HBO Films, when he decided to executive produce with Ed Saxon and Rosie Perez an anthology series focusing on the daily lives of the New York City denizens taking the subway.

In the spring of 1995, ads were posted in New York–based magazines with the headline: "You know that great subway story you've told your friends a thousand times.... It could make a great movie."[4] With the chance to win a paid writing credit, a walk-on credit, a year's supply of subway tokens, and an annual subscription to HBO, hundreds of New Yorkers submitted personal stories about their encounters on the subway. Fifteen writers were chosen, and their scripts fell into the hands of prominent filmmakers.

Gathering fellow New Yorkers Bob Balaban, Israel Horovitz, Julie Dash, Abel Ferrara, and Joe Viola, among others, Demme and crew filmed a mix of comedic, dark, erotic, and humanizing vignettes that became *SUBWAYStories: Tales from the Underground*. Demme directed the opening comedic short *Subway Car from Hell*, in which a street musician tries to make his train. Demme enlisted his fellow Rockland friend and Broadway actor Bill Irwin to deliver a physical performance worthy of Jacques Tati while KRS-One played the knish vendor who serves Irwin a spicy hot dog.

Like many of his projects since *Something Wild*, Jonathan made *SUBWAYStories* into a family affair. His nephew Ted Demme had had a series of substantial hit films under his belt after *Yo! MTV Raps* ended in 1995, such as the Denis Leary–led Christmas comedy *The Ref* (1994) and *Beautiful Girls* (1996). When his uncle asked him to contribute to *SUBWAYStories: Tales from the Underground*, Ted directed the short *Manhattan Miracle*, written by Joe Viola, a harrowing yet silent story of a pregnant woman (Anne Heche) contemplating suicide before hearing the shouts of a concerned citizen on the opposite platform (Gregory Hines). Although it allowed the Demmes to bask in the creative spirit of directing as a family, the show was panned by critics.

Clinica Estetico was gaining momentum and signed a three-year production deal with Universal Pictures in early 1997. Demme's production company was home to a thriving collective of filmmakers: director Nancy Savoca and husband/screenwriter Richard Guay made their *True Love* (1989) and *Household Saints* (1991); Jo Menell and Angus Gibson filmed their inspiring documentary, *Mandela* (1996); and Victor Nuñez was able to make *Ulee's Gold* (1997), the story of a Florida beekeeper that would earn Peter Fonda a Golden Globe for Best Actor in a Drama and an Oscar nomination. The latter was a notable boost for Clinica Estetico as the $2.9 million film would earn a healthy $9 million at the box office.[5]

When he wasn't behind the camera, Jonathan was looking at three hundred photos of his Haitian art collection. "If I'm being honest with myself, it has to be branded an addiction," Demme said. "Because I have an emotional dependence on it. My eyes have got to have it, this is not a joke."[6] Since 1986, Demme's collection of Haitian folk art had grown from shopping in Port-Au-Prince to commissioning artwork by the country's leading artists. With his status as a successful film director, Demme tried to use his industrial clout to promote the work of Edgar Jean-Baptiste, Andre Pierre, Etienne Chavannes, Ernst Prophete, and Jasmin Joseph. While working as an artist-in-residence at Ramapo College in New Jersey in 1994, Demme curated an exhibition of paintings from his personal collection.

Demme's foray into art curation led to starting a book publishing company, Kaliko Press. *Haiti: Three Visions* is an immersive text on contemporary Haitian art. With interviews conducted by Edwidge Danticat, the book captures the political and social strife depicted on Masonite plates. In June 1997, Demme flew in a series of artists for the opening night of his exhibition at New York City's Equitable Art Gallery displaying a hundred collected art pieces. The exhibition, "Island on Fire: Passionate Visions of Haiti from the Collection of Jonathan Demme," coincided with the director's efforts in creating a positive narrative about Haiti. Looking at the companion coffee table book for "Island on Fire" offers the reader a glimpse into Demme's self-professed addiction to Haitian art and also into how the art has been inspirational in his filmmaking ventures. The forged iron sculptures of Georges Liautaud and other inspired artists materialize in the Clinica Estetico logo of Demme's movies.[7]

Jonathan and Joanne Howard struck a balance in their lives as artists raising a family. CDs would pile up on the kitchen table with a variety of music playing in between meals.[8] During the summers, the family would have meals outside on their porch, or Jonathan would note the peregrine falcons flying over the Tappan Zee. When the kids had a babysitter, Jonathan and Joanne would travel to the

Lower East Side, having meals at Buffa's Luncheonette before taking in a show.[9] When Joanne told her husband that British singer-songwriter Robyn Hitchcock was playing at a club in Nyack, Demme got excited.

Paisley shirts and acerbic wit were part of Robyn Hitchcock's repertoire since the mid-seventies. Inspired by the psychedelic lyrics of Pink Floyd's founding member, Syd Barrett, and the breezy acoustic guitar work of Nick Drake, Hitchcock and his first band, the Soft Boys, were cult favorites of music lovers before the raw, anti-authoritarian rage of Britain's punk rock scene stifled the sounds of Hitchcock's gentle humor. Demme was enraptured by Hitchcock and violinist Deni Bonet's set, and afterward, he and Joanne went backstage to introduce themselves. "Jonathan appeared through a trapdoor in the dressing room," Hitchcock recalled. "My girlfriend knew who he was, but I had no idea what he looked like. I guess he appeared that night because I was almost on his doorstep."[10] What first started as a pitch for making a series of music videos led to the idea of making a feature-length film.

Demme was inspired by a performance of the play *Mr. Dead and Mrs. Free* at the Squat Theatre. During a walk in the Chelsea neighborhood in the early eighties, he had wandered into the drape-sheathed storefront on 256 West Twenty-Third Street and was transported. The Hungarian acting troupe the Squat Theatre had enticed and shocked audiences since 1977, using their storefront space as a place for Dadaist expression with the added dimension that the performance was a backdrop to the live action out on the streets.[11] While watching the play, Demme was gobsmacked when a military jeep made a U-turn on Twenty-Third Street and three soldiers ran into the theater, grabbed one of the actors, and drove away. Demme wanted to incorporate the audience into Robyn Hitchcock's performance by filming their reactions outside a storefront, similar to the way the Squat Theatre integrated the audience and the outside world.

Rallying people to watch a free concert wasn't a hard task for Demme. While Hitchcock performed with Billy Bragg at the Beacon Theatre, Demme and his Clinica Estetico staff handed out leaflets promoting two free concerts on Fourteenth Street, bringing in a total of 120 people. Hitchcock was free to stage the performances how he pleased. He recalled, "There were no obstacles that Clinica couldn't overcome. They didn't try to involve me in any practical aspect of staging the show, bless them!" In December 1996, Demme assembled his crew of four cameramen to film two days of performances for his next film, *Storefront Hitchcock*.

Unlike the gymnasium-styled backdrop of the Pantages Theatre in *Stop Making Sense*, the pedestrians walking past the storefront were part of the performance, standing with curiosity akin to those who stopped traffic on Saville Row in 1969 to watch the Beatles' final rooftop performance in Michael Lindsay-Hogg's documentary *Let It Be* (1970). On stage stood three safety cones, a table with a glass of water, a phone, and Robyn's twelve-string acoustic guitar on its stand like a pawn shop display. The familial atmosphere Demme brought to his feature films is present in his performance film: Ed Saxon stands outside holding a photo taken by Ted Demme of Clinica Estetico's father figure, Kenny Utt, who passed away in 1994.

Demme asked cinematographer Tony Jannelli, "What can we do to make every single song look different?" The idea came from the timing of the concerts, which would start in the afternoon while the light was still present before fading into winter's evening: "The lighting really set the trajectory of the film. Jonathan gave me free rein to light the film based on the mood of the songs."[12] One idea Jannelli devised was having a glass grid with different colored gels wheeled outside the store. As the light faded from the windows, the multicolored set would replicate a stained-glass window.

When Hitchcock strums the riff to his gritty love/hate song about writing love songs, "Freeze," the stage is front lit like the end of *Stop Making Sense*. Demme and editor Andy Keir devised the split-screen technique covering all angles of Hitchcock performing, emphasizing the impact of his lyrics and methodical strumming for the filmgoing audience. As the concert ends with "No, I Don't Remember Guildford," Hitchcock leans into the microphone, talking to the director: "JD, was that good? Should we cut it?"

THERE'S NO GOING BACK

Storefront Hitchcock wasn't the commercial success that *Stop Making Sense* had been. The film was released through Orion, the once-renowned haven for directors that was now fading to obscurity. The success of *Ulee's Gold* and the warm reception to *Storefront Hitchcock* were bittersweet grace notes for Orion, with Demme's company providing as much support as possible for the studio that helped revive his career after *Swing Shift*. Warner Bros. Records released the *Storefront Hitchcock* soundtrack to warm reviews, yet it didn't gain the Billboard chart status of *Stop Making Sense*. As Jay Hedblade wrote in the *Chicago Reader*, "Because he isn't Hendrix or Sinatra in either department, the songs are the defining element."[13] The film was shelved until November 1998, one month after the release of Demme's next film, *Beloved*.

From left to right: Evelyn Purcell, Larry Kaplan, and Jonathan Demme at the United Artists Publicity Offices in New York City, 1968. (Courtesy of Evelyn Purcell)

Evelyn in New York. (Courtesy of Evelyn Purcell)

Larry Kaplan, Evelyn Purcell, and Jonathan Demme at JFK Airport picking up the cast of *Yours, Mine and Ours* for a publicity tour, 1968. (Courtesy of Larry Kaplan)

Demme and Purcell in the early seventies. (Courtesy of Larry Kaplan)

Jonathan and Evelyn's wedding day in London, May 1970. (Courtesy of Larry Kaplan)

Evelyn and Jonathan working together on the set of *Crazy Mama* (1975, New World Pictures). (Courtesy of Evelyn Purcell)

Jonathan Demme on the set of *Melvin and Howard* (1980, Universal Pictures). (Courtesy of Photofest Digital)

Melanie Griffith and Jonathan Demme on the set of *Something Wild* (1986, Orion Pictures). (Courtesy of Photofest)

Jonathan Demme and Jodie Foster on the set of *The Silence of the Lambs* (1991, Orion Pictures). (Courtesy of Photofest Digital)

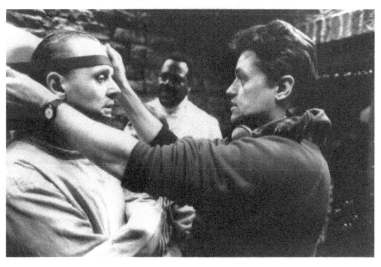

Demme strapping in Anthony Hopkins in *The Silence of the Lambs* (1991, Orion Pictures). (Courtesy of Photofest Digital)

Rev. Robert Castle, aka Cousin Bobby, with Jonathan Demme shooting *Cousin Bobby*. (Courtesy of Photofest Digital)

Robert Demme, Jonathan's father. (*Pan American Clipper* 8, no. 10 [October 1950], Pan American World Airways Records—Digital Collections [miami.edu])

Robert Demme

Robert Demme, Public Relations Representative for the Western Atlantic Region, joined the public relations department of AOA (then American Export Airlines) in 1944 and became assistant director of public relations in 1947.

Prior to joining the airline he was editor of "Skyways" magazine for three years. Earlier he handled aviation and travel accounts in the publicity department of the Erwin Wasey Company, advertising agency, and before 1940 he was a newspaper reporter and free lance writer.

Mr. Demme was born in Cedarhurst, L. I., and was graduated from Duke University in 1935. He is married to the former Dorothy L. Rogers and they have three sons, Rick, Jonathan and Peter.

15

Ghosts at the Door (1997–2000)

Jonathan Demme's life in Nyack had an idyllic hold on him during the mid-nineties. Outside of his cottage and family, Rockland County was a special place for Demme to meditate on his work, as well as to soak up the creative inspiration from the authors who resided in the neighborhood. It wouldn't be surprising to find Walter Mosley or Edwidge Danticat having a steak dinner with the Demmes. Another guest who might have been at the table was Toni Morrison. During the mid-eighties, long before Jonathan moved to Nyack, Morrison had been working on a book in her home on the Hudson River, inspired by an article she came across in an 1856 edition of the *Cincinnati Gazette*.[1]

The pre–Civil War news article reported on Margaret Garner, an escaped slave who had run away from her owner in northern Kentucky. She had been caught and arrested in Ohio after slitting her daughter's throat and attempting to drown her other child. The court was conflicted as to whether Garner should be tried for murder or for damaging stolen property. The book that Toni Morrison had been writing would become *Beloved*, one of the most profound and polarizing novels about slavery in America.

The novel was released to critical acclaim in 1988, and Morrison won the Pulitzer Prize. Beyond the praise received from the American literati, Oprah Winfrey was such a passionate fan of Morrison's book that she tracked her down through her town's fire department

THERE'S NO GOING BACK

since her number was unlisted. When Winfrey told Morrison she would like to buy the rights to make *Beloved* into a feature film for her production company, Harpo Pictures, Morrison was flattered and somewhat skeptical. As Morrison noted before her passing in 2019, "My oldest son said, 'Mom, you'll always have the book. It's not destroying the book, it's just another version.'"[2]

Oprah Winfrey recalled the challenges she and screenwriter Akosua Busia endured while trying to find a director to helm her passion project. "Akosua Busia and I had originally gone to Peter Weir, and he summarily rejected it," Winfrey said in 2022. "I was so involved in the growing height of the Oprah Winfrey Show that I don't remember how many other people we went to."[3]

Winfrey eventually approached Demme to direct *Beloved*, and they met for the first time in Nyack in January 1997. After reading the book, he saw the project as a golden chance to return to the director's chair and make a feature-length epic on a formidable issue, the ghosts of slavery. "It's arguably a subject that the entire world has to come to terms with appropriately," Demme said in 1998. "It's not just that we were a colonial territory where slavery, this horrendous thing between the races, was acted out. It started in other hemispheres. It's a deep, challenging piece that just, to me, had incredibly emotional rewards. And also, it's a ghost story and it has a deeply suspenseful, deeply disturbing, supernatural dimension to it."[4]

In Cincinnati in 1873, Sethe (Oprah Winfrey) encounters Paul D (Danny Glover), a former slave who resided with Sethe at the horrific Sweet Home plantation eighteen years earlier. Paul D enters Sethe's house, which has shaking walls and an ominous red glow coming from some apparition. Much to the skeptical dismay of Sethe's surviving daughter, Denver (Kimberly Elise), Paul D stays with Sethe, rekindling their lost relationship. Days later, a regally dressed young woman with a scarred, slit throat emerges from the Ohio River and sleeps outside Sethe's house: it's Beloved (Thandiwe Newton), the reincarnation of Sethe's daughter whom she had murdered before she was brought back to Sweet Home. Beloved's presence is bittersweet and sorrowful for Sethe as the memories of her incarceration and the killing flood over her. Within those memories, the possibility of redemption is revived by the memory of Sethe's mother-in-law, Baby Suggs (Beah Richards), and her uplifting sermons in the woods. It takes the local community to exorcise Sethe's trauma through incantations as Denver leaves home to work for a wealthy, yet racially sympathetic, white family in Cincinnati.

Danny Glover and Oprah Winfrey would reunite in the lead roles, for the first time since their galvanizing performances in Steven Spielberg's adaptation of Alice Walker's *The Color Purple* (1982). Danny Glover had been friends with Jonathan through their activist work and shared interest in making a film about the Haitian Revolution. Fittingly, Glover's production company is named Louverture Films after the 1804 Haitian revolutionary. Glover, coming off the success of Richard Donner's *Lethal Weapon* franchise for Warner Bros. (1988–1998), saw the Reconstruction Era as an essential period of African Americans living as free citizens. As he told *Jet* magazine in 1998, "We haven't come to terms with that experience, and the relationship that experience has to the moment right after. An enormous wave of humanity comes out of that experience."[5]

Born to a Zimbabwean mother and an English father, Thandiwe Newton, a graduate of Cambridge University, gained attention with roles in director Neil Jordan's *Interview with the Vampire: The Vampire Chronicles* (1994) and James Ivory's *Jefferson in Paris* (1995). She built her résumé acting alongside rap artist Tupac Shakur in *Gridlock'd* (1997) and in Bernardo Bertolucci's *Besieged* (1998). After a successful audition, Demme told Newton to listen to Louis Armstrong records to capture Beloved's jagged timbre and to read literature about young women held in captivity. "I felt like I was playing that children's game where you fall backwards and hope people will catch you," Newton said in 1998. "I had to strip away all of the affections of a civilized person."[6] In many ways, it was kismet that Newton should play the titular role, as *thandiwe* means *beloved* in Zulu.

Beah Richards had been a prominent figure on Broadway and in film since the late fifties. She had plum roles in Arthur Penn's *The Miracle Worker* (1962) and Norman Jewison's *In the Heat of the Night*

(1967) and earned her only Oscar nomination in Stanley Kramer's *Guess Who's Coming to Dinner?* (1967). A poet and lifelong activist for civil rights, Richards endured surveillance from the House Un-American Activities Committee during the Red Scare. Richards's resilience was represented in her four decades of film and television work, but never more so than in the role of Baby Suggs, who lifts the spirits of her family and congregation with her pragmatic views on life. Rounding out the cast was Kimberly Elise, playing Sethe's surviving daughter, Denver, and Albert Hall as Stamp Paid, who tells Paul D about what happened to Sethe when she left Sweet Home.

Before shooting commenced, Oprah had Demme, Morrison, and the cast come to her Indiana ranch to discuss the film. "We spent three or four days talking about the movie, the characters, what we wanted to achieve and how this was something bigger than all of us," Winfrey said. "We weren't just doing this for ourselves, we were doing this for Margaret Garner, her ancestors, our ancestors. We saw this film in a much larger viewpoint since the beginning."[7]

Kristi Zea was tapped as production designer along with cinematographer Tak Fujimoto. The ninety-four-day shoot of *Beloved* started in Philadelphia on a soundstage in the city's center. They built Sethe's house so that the foundation could be hoisted up and the set could tilt to simulate the house shaking, symbolizing the ghosts of Sethe's children. Beyond recreating nineteenth-century Cincinnati in downtown Philadelphia, Demme would travel to Delaware and Maryland, shooting additional footage.

Joe Viola stepped in to help shoot Beah Richards's memorable sermon scene as the camera slowly rotates around the congregation. "Talk about a sequence!" Viola said. "However, Beah could barely walk, so I said to Jon, 'I've been in a similar situation in commercials. What you do is strap her to a hand dolly so she could lean against the back, strap her under her wardrobe, and you can wheel her wherever you want; she'll be comfortable. It will look like she's standing free because she can swivel.' I stood there, and she did the first take straight through. When I looked over at Jonathan, everybody (the camera crew and both of us) had tear-filled eyes. It was so moving and unbelievable."[8]

In preparation for playing Sethe, Oprah Winfrey would light candles in her trailer and read the names of those who were sold into slavery.[9] She even went as far as to be blindfolded and wander around where the Underground Railroad led those enslaved toward salvation. "My goal was that I was going to stay there for a couple of days and figure out which way was north," Winfrey said. "The idea of following stars which way to go. I sat out there for ten hours and had a spiritual revelation understanding what it would be like to be in a space where no one knew where to go."[10]

The on-set chemistry between Demme and Winfrey was joyous during the shoot. Demme would pass notes to Winfrey after a day's shooting with words of affirmation. Winfrey was still working on her television show, organizing for the fall season, and at one point was torn between flying to Chicago or staying on set. As she wrote in her book *Journey to Beloved*, "JD heard about my plans to go to Chicago on my one day off, and a conversation with me which kept me in Philadelphia. Wise decision. He thought Chicago would change my focus and zap my energy."[11]

Winfrey and Demme disagreed at times about how closely they should abide by the book, which led to creative tensions. Winfrey wanted to be faithful to the verisimilitude of Morrison's novel, but there were times when following the book interfered with Demme's visual sense of lighting and use of flashbacks to keep the film's rhythmic pace. The visual and sonic elements of the film were used to augment Morrison's prose, such as when Tak Fujimoto utilizes his trademark pulsating red light during Beloved's encounter with Paul D.

"We couldn't use everything from the book," Demme admitted, "but we didn't make the frequent kind of little 'improvements' that filmmakers often make on books. When you go, 'You know, I know that they are riding up—in the book, it says they're riding up in a Chevrolet in red outfits, but wouldn't it be terrific if they arrived in a big, black Cadillac and had on tuxedos? You know, that would be much more visual, wouldn't it?' We didn't do that kind of thing. We tried to be faithful to the kind of imagery that Toni Morrison was picturing in her mind in the first place."[12] "I was steadfast on representing the essence of what Toni Morrison intended in those pages," Winfrey said, "that we were not going to disrupt that."[13]

On *Beloved*, like his experience on *Swing Shift*, Demme would have his share of worry; once again, the leading actress was also the producer and had the final say about what should be in the film. When Winfrey asked to sit in on the dailies, Demme acquiesced. "I, as a producer, was watching dailies every day," Winfrey said. "Jonathan said only because I was the producer that he allowed me to see the dailies; he would not allow the actors to see them." To avoid being stuck in the same position as he was on *Swing Shift*, Demme asked to stop by Oprah's hotel room the day after one particular incident.

"I was watching the dailies and making comments about my reaction to Thandiwe's scene about the diamonds," Winfrey recalled. "When he came in, I felt like I was eleven years old and had been taken to the principal's office. He read me the riot act about doubting the shots and commenting on the scenes—it was unacceptable, and he banned me from dailies. I was sitting there crying. I was a kid who was never taken to the principal's office, so I was sitting there thinking what it was like to be reprimanded. I wasn't allowed back in dailies for a while."[14]

Winfrey's most challenging day on set was when Toni Morrison visited. "Toni came on set, and we were looking at dailies of the 'stolen milk' scene," Winfrey said.

> I had done various takes on that where Sethe was crying. I remember sitting there in dailies, and Toni turned to Jonathan saying, "Sethe never cried." She just glared at me, and I was so embarrassed. I thought Toni Morrison hated me. Jonathan responded, "You know, she has her vision of it, and you have your interpretation, and we can find the balance because we have many, many takes where she didn't cry." That put the fear of Toni in me for the rest of the film no matter what. Even at the end scene when Sethe is sitting in bed, I was like "Jonathan, does she cry?" He said, "Sethe never cries!"[15]

Ghosts at the Door (1997–2000)

Arguably one of the most difficult scenes for Demme to shoot was young Sethe (LisaGay Hamilton) being abused by the plantation owners. Hamilton was wary about the brutal scene. "She wanted for me to be on set during this milk rape scene," Kristi Zea said.

> I could tell she was in distress about it, and I went over to him and said, "Jonathan, I need to let you know that this is a very upsetting scene for the actress, and she asked me to stay on the set while this goes on." What he didn't want was for me to break the fourth wall in the sense of making sure that she felt supported but not get in his way of directing the scene. Even though she was wearing a prosthetic device, and no one was touching her skin, it was so intimidating for her that at a certain point, she was feeling insecure about it. You must put yourself in a head space of walking that fine line between reality and support.[16]

The realism of Demme's portrayal of violence in the film caught the eye of the Philadelphia Police Department. Michael J. Dennis, the film's office and stage production assistant, had "a bird's-eye view of the production." One of the jobs was to take film stills to be processed. "This was on 35mm still photography, so you have to take it to CVS," Dennis recalled. "One of the PAs got detained because one of the photos was a makeup test for the dead infant. Whoever was processing the film thought that it was real."[17]

Despite the harrowing experiences shooting the violent sequences, the set did carry an emotional warmth throughout production until it wrapped up in Philadelphia. An avid baseball fan, Demme drove up to Cooperstown, New York, to the Baseball Hall of Fame with his son, Brooklyn, buying jerseys for the cast and crew as gifts.[18] Demme's focus on a historical ghost story had some resonance in his personal life. "I believe in ghosts. . . . I believe in spirits and inhabiting," Demme told Charlie Rose. "I think that one thing that it comes from is, as life goes on and—I mean, my grandmother, who's been dead for many years—especially when I'm interacting with my kids—she's always in the room. And I know my parents who have died—their spirits are around."[19]

Beloved was released in theaters nationwide on October 16, 1998. The film received mixed reviews. While Kenneth Turan praised the film in his review for the *Los Angeles Times*, citing the "unsentimental fierceness"[20] in Demme's adaptation of *Beloved*, Joe Morgenstern of the *Wall Street Journal* was critical of Demme's interpretation of Morrison's novel: "It has savored Ms. Morrison's diction but rendered much of it in ponderous Noble Negro-speak. It has swallowed all of those ghosts whole but hasn't figured out how to objectify the author's magic realism, surrealism and primitive supernaturalism without turning drama into an off-putting freak show."[21]

The expectation that a late-nineties American audience would embrace a film like *Beloved* seemed appropriate given the series of World War II films released in the fall of 1998: Roberto Benigni's comedy/drama centered around the Holocaust, *Life Is Beautiful*; Steven Spielberg's intensely violent account of the Normandy landings, *Saving Private Ryan*; and Terrence Malick's adaptation of James Jones's book about US infantrymen on Guadalcanal in *The Thin Red Line*. Incidentally, Spielberg had attempted to capture the slave trade in his epic *Amistad* a year earlier. However, audiences may have been taken by surprise by *Beloved*, expecting something akin to *The Silence of the Lambs*'s tabloid-inspired serial killers. Instead, they were presented with a ghost story, an existential reflection on an America still unable to acknowledge its genocidal past. "I realized that when we were doing the testing for the film," Winfrey said, "we got notes back saying people were so confused; the questions we got back were 'Was she a real ghost, like Casper?' (in reference to Joe Oriolo and Seymour Reit's comic strip and Brad Silberling's 1995 film adaptation). 'If she was a real ghost, why can't she walk through walls?' I think there was a different expectation, a different comprehension from the audience of what it meant to present a spirit in the context of Toni Morrison's story."[22]

Demme would point the finger at the theater chains that released the film in a small window of time. "*Beloved* only played in theaters for four weeks, it made $22 million—I think that's a lot of money—and the only reason it left theaters after a month was because the Disney Corporation that released the picture wanted all of the *Beloved* theaters that were doing well in a number of situations, but those theaters wanted those theaters for Adam Sandler's comedy *The Waterboy* (1998). We were told that they would bring us back at the end of the year, and they didn't. But the picture did very respectably. It was in the Top Ten its whole short life."[23] With an estimated budget of $80 million, *Beloved* was considered a flop. The only supernatural event that topped the box office was Nicole Kidman and Sandra Bullock playing witchy sisters in Griffin Dunne's romantic comedy *Practical Magic* (1998).

Like *Philadelphia*, *Beloved* was made with sincere intentions; Winfrey and Demme wanted to illuminate audiences through the visceral and breathtaking imagery initially penned by Toni Morrison. In many respects, *Beloved* was a film ahead of its time, focusing on the Black experience of the Reconstruction Era. Tak Fujimoto's sumptuous and grainy cinematography emphasized both the horrific and the bucolic in the same way Vittorio Storaro lit Bertolucci's *Novecento (1900)* (1976) or Haskell Wexler used backlight aura for Hal Ashby's film about folk singer Woody Guthrie, *Bound for Glory* (1976).

Some thought if the film had been released on television, as was David L. Wolper's adaptation of Alex Haley's *Roots* (ABC, 1977), it might have become a critically praised epic. "You've got Oprah and Jonathan Demme swinging for the fences to present the subject as accurately as possible to the book," Michael Dennis said. "Had it been made as a made-for-TV-series, it would have been legendary."[24] With the film clocking in at nearly three hours, it seemed like Demme could have made two ninety-minute films like he did during his days with Roger Corman. It had been Corman's ambition to capture segregation in his commercially panned 1962 film *The Intruder*, but Demme realized that social commentary can only motivate an audience to a certain point before the eye becomes distracted.

THERE'S NO GOING BACK

Beloved did find a fan in Sidney Lumet, who wrote a glowing letter to Winfrey about his admiration for the film and her performance. In a letter marked February 3, 1999, Lumet wrote the following:

> I heard all kinds of theories about why people think it failed commercially and artistically. None of the theories deal with the most obvious and simplest truth: our country will simply not involve itself in anything about Black life that moves out of the narrow, preconceived notion of what White America thinks Black life means. There are so many continual gambles in it. Even though *Beloved* is not overtly political, it is, in my view, a very political picture. Any piece of work that deals with black or white life being treated so poorly is in return, per se, political. I found the picture so deeply moving and disturbing, wonderfully acted, and directed.[25]

Over a decade after *Beloved*'s release, Demme contacted Winfrey about the possibility of rereleasing the film. In hindsight, the timing was perfect as the filmgoing audiences of 2012 were more open-minded and receptive to films about racial inequality. *Beloved* had been up against the popular fare of the late nineties, which was preoccupied with the grief of white suburban America, as in Ang Lee's *The Ice Storm* (1997), Sofia Coppola's *The Virgin Suicides* (1999), and Sam Mendes's *American Beauty* (1999). In contrast, films like Lee Daniels's *Precious: Based on the Novel "Push" by Sapphire* (2009), Tate Taylor's *The Help* (2011), and Benh Zeitlin's *Beasts of the Southern Wild* (2012) were now being warmly embraced. However, Winfrey thought otherwise. "There was a part of me that didn't want to relive through the experience of the lack of reception that I decided to attempt to never make a film about slavery again," Winfrey said. "I was hurt by Black journalists asking me, 'Why do we need another film about slavery?' I responded, 'When's the last film we've had about slavery?' I was really surprised to see *12 Years a Slave* (Steve McQueen's 2013 Oscar-winning film) received so well as it was. I thought, 'Maybe the climate has changed.'"[26]

Ghosts at the Door (1997–2000)

While filming *Beloved*, LisaGay Hamilton and Beah Richards developed a strong friendship. Hamilton told Demme she wanted to direct her first project: a documentary honoring Richards's life as an actress, poet, and orator. While Richards was battling emphysema and limited mobility, Hamilton visited her in Vicksburg, Mississippi, with her digital camera. The result is a warm, reflective, and hopeful tribute to the advancement of Black artists in American theater and cinema, which was epitomized by Richards's ceaseless energy. Richards passed away on September 14, 2000. In her final wishes, she asked LisaGay to scatter her ashes over the cemetery honoring the Confederate soldiers of the Civil War as an act of defiance to those who profited off the work of 12.5 million Black people. In 2004, Hamilton would release the Peabody Award–winning documentary *Beah: A Black Woman Speaks*.

Demme continued to be involved with humanitarian efforts in Haiti. In 1995, he received a videotape of a twelve-year-old Haitian boy, Roland Aristide (no relation to the corrupt leader of Haiti), talking into the camera and addressing his missing mother, Lucienne. "That video kicked me into gear," Demme told the *Miami Herald* in 1998. "I had been to Guantanamo a couple of times and all I could see was this great mass of people. Then, I saw the tape of a boy trying to find his mother, and it put a single face on the whole crisis."[27]

The video was given to Demme by attorney Cheryl Little, whom he met when she was interviewed for the 1992 documentary *Haiti: Killing the Dream,* produced and directed by Hart Perry and Katharine Kean after Aristide's ouster. Representing three hundred children for the Florida Immigrant Advocacy Center, Little was invited on Oprah Winfrey's television show to address the topic of displaced families seeking refuge and citizenship status in the United States. After Lucienne reunited with her son, Roland, Florida senators Bob Graham and Connie Mack introduced the Haitian Refugee Fairness Act.[28] The Aristide reunion was a positive affirmation for Demme and his continuing passion toward Haiti.

With any passion comes great loss, and such was the case when Radio Haiti's leading journalist, filmmaker, and activist, Jean

Dominique, was assassinated outside the offices of the station on April 3, 2000. One of the first broadcasters to editorialize his broadcasts and introduce the Beatles to Haiti, Jean Dominique used his platform to call out the authoritarian rulership of the Duvaliers and support Aristide's run for office.

Demme first met Jean Dominique when he was filming *Haiti: Dreams of Democracy* in early 1987. "While making that film," Demme said, "everyone encouraged me to go to Radio Haiti and talk to Jean and Michèle." Their shared love for Haiti, its music, and its canon of cinema culminated in late 1991 when Jean Dominique and his wife, Michèle Montas, left Haiti after Aristide's ouster and after the Tonton Macoutes made several attacks on the station. "He did this amazing thing where he would wrinkle up his nose and sniff the air," Demme told WNYC in 2000. "He would smell what was happening."[29]

Demme would befriend Dominique and Montas when they moved to New York, and he started filming conversations with Jean Dominique with the initial intention of making a documentary about a journalist in exile. "Jonathan was obsessed with the idea of finding the history of Haitian cinema," Edwidge Danticat said, "and part of my job was also research and calling people about finding prints of these missing films. After teaching these classes at Ramapo College, Jonathan would film these interviews with Jean that would be part of *The Agronomist*."[30]

Demme wanted to develop a project exemplifying the importance of Haitian cinema, and then his friend was assassinated: "The only response to the anguish and anger of losing such a dear friend and extraordinary man was to finish the film."[31] As with Juan Botas, Jean Dominique would be honored through a documentary about his upbringing in Papa Doc's Haiti, his advocacy for screening Haitian cinema (much to the chagrin of the authoritarian Duvalier), his self-imposed exile, and his return to Radio Haiti. When asked by Demme about the prospects of reviving his radio station on his return to Haiti, Jean Dominique replied, "Jonathan, you cannot kill the truth. You cannot kill justice. You cannot kill what we are fighting for." The footage of Jean Dominique flashing a peace sign to the sixty thousand people applauding his return to Haiti in late 1986 epitomizes the country's unity and support for a free press in a politically fragile society.

Like *Cousin Bobby*, *The Agronomist* is a reverential portrait of one of Jonathan's personal heroes and friends. In some ways, Demme and Jean Dominique were kindred spirits. Their initial love of cinema in the mid-sixties culminated in individual keystone moments: While Jonathan was cutting his teeth in movie publicity, Jean Dominique's United Haitian Filmmakers collective was dissolved by Duvalier, leading to his first arrest in 1965, three years after the release of his documentary *Et Moi, Mais Je Suis Belle* (1962). After leaving jail, Dominique brought his enlightened perspective on Haiti's politics to the airwaves in 1973, the same year Demme began writing his directorial debut. In *The Agronomist*, Jean Dominique told Demme about the sociopolitical influence French cinema had on him at a young age. "In France," Dominique said, "I discovered that if you seek a good film correctly, the grammar of the film is a political act." After his friend's passing, Demme would find himself in France attempting to reinvent his creativity.

16

Losing Control (2000–2004)

Jonathan described *The Truth about Charlie* as "a receptacle for all this love I had for French cinema and culture."[1] With this remake of Stanley Donen's 1962 espionage thriller *Charade*, Demme wanted to modernize Peter Stone's story of a young woman who becomes entangled in a deadly game of cat and mouse when a trio of assassins try to find twenty-five thousand dollars stolen from them by her dead husband. In Demme's version, six million dollars' worth of diamonds was stolen from Charlie's cohorts during a botched raid in war-torn Sarajevo. Meanwhile, Charlie's estranged mother was hunting down her son's killers.

Jonathan focused on the production of *The Truth about Charlie* like he was shooting his early films for New World Pictures, revisiting the Corman-esque storytelling of his early years—only this time, he would be working with advanced technology and a bigger budget. Rather than shooting strictly on film, Demme embraced digital cameras, seeing the benefit of their time-saving quality to enhance this creative venture. He said, "The idea for us is to try and shoot the kind of movie we would have liked to do fresh out of film school."[2] Like a cinephile auditing classes at NYU, Demme soaked up inspiration watching international capers from Tom Tykwer (*Run Lola Run*), Wong Kar-Wai (*Chungking Express*), and Lou Ye (*Suzhou River*). His trip to the 1999 Sundance Film Festival to see Lee Myung-se's *Nowhere to Hide* inspired him to cast Park Joong-Hoon in his latest film.

Before production began, the unimaginable happened: Clinica Estetico closed shop. Reported in *Variety* as an amicable divorce, the split between Demme and his production partner, Ed Saxon, came at an awkward point when various projects were slated to be produced under the Clinica Estetico banner.[3] As with Orion's bankruptcy a decade earlier, it can be assessed that Clinica Estetico was feeling the financial struggle of keeping afloat in the wake of both *Beloved* and *Storefront Hitchcock*'s tepid box office reception, despite their critical praise. The losses were too much for the company to bear, and they couldn't keep the clinic running. The tension built behind the closed doors of Jonathan's office; the mounting pressure of sidelining projects was anathema to the mellow environment he and Saxon had created fifteen years before. Sodas and chili burgers calmed Demme's nerves as he focused on *The Truth about Charlie*.

Initially helping on the screenplay was one of Demme's biggest fans, Paul Thomas Anderson. In an interview promoting *Boogie Nights*, his 1997 hit film about the San Fernando Valley porno boom of the late seventies, Anderson was asked who his three favorite filmmakers were. Like Orson Welles's response to a similar question sixty years earlier, where he referenced John Ford as his favorite director, Anderson said, "Jonathan Demme, Jonathan Demme, and Jonathan Demme."[4] After seeing *Boogie Nights* and reading of Anderson's admiration for his movies, Demme met with Anderson, and their friendship blossomed over the next two decades. However, schedules got in the way of this collaboration, and Steve Schmidt ended up cowriting *The Truth about Charlie* with Demme while Anderson focused his efforts on *Punch-Drunk Love* (2002), his enveloping dramedy inspired by Blake Edwards's and Stanley Donen's films.

Demme envisioned *Beloved* star Thandiwe Newton and Will Smith as his Audrey Hepburn and Cary Grant. He arranged a screening of *Charade* for Newton, telling her why she would be perfect as Regina Lambert, and she happily accepted. Will Smith was considering playing Lewis Bartholomew (aka Joshua Peters) until Michael Mann cast him as Muhammad Ali in *Ali* (2001), his upcoming biopic for Columbia Pictures.[5] After rewatching *Boogie Nights*, Demme realized Mark Wahlberg was a promising alternative to Will Smith.

Jeffrey Wright was the first actor in Demme's mind to play the deceptive Carson Dyle. Demme had wanted to work with Wright ever since seeing his portrayal of Jean-Michel Basquiat in artist Julian Schnabel's 1996 directorial debut, *Basquiat*. Like Will Smith, Wright had already agreed to work on *Ali*, and Demme turned to his friend and fellow filmmaker Tim Robbins to play Dyle.[6] Alongside Park Joong-Hoon were Ted Levine and LisaGay Hamilton as Charlie's band of thieves. In contrast to *Charade*, the presence of Christine Boisson as the commandant investigating Charlie's killer and Frédérique Meininger as Charlie's vengeful mother is courtesy of Demme's unbridled love for female protagonists who are reliable in a world of lying men.

Shooting in Paris was a breath of fresh air for Demme as he and Tak Fujimoto scouted locations around the city. However, they didn't want *The Truth about Charlie* to look like a dated vacation postcard; paranoia and realism were what Fujimoto envisioned when scouting locations with Demme. "There's a rule that as long as the camera isn't mounted," Demme said, "you can shoot wherever you want without a permit."[7] If the camera was not grounded by a tripod, Demme, Fujimoto, and camera operator Pierre Morel could shoot verité. In the one case where the camera needed to be placed at ground level, they used a deflated soccer ball to prop it up.[8]

Along with keeping the eyeball stimulated, Demme wanted the audience to soak in the soundtrack of thirty-eight songs stitched into the film: "In the cutting room, I started to think of the story like a concert, which builds in momentum then finds a place for a slower number and then builds up again in intensity."[9] Except for Charles Aznavour's performance at the end of *The Truth about Charlie*, Demme's remake had the momentum of a music video; it was cut at a pace that defied the director's love for extended takes. However, wariness over Demme's new project was building in the press. As *Entertainment Weekly* wrote, "Pairing Wahlberg and

Newton feels appealingly fresh, but a yearlong *post-production*? This isn't *The Lord of the Rings*."[10]

Universal ran test screenings of *The Truth about Charlie* over the summer. A two-hour cut played to mixed reception. After three screenings, Demme pared down the film to a solid 104 minutes: "I have final cut, so in theory, I could put out any version I want. But I want a lot of people to see the movie, and one terrific way of finding out how much folks are going to like it is to show it to recruited audiences. So, I embrace that part of the process very much."[11] Despite his pragmatism in putting a positive spin on test audiences, Demme was personally dismayed that his original cut didn't appeal to them.

Released on October 25, 2002, *The Truth about Charlie* opened to a paltry $2.2 million in its first weekend. The film would ultimately gross over $7 million worldwide, not even making a dent in the $60 million budget.[12] While some critics like Andrew Sarris and Peter Travers gave Demme the benefit of the doubt in his intertextual love letter to the Nouvelle Vague, others were scathing in their reviews. The *Chicago Reader* called the film "a flat-footed remake."[13] As a former film critic and publicist, Demme found it hard to avert his gaze from a bad review and not dwell on it, even when he showed off his wide smile during interviews promoting the movie.

The Truth about Charlie can be classified as a meta-Demme film. His New World Pictures approach toward sex, violence, and social commentary is present in the film: Newton's shower scene at the Hotel Langlois—named after the cofounder of the Cinematheque Française—is a nod to Cary Grant's fully clothed shower scene in *Charade*, and Demme's plea for peace is shown in the climactic standoff ending with everyone's guns on the ground. Beyond referencing the French films and actors he admired, Demme used the camera to honor those who had helped him in his career. Kenny Utt's photo hangs outside the garage of the swap meet as the late Monsieur Hyppolite, the stamp collector who had an eye for rarities. After the comedic nod to *The Silence of the Lambs* during the end credits, as Tim Robbins is poisoned by Frédérique Meininger, a shot of François Truffaut's grave appears on the screen; after signing Demme's copy of *Hitchcock/Truffaut* back in 1968, Truffaut was the first filmmaker who told Jonathan that he would be a director.

Demme honored his nephew Ted Demme by featuring "Bigga Man" on *The Truth about Charlie* soundtrack. Written by Ted Demme, the song had a personal resonance for Jonathan after tragedy struck on January 13, 2002. Ted Demme, who had just come off the critical and box office successes of *Blow* (2001), died of a heart attack during a charity basketball game in Santa Monica.[14] He was thirty-eight years old. Jonathan consoled his estranged brother, Rick, and sister-in-law, Gail, over the loss of their son. Rick passed away from cancer three months later in Fort Pierce, Florida.[15]

Despite his personal losses and the commercial failure of *The Truth about Charlie*, Demme continued to work. He rebounded as the executive producer on Spike Jonze's *Adaptation* (2002). Demme and Ed Saxon had acquired the rights to Susan Orlean's book *The Orchid Thief* in 1998, while Clinica Estetico was still in operation. They hired Charlie Kaufman to write a script with Jonze directing. Demme and Saxon expected a faithful rendering of Orlean's story about orchid enthusiast John LaRoche and his life in the Florida Everglades, but Kaufman had such a difficult time adapting the book that he wrote himself into the story. Kaufman visited the set of *Being John Malkovich* (1999) and told Spike Jonze about the new premise, which Jonze loved. However, Kaufman kept this information from Demme and Saxon until after the script was finished.[16]

Starring Nicolas Cage, Meryl Streep, and Chris Cooper, *Adaptation* earned a cool $32.8 million worldwide and four Academy Award nominations in 2003, including Best Screenplay for Charlie and Donald Kaufman. Chris Cooper received the Best Supporting Actor award for his portrayal of John LaRoche.

While promoting *The Truth about Charlie*, Demme wasn't asked about his cinematic ode to French New Wave cinema or his involvement with *Adaptation*. The question on reporters' minds was whether he had seen Ridley Scott's *Hannibal* (2001) or Brett Ratner's *Red Dragon* (2002). The films that followed in the Hannibal Lecter franchise haunted audiences and split critics over Scott's and Ratner's rendering of Harris's novels. Thankfully, Demme didn't want to be associated with either picture. A decade later it seemed like Demme was Clarice Starling: he couldn't stop the screaming of the lambs.

Demme's next film was conceived in the wake of the September 11 attacks, when nineteen members of Al-Qaeda hijacked and crashed planes into the World Trade Center and the Pentagon. President George W. Bush then declared war on Afghanistan before invading Iraq in March 2003. A pacifist since seeing *Far from Vietnam* at the 1967 New York Film Festival, Demme was frustrated at how the hawkish commander in chief was heard at home. His disdain toward the Bush administration was evident when he bought his dogs a squeaky toy that resembled Bush's senior advisor, Karl Rove.[17]

The war on terror would be reflected in Demme's remake of the Cold War classic *The Manchurian Candidate*. John Frankenheimer's 1962 film version of Richard Condon's novel was received with mixed reviews by American critics.[18] The pall over the nation in the wake of the Kennedy assassination and the Cuban Missile Crisis led the film to be pulled from circulation in 1963. Frank Sinatra, who starred in the 1962 version, went so far as to purchase the distribution rights to keep it from being screened. In 1988, the film was rereleased to critical acclaim, being heralded as Frankenheimer's best film.[19] Sinatra's daughter Tina reportedly went to a screening and was so amazed by the audience reception that she called her father to sign off on her producing an updated version of *The Manchurian Candidate*.[20] She brought the project to Sherry Lansing, the CEO of Paramount Pictures.[21] When going over the possible directors to helm the remake, they brought up Demme's name.

At the time, Demme had signed on to International Creative Management, with Robert Newman as his agent. Newman, a fan of Demme's since seeing *Last Embrace* while attending the University of Miami, helped market *The Truth about Charlie* before Demme went to ICM.[22] Showing interest in shooting another remake of another film from his youth, Demme flew out to Los Angeles and met with Lansing and coproducer Scott Rudin to go over casting decisions.

THERE'S NO GOING BACK

The film substitutes the Gulf War for the Korean War as the setting for the story of former prisoner of war Maj. Ben Marco. In the original, Marco has recurring nightmares of his fellow captive Sgt. Raymond Shaw, who was brainwashed into killing two members of his platoon. While Marco is investigating these dreams, he tracks down Shaw, whose domineering mother, Eleanor Shaw Iselin, is supporting her husband, Senator John Iselin, in his run for the presidency. When Eleanor reveals a queen of diamonds from a pack of cards, Raymond is ordered to assassinate her husband's opponent. On realizing this hypnotic chicanery, Marco is unable to resist the queen of diamonds and assassinates Raymond before turning the gun on himself.

Meryl Streep wanted to work with Demme after coming off her performance in *Adaptation*. Denzel Washington, whom Demme was excited about reuniting with for the first time since *Philadelphia*, would play Marco. They had recently reconnected at a Director's Guild New York screening in December 2002, where Demme praised Washington's directorial debut, *Antwone Fisher*.[23] For the role of Raymond Shaw, Liev Schreiber was a favorite for Demme and Lansing; his physique and intensity were reminiscent of Laurence Harvey's in the Frankenheimer film. Additionally, Schreiber and Washington had worked together before on Norman Jewison's 1999 film *The Hurricane*.

Kristi Zea accompanied Jonathan to LA to show Sherry Lansing the artwork Denzel Washington's Ben Marco would have in his notebook. "We had a bunch of illustrations to show Sherry to get her on the same page," Zea recalled. "In the middle of all that, Jonathan basically said, 'Scott [Rudin] is not helping. Either it's him or me.' That's when they worked out some sort of deal, and Scott got off the show."[24] Rudin was out of his way, but it was the first of many difficulties that would rest on Demme's shoulders throughout production. Few details were given by those interviewed about Demme's sudden decision to separate himself from Rudin, but it can be inferred that, similar to his contention with Freddie Fields and Paramount while making *Citizens Band*, Demme didn't want to revisit the anxiety he had felt with Rudin after the release of *Philadelphia*.

Jonathan had a budget of eighty million dollars and was on a tight schedule of three months to shoot and edit the film before the runup to the Democratic National Convention.[25] Daniel Pyne, who co-adapted Tom Clancy's *The Sum of All Fears* (2002) for Paramount, was brought on to turn *The Manchurian Candidate* from a Cold War thriller into a film that reflected the post-9/11 zeitgeist. Eleanor Shaw would be written as a senator, rather than a senator's wife, assisting her son's run for public office with her nefarious supporters at Manchurian Global, a Halliburton-inspired arms manufacturer. Pyne suggested to Demme that Eugenie Rose Chaney, Marco's love interest, who is marginalized in the original film, be involved in tracking Marco's activities as a covert agent who cleans up politically motivated assassinations. According to Demme, "Dan's idea was that if Marco is going to have a much more difficult journey, then someone has to function the way Marco does in the original film and be the force of good rising to the rescue."[26] Demme suggested *Beloved*'s Kimberly Elise as the perfect actor to play Rosie.

Shooting commenced on September 22, 2003,[27] six months after the start of the US-led invasion of Iraq. Thus, recreating Operation Desert Storm in the Middle East was a risk Paramount didn't want to take. Frankenheimer had shot the fighting scenes of the Korean War in Griffith Park. In this version, Demme used the sandy vistas of Jacksonville, Florida, and the salt mines of West Creek, New Jersey, to replicate war-torn Kuwait. As in *The Truth about Charlie*, Demme and Tak Fujimoto shot the battle sequences in digital with night vision optics, mirroring the battle footage of the Gulf War.[28]

On most films, Demme would dress in his tropical apparel or tourist-trap sweatshirts, yet during the production of *The Manchurian Candidate*, he wore wingtips, pressed pants, a dress jacket, and a tie with a Windsor knot. Though he had a smile on his face with his actors, the tension and stress were getting to Demme. He recalled Ben Marco being "like a receiver picking up all this information," and Demme's obsessive nature of immersing himself into a film like it was a heated pool felt more like he was getting caught up in a riptide.[29] There were constant rewrites to the script as news broke about the inhumane treatment of prisoners at Abu Ghraib, which was orchestrated by US soldiers stationed with the 327th Military Police. But Demme pushed ahead, exhausting himself in the process.

Tak Fujimoto was concerned about Demme's irritability in between setups. "It took a lot out of him," Craig McKay observed as he and Carol Littleton edited the film. "He thought it was a miserable experience; he wasn't behaving like himself. Jonathan wondered if he had lost a part of himself making that film."[30] Demme pined for the wisdom and stoicism of his departed friend and producer, Kenny Utt, whose photo was again on the set, this time displayed in Rosie's apartment.

Despite the anxiety, Demme savored the time he had working with Meryl Streep. Neither Washington nor Streep watched the original film before shooting commenced, and she brought her own ideas of how Eleanor Shaw should be presented. She studied the rhetoric and nuances of Nancy Reagan and General George Patton. While watching Streep ask Dean Stockwell, "Where are all the men anymore?" after the assassination of Senator Thomas Jordan, Demme couldn't help but smile behind the monitors. Streep's impromptu chewing of the ice from her drink at the Compass Restaurant assured Demme that she was not a woman who needed to take direction. "Arguably there's no character Meryl has ever played who is so completely removed from who she is as a person," Demme told David Thompson. "Yet, we were able to capitalize on some of her real-life characteristics: how rampantly smart she is, and how sexy and charismatic."[31]

One thing Demme was adamant about was not recreating the memorable scenes from Frankenheimer's film, namely the solitaire game with the hypnotic queen of diamonds and the ending. Solitaire is replaced by microchips inserted into Marco and Shaw, which are activated by a phone call ordering them to kill. Demme uses an extended take in the dream sequence (in which Shaw strangles one of his fellow soldiers) to deliberately present the audience with gritty and stylized violence that was not present in the original Hays Code–era film and to address the trauma sustained by war-weary soldiers.

Demme said, "We felt that a scene with Raymond strangling somebody surrounded by a lot of technology is enough to haunt a guy for a long time."[32]

The election victory party scene was shot at the Cipriani Club on Wall Street. Inspired by Richard Sylbert's prophetic use of televisions and news broadcasters in Frankenheimer's production, Demme and Kristi Zea used jumbotron plasma-screen televisions in their design for Shaw's campaign headquarters and the victory party. As in most of his films, Demme wanted to record a live musical performance. He'd seen the Fountains of Wayne perform the Kinks' "Better Things" on the NBC talk show *Late Night with Conan O'Brien*. Demme wanted the band to perform on the stage in Uncle Sam costumes as Marco carries out the assassinations of Raymond and Eleanor Shaw as a darkly satirical note on post-9/11 America.[33]

The live performance never came to fruition. Instead, the music is cued up as Washington steadies his aim for the sniper's nest shot at a separate location in Yonkers. Rather than Marco committing suicide after shooting the Shaws, Rosie runs up to the sniper's nest to shoot him in the arm before he attempts to kill himself. The ending reveals complex contradictions and hypocrisy within corporate and media realms. Before a broadcast by cable news, Rosie and her fellow agents are shown doctoring surveillance footage of Marco entering the Cipriani Club to target Manchurian Global for its involvement in the assassination. It was a significant scene for Demme—his comment on the wag-the-dog attitude of the US media during the lead-up to the Iraq War. "The newscaster says that another former employee was arrested, and the authorities are pursuing any other links that might exist," Demme said. "In other words, it's not the media who is pursuing it—they'll report what the authorities tell them. So, our anger isn't a copycat, recycled anger from Richard Condon's book or Frankenheimer's movie: there's a lot to be enraged and frightened about today."[34]

Demme's current frustrations with Paramount reopened wounds from the struggle he had with Freddie Fields on *Citizens Band* over twenty-five years earlier. During postproduction, the studio rejected

Rachel Portman, the composer who had scored *Beloved* and *The Truth about Charlie*, as the best choice to score the film. "It never occurred to me that I would hear back from Paramount Pictures, 'We veto Rachel Portman.' Fortunately, I had power of veto, too, but I couldn't proceed in the presence of it."[35] After listening to samples and temp tracks from other composers, Demme was insistent that Portman score the movie.

With the Democratic National Convention months away and time being of the essence, Paramount went with Demme's decision on Portman. But his frustration seeped through, even to his own choice. Demme sent notes to Portman's home in England saying that the music "wasn't dark enough." Consulting with his longtime musical editor, Suzana Perić, Demme wasn't sure that Portman "had a dark side" and thought perhaps he'd made the wrong decision. Perić assured Demme, "Rachel has a dark side. Wait until you see when you tell her." When Demme told Portman he needed something that would "scare the shit out of everyone," Portman sent in a trove of music that fit the dark and terrifying mood of *The Manchurian Candidate*.[36]

Filming wrapped on January 31, 2004. An exhausted Demme retreated to his living room back in Nyack and watched the hawkish actions of Operation Iraqi Freedom. When promoting *The Manchurian Candidate* the following year, Demme didn't hide his personal disdain for politicians profiting off business interests. "In this movie, I've tried to ask the questions 'Is this okay? Is there something morally wrong with this?' . . . And I firmly believe there is something profoundly wrong with this—it takes a notion of conflict of interest into an Armageddon dimension—but infuriatingly no one is talking about it."[37]

There were other filmmakers equally frustrated with the false-flag narrative from the Bush administration that Saddam Hussein having weapons of mass destruction is what led to the invasion of Iraq.[38] Trey Parker and Matt Stone, the creators of Comedy Central's controversial animated series *South Park*, made a marionette-led satire about the war on terror titled *Team America: World Police*, which was slated for an October release by Paramount. And one week before the theatrical release of *The Manchurian Candidate*, Michael Moore's *Fahrenheit 9/11*, a scathing and controversial critique of George W. Bush, came out and was a critical success. When it was released on July 30, 2004, *The Manchurian Candidate* didn't prove to be as incendiary or revealing as Moore's documentary. Demme's film earned twenty million dollars in its first week, trailing behind Paul Greengrass's *The Bourne Supremacy* and M. Night Shyamalan's *The Village*. The day before the release of *The Manchurian Candidate*, the Democratic National Convention ended with Massachusetts senator John Kerry securing the nomination as the presidential candidate; he would be defeated in the election by George W. Bush the following November by a slim margin of thirty-five electoral votes.[39]

As with *The Truth about Charlie*, critics and audiences were divided over Demme's (second) remake of a sixties movie. David Ansen of *Newsweek* called Demme's version of *The Manchurian Candidate* "doggedly, wretchedly earnest,"[40] while Roger Ebert praised Washington's and Streep's performances and acknowledged that the film "makes timely implications about corporate influence on the White House, on terrorism, and on war."[41] If box office numbers are an indicator of the average American filmgoer, faith and superheroes were guiding them to the megaplex. The *Shrek* and *Spider-Man* sequels and Mel Gibson's *The Passion of the Christ* were the top three films of 2004.

Jonathan Demme didn't want to make another studio picture again. Even though he had final cut and squeaked by with *The Manchurian Candidate* (which grossed ninety-six million dollars—just sixteen million dollars over Paramount's eighty-million-dollar budget[42]), it was hard for him to be an independent filmmaker while at the mercy of the studio, no matter how many accolades or awards he had received.

In times of crisis, Demme would refer to a proverb he heard when he was in Haiti seventeen years earlier: *petit à petit, l'oiseau fait son nid* ("little by little, the bird makes its nest").[43] Demme chose to sequester himself with his family in his Rockland nest, far from the reaches of Hollywood.

17

Heavy Winds (2005–2006)

After *The Manchurian Candidate* failed to be the politically influential blockbuster Jonathan had hoped for, he found peace up in Lovell, Maine, far away from the hurly-burly of Hollywood and New York City.

Demme had an epiphany during the press tour for *The Manchurian Candidate* when Denzel Washington told him about *Napoleon Dynamite* (2004), a movie his kids couldn't stop talking about. Jared Hess's $400,000 film about the comedic and heartfelt adventures of the titular gawky Idaho teenager grossed $44.5 million at the domestic box office. At first, Demme was hesitant when he looked at the PG rating, "the kiss of death," before watching the movie with his kids.[1] But he was struck by the humor and heart of a film shot on a shoestring budget; it was a reminder of how he started behind the camera when working for Roger Corman and of the colloquial charm of *Citizens Band*. If anything, *Napoleon Dynamite* was a sign to the sixty-year-old director that he could make the films he wanted to make without any excessive budgets from the studios.

During his time away from the camera, Demme served as a mentor to aspiring filmmakers. One of them was US Army Sergeant Gonzales R. Joseph. The Haitian-born Joseph emigrated to Florida in 1989 and served three years in the army. Before his enlistment ended, the September 11 attacks prompted him to serve in Operation Iraqi Freedom. "We became avid email pals," Demme said. "He had read about *The Agronomist*. Somehow or other, he managed to see that

Heavy Winds (2005–2006)

film in Iraq and he loved it, it spoke to him."[2] They would correspond until Joseph returned from his tour of duty.

Demme's trips to the movies hadn't slackened since his teenage years in Miami. It was only a twenty-minute ride over the Cuomo Bridge leading to Pleasantville, home of the Jacob Burns Film Center. Prior to the theater's opening in June 2001, JBFC founder Stephen Apkon offered Demme a spot on the advisory board. He declined, saying that "he was so busy and didn't want to just lend his name to something and not be involved. I joked that he was the only person in the industry I reached out to that didn't say yes," Apkon said. This would quickly change.[3]

Demme and his wife, Joanne, were frequent visitors to the theater. They began volunteering in its educational programs, helping elementary school students create animated films in the JBFC's Animation: Minds in Motion program. Demme called Apkon to say that he loved what they were doing and regretted not saying yes earlier and asked if he could join the advisory board. He was offered a position in the board's leadership, which he happily accepted.

The film center was one of the few theaters that wasn't a multiplex catering to mass audiences, and Demme was captivated by the education center, which encouraged children to make movies. Apkon remembered that "Jonathan would come to the red-carpet premieres of fourth-graders' Animation: Minds in Motion films and be cheering them on like it was a Hollywood opening. He located himself within the film center community not as somebody outside or above it but somebody intimately connected to it at its core."[4]

Demme curated his weekend series Rarely Seen Cinema as a way to lure audiences to see films outside the conventions of mainstream cinema. The film that kicked off the series was Conrad Rooks's 1966 *Chappaqua*, a semi-autobiographical psychedelic odyssey through New York. "That was fun to do because the next town over is Chappaqua," Apkon said. "It was clear right from that first night that people wanted to be challenged. They enjoyed it and loved the conversation. In typical JD style, we showed the film, and it wasn't him sitting up on stage playing the Hollywood director.

He would stand at the front with whoever was there and just exude love for the films and the people who created him."⁵

Demme treated audiences to heartfelt anecdotes about his friends whose films he screened, from Bertolucci's 1981 dramedy of a wealthy industrialist hesitant to pay a ransom to save his son (*Tragedy of a Ridiculous Man*) to Hal Ashby's *Coming Home* (1978). Jonathan enjoyed the communal experience with audiences; he called it "fertilizing the air."⁶

On March 15, 2005, Neil Young was in his Central Park hotel suite. The night before at the Waldorf Astoria, he inducted the Pretenders into the Rock and Roll Hall of Fame. When Young woke up after the ceremony, he saw shards of broken glass in his eyesight. The pain grew as Young consulted doctors and neurologists. Young saw a Florida-shaped image in one of the X-rays, which a neurosurgeon told him was a brain aneurysm that needed to be removed within the week. Rather than waiting in his New York hotel room, Young flew down to Nashville; songs would fill his notebook in fifteen- to twenty-minute spurts. He booked some time at Masterlink studios, recording what could have been his last album, *Prairie Wind*.⁷

Young made a full recovery and finished the recording sessions on *Prairie Wind*. Out of nowhere, he got a call from Demme saying he had a year off and wanted to collaborate on a new film. After *Philadelphia*, Demme had made *The Complex Sessions* (1994), filming Young with the band Crazy Horse as they performed four songs from their *Sleeps with Angels* album, and he nearly got involved in making an adaptation of Young's 2003 environmental rock opera, *Greendale*. Young ended up financing and directing *Greendale* through his film production company, Shakey Pictures ("Shakey" was the nickname Young's father used to call him as he struggled with childhood polio). As they were sitting in the restaurant of the Hermitage Hotel, Demme was excited about working again with Neil Young.⁸

It made sense to make a live concert film to debut Young's *Prairie Wind* album. Ideas floated across the table about the appropriate venue for the performance. Two blocks east of the hotel stood the Ryman Auditorium, formerly home to the Grand Ole Opry, the weekly country music showcase broadcast on WSM Radio. Young and Demme thought it would be fitting to model the concert after the Opry shows by having cloth backdrops and using different colored lights to illuminate the stage for each song from *Prairie Wind*. At dinner one night, Neil surprised Demme by telling him that he hired Manuel Cuevas, the man who designed the illustrious Nudie suits for Salvador Dalí, Elvis Presley, and Gram Parsons, as the costume designer. Performing alongside Young would be his wife, Pegi; Emmylou Harris; and the Fisk University Jubilee Singers.

Indie film veteran Ellen Kuras was brought on as cinematographer, with Tony Jannelli and Declan Quinn as camera operators. For Kuras, lighting the stage was a logistical challenge right up to the day of the concert. "Unlike most concert films where the drummer stays in the same spot, or the bass player, you can just put lights in those particular areas," Kuras said. "Every time a song would change, the staging would change; the hammer dulcimer player might be five feet downstage or ten feet stage left for each scene. For me, it was tricky to create these looks and be able to light for each of the songs."[9] While Kuras and the crew worked out the lighting, Demme would take some of the musicians on break from twelve-hour rehearsals for a drive around Nashville to record interviews on his Hi8 definition camcorder.

The curtains rose on August 18, 2005, as Neil Young strummed Hank Williams's sun-burnished Martin D-28 acoustic guitar, opening with "The Painter." Demme was watching the concert from a booth with monitors while Ellen Kuras coordinated with the camera crew. "We were both there working side by side—it was a live show, but we were recording on film," Kuras said. "I had to coordinate with all the camera crews and assistants to stagger when they would roll so that we wouldn't roll out all at the same time, missing critical parts to the songs."[10] The Parcan and Leko lights hung over the stage added a warm aura while Young and his band dug into each song from *Prairie Wind* album. The second half of the show featured Young performing his renowned songs like "Old Man," "Heart of Gold," and "Comes a Time."

For two nights, Neil Young and his band performed to glowing praise from the fans and critics. Writing for the *New York Times*, Jon Pareles noted that Young's "lyrics are infused with feelings of mortality and are full of benedictions and farewells."[11] Contemplative and soulful, Young was savoring his new lease on life through a celebration of life. Thankfully, Demme was there to record this spirited revival. "The reason why the film works is because Jonathan understands feeling," Kuras said. "He understood the emotion and meaning. It's not just that you're documenting the songs being sung; you're capturing the moment. You're creating a sensibility."

Filming these performances for what would be titled *Neil Young: Heart of Gold* brought a much-needed sigh of relief for Demme, who dug his heels into the music and cinematic attributes of the stage. It was also a family affair, with his children working on the film in various capacities and Neil's daughter designing the titles for it. After the two-night residency at the Ryman Auditorium, both artists would keep in contact, with the possibility of Demme making a documentary on the annual concerts created by Neil and Pegi Young to help finance the Bridge School in San Mateo, California.[12]

Ten days later, on August 29, 2005, Hurricane Katrina hit southeast Louisiana. At winds up to 145 miles per hour, the storm left a path of devastation, leaving 1,833 casualties, 850,000 homes ruined, and almost 7,000 people missing.[13] Before the FEMA (Federal Emergency Management Agency) trailers rolled into New Orleans, people waited in lines for food, shelter, fresh water, and phones to call their families. As news organizations projected images of flooded houses, people seeking help from their rooftops, and Interstate-90 clogged with outgoing traffic, Jonathan Demme got a call from his friend Cyril Neville and decided to visit him in New Orleans.

Demme had just finished the postproduction work on *Neil Young: Heart of Gold* before he flew down to New Orleans with his digital camera in January 2006. After arriving at the Lower Ninth Ward Holy Cross neighborhood, Demme watched and listened to the stories of resilience from those trying to return to their homes.

One person who had caught Demme's eye on his first visit to New Orleans was Carolyn Parker, a sixty-year-old woman living in a FEMA trailer. By chance, Demme was walking around with his camera when he met the benevolent woman. Her upbeat attitude and candor with the local mail carrier left an impression on Demme. Before parting ways, Parker said to Demme, "I'm glad I met you today, cameraman!"[14] Demme would become friends with Carolyn and her family, and for the next three years, he chronicled her David-and-Goliath fight to return to her home. Parker's determination to return home struck Demme when she attended a conference held by the Bring New Orleans Back commission, presided over by Mayor Ray Nagin. When Nagin and the panel announced that New Orleanians couldn't return to their homes for another four months, Parker went up to the microphone and told the mayor, "I don't think it's right that you take our properties, over my dead body. I didn't die with Katrina!"[15]

Parker's open spirit, devotion to her church, and history struggling with oppression made Demme and producer/journalist Daniel Wolff frequent flyers to the Crescent City, with their camera in tow. One of the affectionate scenes in Demme's film *I'm Carolyn Parker: The Good, the Mad, and the Beautiful* shows the family sitting in their newly renovated house, having Thanksgiving dinner, and talking about change and progress in America. Ever the soothsayer, Parker tells her children, "When y'all keep shipping those goddamn computers and all this other bull crap, that same thing is what's coming back to bite you in the butts." The film ends with Demme eating a homecooked meal at the Parker homestead and watching the New Orleans Saints' wild-card game against the Seattle Seahawks.

When PBS and its documentary-production division, P.O.V., saw Demme's assembly cut of *I'm Carolyn Parker: The Good, the Mad, and the Beautiful*, they assisted with the postproduction and editing costs. Demme brought on Ido Haar, international filmmaker-in-residence at the Jacob Burns Film Center, to edit the movie in the center's media labs. Haar suggested that Demme narrate portions of the film for the sake of the audience being in concert with the filmmakers, both being invited into Parker's neighborhood and witnessing the six-year revitalization process of her home. "As far as Ido was concerned," Demme said, "this was a relationship film, or a relationship with Carolyn and these visitors from New York who kept showing up year after year."[16]

Parker and the documentary would tour the film festival circuit from Venice to Toronto in 2011. For Demme, the end goal of his film was like that of *Cousin Bobby*, highlighting a profile in courage. "This is a film unlike anything I've made before," Demme said. "Because here's an opportunity for me to introduce to people this amazing friend of mine, this person I've fallen madly in love with, Carolyn Parker, who I believe has the capacity to inspire others in the same way she inspired me."[17]

A year after Katrina, the public interest in rebuilding New Orleans petered out. This only heightened Demme's determination to chronicle the revival of the city. He created a series of shorts, *Right to Return: New Home Movies from the Lower 9th Ward*, which aired on the PBS news program *The Tavis Smiley Show* (2004–2017). "Once the water subsided and the imagery wasn't fresh anymore, we stopped knowing what was going on down here," Demme told the Associated Press. "The hurricane, the floods got our attention. The big question is, 'Then what happened?'"[18] Demme attempted to answer that question in the following years with his new film, *My Favorite American*.

While chronicling the revitalization efforts in New Orleans, Demme reunited with one of the earliest supporters of *Citizens Band*, President Jimmy Carter, who was hard at work building new housing in the city. Since leaving the White House in 1981 after serving his only term in office, Carter was ceaseless in his humanitarian efforts. He and his wife, Rosalynn, got involved in 1984 with Habitat for Humanity, which has built homes for countless low-income families. Carter's efforts extended to building homes for those affected by natural disasters and economic hardships, and he was vocal about his support for Palestine after the 1977 Camp David Peace Accords. However, when promoting his 2006 book, *Palestine: Peace Not Apartheid*, Carter faced backlash from pro-Israel organizations, conservative news outlets, and prominent Democrats like Nancy Pelosi and Howard Dean. Harvard Law professor and controversial firebrand Alan Dershowitz challenged the former president to a debate at Brandeis University, which Carter declined. Demme and producer Neda Armian covered Carter's book tour for the documentary *Jimmy Carter: Man from Plains*.

One of the key shots in the film is of the former president drawing a map to explain the ongoing plight between Israel and Palestine. Demme wanted to shy away from saturating the audience with graphs and statistics through a verité lens. "When faced with the need to visualize the territorial dimension of Palestine in regard to Israel and the other surrounding countries," Demme recalled, "it occurred to me that maybe Carter can make a little map. Little did I realize how incredibly powerful it would be if he sketched it out."[19] Demme was given the map as a gift, which he would hang in his office.

While following the thirty-ninth president across the country, Demme saw him as Gary Cooper's town marshal from Fred Zinnemann's western *High Noon* (1952). "Right off the bat," Demme said, "I can see all this energy went into trying to make the film feel like the kind of proto-western that Carter's journey suggested it could be. Him being such a cowboy, pinning on his badge one more time to go forth and get the feuding parties, the sheepherders, and cattle ranchers to make peace so everybody can live in a more harmonious world."[20] Traveling alongside Carter was an immersive experience. The joy was evident when Demme, cinematographer Declan Quinn, and the crew put down their cameras at a barbeque in Carter's hometown of Plains, Georgia, to have a quail dinner.

Beyond Carter's resemblance to his childhood western heroes, Demme saw similarities between Carter's church sermons and his cousin Bobby's work in serving the community. In Demme's eyes, it was a refreshing contrast to the politically charged rhetoric of the Religious Right, which came to power under Carter's successor, Ronald Reagan. According to Demme, "So much of Christianity and maybe many religions here in America have been so co-opted and turned away from the kind of basic ideals that Carter talks about that for an agnostic like me to hear him talk in these terms about Jesus and God gives me great renewed respect for people of faith."[21]

While in Phoenix, Arizona, Carter met with a caucus of rabbis who wished to privately debate the former president. Initially, Demme was given permission to film the eight-minute meeting by convincing the rabbis that the recording would be impactful for the film and the ongoing Israel-Palestine debate. But when Demme attempted to reach the rabbis for an advanced screening, he was surprised by their response. "A very terse email came back saying, 'Permission will never be granted to use any of the footage from the film. Do not attempt to contact us again and our lawyers now have a copy of this correspondence,'" Demme said. "We never found out what exactly it was that motivated them to not even want to look at what had happened, but it created a tremendous quandary because I was really banking on that scene. I had grown very attached to it . . . in the interest of balance and really making sure that we fully honored both sides of the argument in order to shed light on things, [and] we were suddenly deprived of it."[22]

The last major hurdle for Demme was when he was barred from filming Carter's speech at Brandeis University. Demme called the president of Brandeis, along with elected officials from Massachusetts, to intercede on his behalf; even Jeff Berg, the head of ICM, contacted the university. In the end, Demme managed to acquire footage from Carter's lecture thanks to the student organizations on campus. After Carter's lecture at Brandeis, he and his wife flew to Sudan to oversee the eradication of Guinea-worm disease, which is transmitted through the water supply.[23]

Jimmy Carter: Man from Plains was released in 2007. Demme and editor Kate Amend had whittled the film's initial seven-and-a-half-hour cut down to two hours. For Demme, the experience of following Carter with a camera, from press junkets to his homestead, was a sort of visual affirmation of the imminent need for a politician who was running for public office on a platform of nonviolence, the antithesis of George W. Bush's actions during his presidency. "I feel like this film winds up becoming a certain kind of reference point in the search for a new president," Demme said. "It sets a very high standard, I think, for what a president can and should be like even though it is a 120-minute constant rebuke to the way the current president conducts his business."[24]

Working on this string of documentaries was a holistic experience for Demme. Money was never an issue for him, as he funded his projects based on the desire to celebrate those he respected, and these projects allowed him to expand his talents at shooting on a digital camera. Furthermore, his volunteer work at the Jacob Burns Film Center created once-in-a-lifetime opportunities for aspiring filmmakers. "I'm a terrible camera person," Demme said in 2008, "but I'm getting better—but the new technology, it's always in focus, and if I point it in the right direction, and the subject matter is strong enough, I can get it on television. And that's great. If I can get people to help me for free, I can make it for practically nothing."[25]

In May 2007, Demme wrapped up filming *Jimmy Carter: Man from Plains* in New York City. He shot footage of the musicians recording the film's soundtrack, a cross-section of artists from trumpeter and santur player Amir El Shaffir to bluegrass musicians Gillian Welch and David Rawlings. Although the footage didn't make it into *Jimmy Carter: Man from Plains*, it did offer another glimpse into Demme's passionate response to the organic process of recording music. The camera catches Demme and longtime music supervisor Suzana Perić exchanging excited nods as the music plays. This marriage of music and documentaries would lead Demme to make his next film—his return to narrative features.

18

A Creative Marriage (2007–2009)

Once again, scripts had piled up on Demme's desk, but the thought of making another major motion picture didn't seem to jibe with him. There was no need for him to tangle with the studios like he had with *The Manchurian Candidate*. He was enjoying his period as a documentarian, shooting films centered around those he admired musically, spiritually, and politically. Plus, they were opportunities for his children to experience the communal efforts of working on a film. Ramona and Jos earned assistant and production associate's credits on *Neil Young: Heart of Gold*, while Brooklyn worked with the stagehands at the Ryman Auditorium. It would take the encouragement of a fellow New Yorker to sway Demme back to making a feature film.

Sidney Lumet showed no signs of leaving the director's chair after being honored by the Academy of Motion Pictures Arts and Sciences with a Lifetime Achievement award in 2005. The iconoclastic filmmaker of *12 Angry Men* (1957), *Serpico* (1973), *Dog Day Afternoon* (1975), and *Network* (1976) was directing his final film, *Before the Devil Knows You're Dead* (2007), when his daughter, Jenny, showed him her first screenplay. Lumet knew Demme socially via his letter of support after *Beloved*'s theatrical release and his cameo appearance in *The Manchurian Candidate*. Lumet called him about the prospect of directing Jenny's screenplay. A surprised Demme asked Lumet to mail him the script.

A Creative Marriage (2007–2009)

Meeting with Jenny Lumet in early 2007, Demme saw promise in her screenplay but didn't see himself directing the film—just helping to make the story, in his words, "seasoned."[1] Demme was wary of jumping back into directing and initially turned down Sidney's offer. But he couldn't stop reading Jenny Lumet's script, then titled *Dancing with Shiva*. The women in the story reverberated with the stoicism and joie de vivre of Demme's past protagonists. "It reminded me in a way of *Something Wild*, because everything to me seemed so unexpected," Demme said. "Predictable, set-up, but then, it's always surprising in the way real life can so often be quite unpredictable and surprising. So, I couldn't forget it."[2] Lumet's tale of a woman in recovery attending her sister's wedding while confronting her past triggered memories from Jonathan's personal life. His mother Dodie's struggles with alcohol reverberated off the page. The more Lumet and Demme refined the screenplay, the more Demme wanted to direct the newly titled *Rachel Getting Married*.

Lumet had felt a cosmic connection to Demme since seeing him win his first Oscar fifteen years earlier for *The Silence of the Lambs*. She knew the script was in good hands, sensing his empathy with complex women and seeing how he'd put them in the forefront of his films. "Every single one of them is a pain in the ass," Lumet said about the women in her script. "Some are improbable, and some are straight up impossible. And I thought if you have a screenful of improbable and impossible women, who on the planet is going to keep the audience in their seats? And that would only be him."[3]

Casting Kym was a no-brainer for Jonathan. He'd seen Garry Marshall's *The Princess Diaries* (2001) with his children and was mesmerized by Anne Hathaway's gleaming, bright-eyed energy. Demme said, "From the moment I saw her in her first film, I wanted to work with her."[4] At the time, Hathaway was branching out from the family-friendly fare for Disney with daring performances in Barbara Kopple's *Havoc* (2005) and Ang Lee's *Brokeback Mountain* (2005). Demme first attempted to approach her at an awards ceremony but couldn't make it to her table, which was crowded by people drawn to her like a moth to flames: "I said to myself, 'My God, she's got tremendous presence with lots of luminaries all over the place.' So, I knew that she had it, I knew that the camera loved her, and that she had an energy that was alluring."

Hathaway received the script with a personal note from Jonathan Demme. She was able to see past the exposition of Kym's past with drugs, alcohol, and family tragedy. She saw an opportunity to dive into the complexities of a character far removed from her own life. "I've been asked a lot about Kym, what it was like to play a troubled character, what it was like to play a tortured character, to play a character so consumed with the darkness. I never saw her in any of those ways," Hathaway said. "I just thought, she's a girl struggling to live an honest life. She is honest; fiercely, painfully, and impolitely honest."[5] One week later, Demme met with Hathaway over lunch, where they excitedly discussed the film.

Hathaway's early involvement in *Rachel Getting Married* helped the film's producer, Neda Armian, secure a distribution deal with Sony Pictures Classics. In 2006, Sony Pictures Classics boasted a cadre of award-winning films like Bennet Miller's *Capote* (2005), which earned an impressive fifty million dollars worldwide.[6] It was also seen as a safe haven for international filmmakers like Pedro Almodóvar (*Volver*), Wong Kar-Wai (*2046*), and Michael Haneke (*Cache*). After his meeting with Sony Pictures Classics copresident Michael Barker, Demme felt like he was in safe hands and entrusted his film to the studio. It was a far cry from what he endured with Paramount on *The Manchurian Candidate*.

The role of Kym's sister, Rachel, required an actor who projected authenticity. Rosemarie DeWitt was one of five actresses shortlisted to play the part. The granddaughter of boxing legend James Braddock, DeWitt got her first film role in 2005 in Ron Howard's *Cinderella Man*, the film based on Braddock's life in and out of the ring. On stage, her performance in Craig Lucas's *Small Tragedy* earned her an Obie Award for Best Performance by an Actor. When Demme invited her to have lunch with Anne Hathaway, he was so amazed by the naturalistic energy between the women that he said to himself, "I wish I had a camera with me!"[7]

A Creative Marriage (2007–2009)

Rounding out the cast was Demme's friend and fellow Rocklander Bill Irwin as Kym and Rachel's doting father (Sidney Lumet had turned down the role); *Philadelphia* alum Anna Deavere Smith as Bill's second wife, Carol; and Debra Winger as Abby, Kym and Rachel's estranged mother. Another friend of Demme's, Paul Thomas Anderson, was initially chosen to play Rachel's fiancé, Sidney, but at the time, Anderson was busy with postproduction duties on *There Will Be Blood* (2007), his turn-of-the-century epic filmed in Marfa, Texas. Musician/actor Tunde Adebimpe, cast as Sidney, also knew Demme. The director had used the song "Satellite" by Adebimpe and his band, TV on the Radio, in *The Manchurian Candidate*.

Adebimpe's musical background played a significant role in how Demme would film *Rachel Getting Married*. Demme and Lumet agreed that Rachel and Kym's father was in the music business, making it natural for their wedding guests to be musicians. Jonathan contacted his friends Robyn Hitchcock, Fab 5 Freddy, Sister Carol East, and the musicians he had met with during the recording of *Jimmy Carter: Man from Plains* to balance out the music-to-drama ratio. "It would be utterly normal for there to be many musicians at the house, many instruments lying around the house," Demme said. "I thought that if we got the right musicians that would be the friends of the couple, that they would make some very beautiful music in the moment."[8] The combination of professional musicians and actors under Demme's direction felt like home away from home.

The forty-day shoot began in Fairfield, Connecticut, on September 19, 2007.[9] Rather than working at a breakneck pace, the crew worked six days a week for the next five weeks. Like Demme, the cast and crew were emotionally invested in the characters. After the scenes where Kym is awkwardly confronting her family, when Jonathan called, "Cut," crew members would respond by saying, "That's what it's like at my house."[10]

For the twelve-step recovery meetings in the film, Demme cast a cadre of theater actors and close friends. Presiding over the first meeting was Pastor Mel Jones, director of the Bethel Colony South drug rehab program in Louisiana. Jones had met Demme while he was filming in the Lower Ninth Ward and was featured in *I'm Carolyn Parker: The Good, the Mad, and the Beautiful.* "We would get into the room, and the actors would be ready," Demme explained. "Declan (Quinn, cinematographer) was using very little light [and] lit the room in such a way that he could point the camera in any direction. And I would be sitting in my chair, having not said anything to the actors, looking at my monitor, and I'd say 'Action!'"[11] Without any major announcement for setting up shots, Declan Quinn was able to capture Hathaway's tearful monologue describing her little brother Ethan's accidental death and how she is unable to accept that God can forgive her.

The tension and humor in Lumet's script flowed like prop wine in the rehearsal dinner scene as each person went around the room delivering well-wishes to Rachel and Sidney. Guests included Demme's closest friends Jim Roche and Paul Lazar as well as Carolyn Parker's daughter, Kyria Julian. Unlike his previous films, which used subjective cameras or elaborate tracking shots, Demme and cinematographer Declan Quinn let the cameras roll, giving the audience the feeling of being right there at the dinner table. Demme said, "Let's get a cast that is ready to work without knowing what the shot is, that will let us shoot this documentary style. And truly, the actors, there was never a planned close-up, there was never any planned shot."[12] There were very few cuts. The takes ran up to forty minutes.

Demme relished the free-flowing, low-stress environment he created for his crew. However, when it came time to shoot the family fight scene after Rachel realizes Kym was lying about her past in rehab, Demme asked violinist Zafer Tawil and his friends to play during the take. When the cameras started rolling after the second take, a frustrated Hathaway asked if the musicians were going to keep playing all weekend. Bill Irwin and Anna Deavere Smith tell the band outside on the porch to stop playing. Demme let cameras roll as the actors continued performing the scene. Seeing his actors emotionally depleted in the monitor, Demme realized he had enough footage for the day. The day's shoot ended at 12:15 p.m., with the director driving from Stamford to Manhattan to catch an afternoon matinee at the movies.[13]

During production, Demme was sending dailies to Robert Altman and Ang Lee's editor, Tim Squyres, who edited the film as it was being shot. Demme was amazed by the latitude Squyres had in choosing what would be the right shots for the final cut. Rather than poring over hours of footage in the editing room, the email exchanges between the editor and director streamlined the production.

Shooting the wedding was a jovial experience for Demme and the crew, who had come to feel an emotional osmosis starting from the beginning of production in the Buchmans' kitchen. The wedding was a celebration of their fruitful labor. Anne Hathaway stayed in character during the shoot, brooding on Kym's bleak worldview while still being charming to those who talked to her between setups. Demme's list of wedding participants included his family; Jos was a guest, and Brooklyn and his friend Barry Eastmond Jr. were the wedding band playing "Here Comes the Bride."[14] Cousin Bobby Castle played the priest who married Rachel and Sidney while Roger Corman filmed the ceremony with a camcorder. Originally, Jenny Lumet wanted to cast her dogs in the film, but Jonathan brought along the family poodle, Olive, to play the Buchmans' dog. After thirty-three days, the film wrapped.

Not long after the shoot, Demme got a call from Neil Young's manager, Elliot Roberts, telling him that Young's recent tour with Crazy Horse had a cinematic quality that needed to be captured on film. In December, Demme shot two nights of Neil Young and Crazy Horse at the Tower Theatre in Upper Darby, Pennsylvania. After his health scare two years earlier, Young bowled audiences over with his soulful performances. Unlike the reserved, southern tableaus in *Neil Young: Heart of Gold*, *Neil Young: Trunk Show* (2009) is a grainy, freewheeling revival of Young's hard-rock catalog mixed with unreleased songs. In Demme's words, "This film is a reaction to *Heart of Gold*. Totally punk."[15] Creatively, it was a blast for Demme to shoot on digital and film. One of the heartfelt sequences in *Neil Young:*

Trunk Show is Young's performance of "Sad Movies," a reflection on the emotive and communal connection of being in a movie theater.

In May 2008, while in postproduction on *Rachel Getting Married*, Demme was tapped by Martin Scorsese to replace him as director on a Bob Marley documentary he had been attached to. Scheduling got in the way when he committed to direct *Shutter Island* (2010) for Paramount. Scorsese handed the film over to Demme with the hope it would be released on what would have been Marley's sixty-fifth birthday.[16]

Demme used a similar blueprint for the Marley documentary as for *Haiti: Dreams of Democracy*, interviewing people from Cape Ann to Kingston. Demme flew to Jamaica with Sister Carol East, visiting Marley's aunt in Cape Ann. "Bob's aunt was very much into her church and brought these instruments from the church that they needed for the documentary," East recalled. "He didn't look for stars," East said. "He looked for real people. Jonathan would meet some Rasta children on the street, ask them where their parents were, and they appeared in the film."[17] As with his voyages to Haiti, Demme couldn't help but purchase Jamaican folk art before flying back to New York with his footage and preparing for the fall rollout of his latest film.

Rachel Getting Married opened to rapt applause at its premiere at the 2008 Venice Film Festival. Anne Hathaway extended her arms, motioning for the audience to sit, but their enthusiasm persisted as she held back tears of joy. While Demme hugged his cast and crew, someone working for the international distributors held a chronometer measuring the length of the applause. After clocking in the ten-minute standing ovation, the distributor would widen the film's release ahead of the awards season.[18]

Demme was riding on a personal high until someone told him, while leaving the theater, that the film was about an interracial marriage. At the press conference, Demme wasted no time in explaining his choice of having a diverse cast. "The truth is, this kind of group of people that are present at the wedding, that is the America that I feel very deeply connected with. That's the America that I know, it's the America that I love."[19]

After the warm reception in Venice, Demme flew to Spain to chair the official jury of the San Sebastian Film Festival. During the promotion of *Rachel Getting Married*, he screened an assembly cut of *Neil Young: Trunk Show*. The audience was getting into the film until Young performed a twenty-minute version of "No Hidden Path." Eight minutes into the song, people started walking out of the three-thousand-seat theater. "I counted and eighty people left the screening, which means that two thousand remained," Demme said pragmatically.[20] Despite the agitation of a few audience members, *Neil Young: Trunk Show* was briefly released to mixed reviews and has yet to be distributed on DVD.

Rachel Getting Married was considered a sleeper hit when it appeared in theaters in September 2008. In a year that encompassed blockbuster comic-book franchise films like Christopher Nolan's *The Dark Knight* and Jon Favreau's *Iron Man*, the film wasn't the financial runaway hit that *The Silence of the Lambs* was, yet *Rachel Getting Married* received warm reviews and had a sixty-five-week run in theaters, racking up $16.9 million worldwide.[21] A. O. Scott of the *New York Times* wrote, "It's a small movie, and in some ways a very sad one, but it has an undeniable and authentic vitality, an exuberance of spirit, that feels welcome and rare."[22] Anne Hathaway would earn her first Oscar nomination for Best Actress in a Lead Role. For Demme, it was a refreshing return to feature films while operating on the level of an independent filmmaker. However, he still had to deal with the powers that be when his vision didn't stimulate certain people.

When producer Steve Bing saw Demme's rough cut of the Bob Marley documentary, he wasn't happy. By 2009, the documentary was, in Demme's words, "on absolute hold." "The portrait that I fashioned from all the archival footage of Bob Marley is one that I love very much," Demme said at the Toronto International Film Festival. "But [that love] is not shared by the financiers and the project is on complete hold at the moment and there's a lot of discussion going on geared to try and find the most positive possible resolution to this situation."[23] From Sister Carol's perspective, it was the first time

THERE'S NO GOING BACK

she had seen Demme sad: "Whatever he put together, they weren't pleased, didn't accept it, and it hurt him a lot."[24] Eventually, Kevin MacDonald, the Oscar-winning filmmaker of *One Day in September* (1999) and *The Last King of Scotland* (2006), would helm the project; it wouldn't be released until April 2012.

Years after Hurricane Katrina, New Orleans kept calling for Demme. In addition to *I'm Carolyn Parker: The Good, the Mad, and the Beautiful*, Demme had tried to make a full-length film about Pastor Mel Jones that didn't come to fruition. Jonathan's son, Brooklyn, had just finished reading a copy of Dave Eggers's *What Is the What*, a story of survival during the Sudanese Civil War.[25] Demme read the book and became an instant fan of Eggers's reportage. Demme was particularly amazed by his book *Zeitoun*, the story of a Syrian American contractor, Abdulrahman Zeitoun, who tried to save his fellow New Orleanians by canoe after the levees broke. One month after the storm, Zeitoun was arrested on the unsubstantiated claims of looting. He and a few Syrian Americans were detained by the National Guard, caged at "Camp Greyhound"—a series of human-size cages outside a Greyhound bus station—and subjected to post-9/11 Islamophobia by the guards. Eventually, Zeitoun was released, and the charges of stolen property were dropped. Eggers's book was a searing indictment of the failed policies of the Bush administration and how the war on terror seeped into the relief efforts during Hurricane Katrina. It would win the American Book Award that year.

Demme met with Eggers in New York to talk about the possibility of making *Zeitoun* into an animated film. Afterward, he flew to New Orleans to get consent from the Zeitoun family. However, one thing Jonathan didn't want to get involved with was a big-budget recreation of Hurricane Katrina. According to Dave Eggers, "That was driven by the book's cover itself, which was an artist's vision of Abdulrahman canoeing alone after the storm. Making a live-action film would have required tens of millions of dollars, a CGI flood, and the re-creation of neighborhoods and homes that were underwater. It all seemed wasteful and wrong. *Taxi to the Dark Side* (2007) had been released around then, so there was a recent example of a film made for adults that used sophisticated animation to depict a recent human rights crisis ethically and artistically."[26]

Rachell Sumpter's cover art for the book, with Zeitoun in his canoe, would form the basis of storyboards laying out the film. However, like Demme's Bob Marley documentary, *Zeitoun* never got made. As the film sat on the back burner, Abdulrahman Zeitoun went from page-turning hero to pariah when his wife filed for divorce on the grounds of domestic abuse, and he was arrested in August 2012 for attempting to murder his ex-wife, son, and someone who claimed to be his wife's ex-boyfriend.[27]

Eggers's time spent with Demme was an education for the bestselling author, who was making strides as a screenwriter for Spike Jonze (*Where the Wild Things Are* [2009]) and Sam Mendes (*Away We Go* [2009], cowritten with Vendela Vida). "It was instructive to me to see how Jonathan had this unexpected success with *The Silence of the Lambs*, which thrust him into the mainstream, and how clearly he learned that he absolutely needed to be operating in the indie world—that making art in the corporate world is very, very difficult, and not for everyone," Eggers recalled. "So, he abandoned all that and did things his way, albeit on a much smaller scale. He was one of the most open and loving people I've ever met. He really led with a radical openness that is truly hard to maintain."[28]

In the following years, Demme would try to maintain his creative flow even when his health was at stake. When his friend and creative comrade since the seventies, Hercules Bellville, died of cancer in February 2009, it spurred Jonathan to stop smoking cigarettes.

19

Burning Desires (2010–2013)

In December 2009, Demme was planning to fly to Haiti with the band Arcade Fire to make a music documentary set during carnival season in Jacmel.[1] On January 12, 2010, one week before the intended trek, an earthquake with a magnitude of 7.0 struck the island. At the time, Demme was being honored at film festivals with lifetime achievement awards. After the earthquake, the festival coordinators requested screenings of *The Agronomist*. His correspondence with Sgt. Gonzales Joseph had continued over the years, and Jonathan bequeathed him a handheld camera to film the relief efforts of the military and aid workers. "I'm hoping to go later this year with the idea of shooting *The Agronomist's Wife*," Demme said in May 2010.[2] Despite his desire to fly down to Haiti, it was a risk he didn't want to take due to his flagging health.

Among the many gifts handed down from Demme's lineage of storytellers and fixtures in American history, one of the few curses was the risk of cancer. All the days and nights that Jonathan spent in the editing room, looking at dailies with a pack of cigarettes and a soft drink, came back to haunt him in 2010 when he was treated for esophageal cancer.[3] Luckily, doctors intervened, and Demme went into remission. He celebrated his sixty-sixth birthday resting at home in Nyack and looking over Jos's homework.[4]

One year after this health scare, Demme went back to work, keeping the ailments between himself and his family. Jonathan and

Joanne split their time between Nyack and Manhattan. Joanne would attend graduate school at Hunter College, while Jonathan spent his time on Christopher Street.[5]

Beth Henley and Demme had collaborated on *Trying Times* for PBS and together attempted to bring *The Stopwatch Gang*, the story of serial bank robbers, to the big screen.[6] They had always wanted to work together again, and that chance came up as Henley was reprising her 2000 play *Family Week* and needed a director for the stage production. Like *Crimes of the Heart*, *Family Week* revolved around a dysfunctional family reuniting at Pastures Recovery Center and confronting their issues with dark humor. Noting the similarities between Henley's play and *Rachel Getting Married*, Demme leaped at the chance to direct his first off-Broadway production. As he told the *Los Angeles Times*, "I love filmmaking and editing and all that stuff, but this is the essence of what I love most about filmmaking."[7]

At the end of the first day of rehearsals, Demme turned to Henley: "Is that what y'all do? You gather and rehearse scenes and then talk about it and go home?" After a pause, Demme's smile widened, and he told the Pulitzer Prize–winning playwright, "I like this job! I wish we didn't have to stop!" Sitting in the wings of the Lucille Lortel Theatre, Demme would react to the performances as if he were watching his films at dailies: "It's like a gunfight at the OK Corral. It's so intense. It's not funny anymore; it's deep."[8]

Family Week opened on May 4, 2010, to scathing reviews. The *New York Daily News* wrote, "Unlike that 1981 Pulitzer Prize winner (*Crimes of the Heart*), the characters are too shallow to stir interest or empathy, even with four fine actors on stage."[9] *Newsday* described the play as "puzzling" and said that "Henley's message, alas, is less clear, but the relationships have a persuasively offbeat impact."[10] After nearly three weeks, the play closed on May 23. It signaled the end of Demme's directing for the stage, and he swiftly returned to his place behind the camera.

Demme next signed on to direct the pilot of the TV drama *A Gifted Man*. Susannah Grant, cocreator of the Fox Television drama *Party of Five* and the Oscar-nominated screenwriter of Steven

Soderbergh's film *Erin Brockovich* (2000), created the television series about a high-profile surgeon (Patrick Wilson) who communicates with the spirit of his late wife (Jennifer Ehle); she persuades him to work at a clinic for destitute patients. Demme would executive produce with his longtime Clinica Estetico colleague Ron Bozman and reunite with cinematographer Tak Fujimoto on the pilot. Despite some positive reviews of Wilson's and Ehle's performances, CBS canceled *A Gifted Man* after one season.

Since leaving Clinica Estetico in 2000, Ed Saxon had become an independent producer for films directed by Richard Linklater (2004's *Fast Food Nation*) and Sam Mendes (2009's *Away We Go*). Saxon was now working in television as a coexecutive producer of *Enlightened*, the Emmy-nominated HBO series cocreated by Mike White and Laura Dern, and he brought on Demme to direct two episodes.

While visiting his children Ramona and Brooklyn at Oberlin College in Ohio, Demme was taken by one of the town's oldest movie theaters, the Apollo. He became a committee member of Friends of the Apollo, which created fundraising activities to benefit the renovations of the theater as both a performance space and a series of classrooms for Oberlin's media studies program.[11]

He had a new lease on life after his cancer scare and developed another project with Neil Young, *Neil Young Journeys*. In May 2011, both artists took a road trip from Ohio to Canada, heading for Neil Young's hometown of Omemee, Ontario. Demme rode shotgun in his 1956 Ford Crown Victoria, recording a guided tour before trekking down to record Young's performance at Toronto's Massy Hall. The footage of Young spinning yarns is reminiscent of Demme's re-creation of Melvin Dummar's mythical ride with Howard Hughes thirty years earlier. From memories of catching fish in his Radio Flyer wagon to reflecting on his father as he drives past the school named after him, Young confides to Demme and the audience about his life experiences.

Half travelogue and half concert, *Neil Young Journeys* was released through Sony Pictures Classics in 2012. Although the film wasn't a financial success on the scale of *Neil Young: Heart of Gold*, money was the last thing Demme worried about. For him, *Neil Young Journeys* wasn't just another performance film; it was Demme's cinematic rendering of Young's story from north Ontario to stardom. "He's a human fountain of cinema," Demme said about Young, "All these stories in these songs are different, and the characters he assumes are so different, he never repeats himself in the way he presents himself in the music."[12] Additionally, Young's presence on screen was more intimate than in the last two performance pieces directed by Demme, courtesy of a ten-thousand-dollar clip camera installed on the microphone. In his positive review of the film, Mark Kermode noted "watching Neil Young through his spit."[13]

Demme also wanted to emphasize the timeliness of Young's song "Ohio." The piece had been written in the wake of the Kent State shootings, in which four students were gunned down by the National Guard on May 4, 1970, while protesting at the height of the Vietnam War. The song struck a chord with Demme regarding the rise of gun violence in America since the Columbine massacre in 1999, when twelve high school students and one teacher were gunned down by two disturbed teenagers in Littleton, Colorado. Demme had coproducer Shane Bissett track down the families of the Kent State four, asking for their consent for the use of archival footage and photos that would be edited into the film with Young's performance. Bissett was told by the sister of one of the four students that history had erased Kent State from the collective memory and that the US government had never apologized for the actions taken by the National Guard in quelling the expression of opposition to America's involvement in Vietnam.[14]

Demme further sensed a revival of the activism from his youth on September 17, when thousands of New Yorkers angry with the financial cuts in the city's education programs and with the mounting debt since the 2008 recession marched to Zuccotti Park. One of the first protesters who camped in the park, Brandon Watts, hit his head on the concrete as police officers wrestled him down. His bloody face made the cover of the *New York Daily News*. For the next two months, Jonathan would visit the park with his dogs, wearing his baseball cap and bright-green Ethiopia sweater and waving a sign saying "Do You Know Brandon Watts?" with the *Daily News* photo of Watts's bloody face. On other weekends, he would bring his camera to capture the drum circles, lending libraries, and campsites set up by the Occupy Wall Street movement. "Our generation actually had the opportunity to see our beliefs effect massive change in this country at that time," Demme told a reporter in Zuccotti Park. "My hope and belief are that this could happen again."[15]

Jonathan passed his love of film on to his children. He and Brooklyn went to the 2012 Marrakesh Film Festival and were stunned by Nabil Ayouch's film *Horses of God*.[16] Demme befriended Ayouch and helped arrange distribution for the film, including a theatrical run through Kino Lorber. He had also shown support for preserving world cinema over a decade earlier, when he, Milestone Films, producer Neda Armian, and Dustin Hoffman had distributed for theatrical release Gillo Pontecorvo's 1957 film *The Wide Blue Road*.

Demme lectured at Oberlin and told students about the endless opportunities for filmmaking and distribution through YouTube.[17] Returning from Ohio, he leapt at the chance to film country musician Kenny Chesney's concert at Wildwood, New Jersey, for Vevo-YouTube's Concert Series. Before Chesney took the stage, the shaggy-haired Demme looked out at twenty thousand people as if he were about to perform. A warm smile at his camera crew signaled they were ready to shoot. Recording and broadcasting live was new territory for Demme, but like his autodidactic approach to digital cameras, he conducted his education in public, and it paid off.

On one of his drives back over the Washington Bridge from Manhattan to Nyack, Demme switched the dial over to DJ John Shaefer's late-night program, New Sounds, on WNYC. As he listened to the soulful saxophone and Italian vocals of Enzo Avitabile, Demme said to himself, "This is the score to life."[18] He booked a trip to Naples to meet up with the producers Davide Azzolini and Antonio Monda, whom he had met when the Naples Film Festival screened Demme's films. They set up a meeting with Enzo Avitabile, and Demme talked for an hour to Enzo about the prospect of making a documentary about him. Despite the language barrier between the Neapolitan Avitabile and Demme, the musician took the director on a weeklong tour as he gathered the musicians who would perform with him. "I didn't know what was going to happen day by day," Demme said. "We just picked him up, went somewhere, and wound up with this film."[19] Avitabile would walk around Naples with his saxophone as Demme scampered from behind with his handheld camera. The jam sessions between Avitabile and his friends were recorded with the musicians sitting in a circle, a visual approach Demme's friend Paul Thomas Anderson would take when he went to India to capture Israeli musician Shye Ben Tzur and Radiohead guitarist Jonny Greenwood with the Rajasthan Express for his 2015 film *Junun*.

While Demme was in postproduction for *Enzo Avitabile: Music Life*, Hurricane Sandy ravaged New York and certain areas of the East Coast. Residing in bed at his Vermont farmhouse as the storm progressed, Rev. Bobby Wilkenson Castle passed away on October 27, 2012. Demme paid homage to Bobby, a spiritual advisor and close cousin, in an op-ed for PBS's P.O.V. website, expressing admiration for how he influenced Demme's son, Brooklyn, to read his "Prayers from the Burned-Out City" in his college studies and noting that Bobby had witnessed the inauguration of Aristide, who would be Haiti's first preacher-turned-president: "He has turned on a million lights for me over the years and has always been a complete and utter stone blast to work with, play with, to hang with, to get arrested with, just to be with."[20]

In May 2013, shooting began on Kate Barker-Froyland's directorial debut, *Song One*. Two years earlier, Demme received a script written by Barker-Froyland about Brooklyn's thriving music scene. While writing the script, Barker-Froyland was an assistant to director David Frankel on *The Devil Wears Prada* (2006), where she first met Anne Hathaway. Demme passed along the script to Hathaway and her husband, Adam Shulman, to produce. Kate dubbed Jonathan "the creative godfather of the film" when he brought along *Rachel*

Getting Married sound mixer, Jeff Pullman, and Suzana Perić and John Carbonara as music editors.[21] Despite mixed reviews from the critics, *Song One* was an immersive experience for Barker-Froyland thanks to Demme's love for her script. Before shooting began, he invited Kate, Hathaway, and Schulman to Webster Hall to see Robyn Hitchcock perform. Barker-Froyland wrote, "Moments like that were a reminder of how all of us came together in the first place and of the musical center of the film."[22]

Jonathan's appreciation of theater never waned, going all the way back to when he was an arts and entertainment critic for the *Coral Gables Times*. Despite the less-than-stellar reviews for his direction of *Family Week*, Demme continued to strive to blend the qualities of a staged play into a feature film. An opportunity for this came up in 2011 when Demme was one of twenty-seven who saw Andre Gregory and Wallace Shawn's production of Ibsen's *A Master Builder* in Greenwich Village at the Pen and Brush Club.[23] Demme watched the performance with rapt attention. "Part of my experience was I saw Andre once he completed his part as old Brovick," Demme told David Edelstein. "Andre kind of joined the audience and was close to the action as you were describing before. I saw how he was creating an energy field between himself and the actors; just feeling that it was going great. I don't know if this sounds insane or not, but you could feel this encouragement—'Yes, yes, yes, exactly right!'—flowing out of Andre."[24]

One might argue that Demme saw a connection between himself and Ibsen's semi-autobiographical protagonist, Solness. Both were retired lotharios searching for some semblance of their youth in their respective autumn years. Demme saw the play and envisioned his close encounter with death. He didn't want Solness mulling over his life from his office desk; he saw him lying in a hospital bed, reflecting on luck and obsession both playing a part in his success as an architect, along with his failure as a devoted husband. Solness's fixation on Hilde, the vivacious assistant who wants him to fulfill a ten-year-old promise of building a castle for her, leads to his literal and metaphorical downfall.

Demme saw *A Master Builder* (initially titled *Fear of Falling*) as an opportunity to create a cinematic presence akin to Mike Nichols's 1966 directorial debut, *Who's Afraid of Virginia Woolf?* To Demme's credit, while he didn't understand the play on an intellectual level, he saw it had a supernatural quality that carried over to the screen. "Malle filmed *My Dinner with Andre* as a film 'about' a meal, and *Vanya on 42nd Street* as a documentary that turns into Chekhov's play Uncle Vanya," Demme said. "We decided to do the reverse this time, taking the Ibsen and turning it into an old-fashioned haunted house movie, and pitting the convivial diners of *My Dinner with Andre* as desperate Ibsenesque architects, fiercely confronting each other on the brink of their deaths."[25]

Rather than confining *A Master Builder* to one room, which was the initial approach to filming, Demme and cinematographer Declan Quinn staged the film in the same Greenwich Village house where Gregory and Shawn performed their play. Quinn had experience working with the duo before when he was the cinematographer for *Uncle Vanya on 42nd Street*. Shot on two cameras and in wide cinemascope over the course of one week, the play became a visual revival of the domestic tension of *Rachel Getting Married* combined with the tight close-ups from *The Silence of the Lambs*, as when Hilde's bright-eyed optimism clashes with the stoicism of Solness's long-suffering wife, Aline.

"I thought that this was going to be the easiest job of my life," Demme said. However, in between takes, Demme would have Andre Gregory act as codirector to find the balance between the theatrical and cinematic elements of Ibsen's play as written by Wallace Shawn. Shawn was concerned that Demme and Gregory were seeing "grotesque acting" on the monitors. Demme said, "I was looking at the monitors and the performances were coming across on a theatrical level and you just can't tell a story like that when the camera's that close, so it was like, 'Oh, we had to make adjustments,' and I think that was exciting for the cast."[26]

Gregory and Shawn wouldn't talk about the play, but Gregory would note to Demme that he didn't want *The Master Builder* to be seen in medium shots but with close-ups. "Everybody's performance invited close-ups," Demme said. "I really thought it was important and exciting to imagine the audience were in the room with everybody at all times."²⁷

Julie Hagerty, who played Aline in both the film and stage versions of *The Master Builder*, balanced the stoicism and beleaguered energy of Aline with poise; it was a far cry from her comedic performances in the Jim Abrahams / Zucker Brothers' comedy, *Airplane!* (1980); Albert Brooks's *Lost in America* (1985); and Frank Oz's *What about Bob?* (1991). As Gregory noted, "She's an example of the weight in the American theatre and American film because Julie could play the mother in Eugene O'Neill's 'Long Day's Journey Into Night,' she could play the wife in Arthur Miller's 'Death Of A Salesman'; there is no tragic role that she couldn't play amazingly, but because in a way she was typecast I suppose as a comedienne, funny actress, nobody thought of going there."²⁸

A Master Builder was released in July 2014 to positive reviews but a small return at the box office. It was evident that Demme didn't focus as much on the $46,874 as he did on the reception of audiences when it premiered at the Rome International Film Festival.²⁹ Michael Phillips of the *Chicago Tribune* hailed the film as "an odd success" while cautioning readers in his first paragraph that it "will likely appeal more to theater people than to film people." Peter Keough of the *Boston Globe* noted Demme's horror film ethos as the townhouse "intensifies the impact" of the film.³⁰

Jonathan saw Sandy McLeod in the audience at a screening of *A Master Builder* in New York City. After their separation, McLeod went on to become an Oscar-nominated documentarian covering climate change and its impact on American farmers. "I wanted to let him know that any past differences had dissolved," McLeod said. "I complimented him on the movie, and he was sweet."³¹ It would be the last time she would see Jonathan.

20

Flash and Dance (2014–2015)

Documentaries were Demme's solace from his conflicting issues with the film and television industries. His next one was inspired by a February 2014 article by Rachel Aviv of the *New Yorker* about UC Berkeley biologist Dr. Tyrone Hayes. Demme traveled from Columbia, South Carolina, to Oakland, California, that June to profile Dr. Hayes, who was discredited by agribusiness Syngenta after he had concluded that the company's herbicide, atrazine, led to the mutation of the reproductive organs in frogs. After paying $105 million in a class action lawsuit to filter the water for Holiday Shores Sanitary District after runoff water affected the midwestern farmland, Syngenta denied any wrongdoing.[1] Like *I'm Carolyn Parker: The Good, the Mad, and the Beautiful*, *What's Motivating Hayes* is a warm and engaging look at an advocate's struggle to protect his home and environment.

One day, Demme got a phone call from Marc Platt, who wanted him to direct a script penned by the Oscar-winning screenwriter Diablo Cody, who had written Jason Reitman's dramedies *Juno* (2007) and *Young Adult* (2011). Meryl Streep was attached to star in the film, *Ricki and the Flash*, the story of a Southern California rock star (Meryl Streep) who flies back to Indianapolis to see her ex-husband (Kevin Kline) and three estranged children: a daughter recently dumped by her fiancé (Meryl Streep's daughter, Mamie Gummer), a son who is about to get married (Sebastian Stan), and another son (Marc's son, Ben Platt) who hasn't been completely accepted by his mother because he is gay. Pete's current wife (Audra McDonald) is the ballast that attempts to reconnect the conservative Ricki with her family. As Platt told Demme over the phone, "If there's one person to direct this script, it's you."[2]

The prospect of working again with Meryl Streep delighted Demme. Unlike the pressure he was under filming *The Manchurian Candidate* nearly a decade earlier, he was in a more relaxed position directing Streep this time. The process was even more satisfying because he was filming Streep acting alongside her daughter. It was the first time they had shared the screen since Mamie was an infant carried around by her mother in Mike Nichols's *Heartburn* (1986).

Six weeks before filming, Streep was learning how to play rhythm guitar from composer and bandleader Neil Citron. It was Citron who would suggest Rick Springfield as Streep's bandmate and current lover in the film. At the Jacob Burns Film Center one day, Neil Young was in the studio and showed Streep how mechanics of feedback and distortion are instrumental when playing electric guitar. Stephen Apkon caught the lesson on his iPhone camera as Streep, Demme, and his pet dogs listened to Young jam on a black Telecaster that was lying around the office.[3]

As in many of his films where music plays a role, Demme wanted to film live performances. Weeks before the shoot, Streep, Springfield, and the Flash band performed at the abandoned Rodeo Bar located in the Murray Hill neighborhood in Manhattan. Bernie Worrell manned the Hammond organ with Leslie speakers; Joe Walsh's drummer, Joe Vitale, was on the DW kit; and Neil Young's bassist, Rick Rosas, filled out the rhythm section. Production designer Stuart Wurzell modeled the interior of the fictional Salt Well bar after the real Rodeo space. Present during the shooting of the live performances on Stage A of the East of Hollywood Soundstage in Brooklyn was executive producer Gary Goetzman.

Goetzman had achieved acclaim as an award-winning producer for projects for HBO (*Band of Brothers, The Pacific, John Adams, Game Change*) in addition to being cofounder of Playtone

Flash and Dance (2014–2015)

Productions with Tom Hanks. When Goetzman arrived on the set to help out Demme with the live performances, their energy was as rewarding as Goetzman remembered it being on *Caged Heat* forty years earlier. Demme insisted on not having microphones or the stands blocking the band while still capturing the verisimilitude of a live performance. Goetzman placed a call to get AT450 microphones to place on Vitale's hi-hat cymbals and AT4050 mics on Worrell's organ, while the sounds of the revelers at the Salt Well bar were picked up on AT4080 ribbons.[4]

Shooting commenced in July 2014.[5] In Jonathan's eyes, the film was a home movie like those he shot in Brooklyn, Westchester, and Rockland County. Wide-eyed and engaged, Demme and the crew made the film into a musical experience. He contacted musicians Jenny Lewis and Jonathan Rice, whom he'd worked with on *Song One*, to write an original track that was meant to be Ricki's signature song, and they were thrilled when they visited the set to hear Streep perform their haunting ballad "Cold One." Shooting close to home, Jonathan had his family and friends present on screen during the climactic wedding reception, with Streep belting out a soulful rendition of Canned Heat's "Let's Work Together."

Ricki and the Flash received mixed reviews when it was released in August 2015. Critics noted the praiseworthy performances, and the film made a solid $41.3 million worldwide at the box office on an $18 million budget.[6] However, the Associated Press thought that the camera should have spent more time on Streep, Gummer, and Kline and felt the wedding reception was contrived.[7] Writing for RogerEbert.com, Glenn Kenny highlighted the sentimentality of the family reminiscing while Ricki strums her guitar in the living room.[8] It can be argued that Demme wanted to recreate the kind of feverish musical vibrancy found in his earlier films and to reflect his eternal love for *Black Orpheus*, a film where myth and music are a hallucinogenic celebration.

The celebration continued in the desert. In December 2014, Jonathan traveled to Las Vegas with Gary Goetzman, who had just seen Justin Timberlake with the Tennessee Kids at the MGM Grand in

THERE'S NO GOING BACK

Las Vegas closing out their two-year 20/20 Experience World Tour. Demme had heard the former teen idol on the radio while driving his kids to school and had also noticed Justin Timberlake's cinematic potential when he saw his performance in David Fincher's film *The Social Network* (2010).

Timberlake was a fan of *Stop Making Sense*, and at his initial meeting with Demme, he looked at the seventy-year-old filmmaker as if he were a rock star. They had initially talked about the prospect of Timberlake starring in a film, but when Timberlake asked Demme to direct his final performances in Las Vegas, Demme agreed. It was a far cry from thirty years earlier, when the director had to convince David Byrne to let him direct the Talking Heads' final concerts. Watching Justin Timberlake charm and delight fans with his dancing, Demme felt it was a surefire hit, and it revived his delight in bringing the concertgoing experience to film audiences.

The nods to *Stop Making Sense* were deliberate, with backlit shadows of Timberlake dancing in tuxedos designed by Tom Ford. With the Tennessee Kids playing their brass instruments and a dance troupe behind him, Timberlake was nimble on his feet and had a visual presence that Demme praised as "adorable."[9] The audience was filmed on aerial cameras suspended over the stage as concertgoers illuminated the screen with their cell phones hoisted into the air like cigarette lighters. As with *Neil Young: Heart of Gold*, Demme and Declan Quinn turned their camera on the road crew building up the sets hours before the show. A humbled Timberlake walked around expressing his gratitude to the crew who had toured with him for the last two years.

Justin Timberlake + The Tennessee Kids was initially set for theatrical release through IMAX until Netflix, the mail-delivery DVD-rental turned television-streaming service, bought the film from the investors. It was an unfortunate blow for Demme to see his film slated as strictly for television. Despite the film's glowing reviews and impressive streaming viewership numbers, Demme had to endure the never-ending battles with and the conflicting natures of the studios and distributors.

Flash and Dance (2014–2015)

When *Ricki and the Flash* was released in August 2015, Jonathan was chagrined by the mixed reviews; he felt that the blame for the film's critical and financial shortcomings rested with its marketing and distribution, an ever-protruding thorn in his side. "You work for a year or two on these things, and then it falls into the hands of the 'idea' people who just take your movie and run with it," Demme said. "And it's like 'Sorry—oops, that was a bad marketing approach.'"[10] Subsequently, the passing of Rick Rosas in November made the post-*Ricki* experience even more wounding for Demme.

Returning to Nyack after the shoot, Demme searched for more satisfying work. Then *Rolling Stone* founder and Rock and Roll Hall of Fame chairman Jann S. Wenner called Demme about directing a twelve-minute film for the Connor, a new movie theater being built at the Rock and Roll Hall of Fame Museum in Cleveland, Ohio.[11] Demme, a longtime supporter of the Hall of Fame and an attendee at the annual ceremonies held at the Waldorf Astoria, agreed to direct. Working with designers BRC Imagination Arts, Demme and members of the museum took a tour bus to Detroit to visit the Henry Ford Museum. Sitting in the theater, Demme concocted the idea of having three-panel screens to create a panoramic view of a succession of archived performances from past Hall of Fame concerts. Eight weeks later, the Hall of Fame Museum's creative director, Christian Lachel, received a cut of Demme's film.[12]

Demme then received terrible news from his doctor; his esophageal cancer had returned, and he would have to undergo chemotherapy. He would describe the experience as both debilitating and spiritual: "During that time, it's been a nice taking stock time."[13] Afterward, even though Demme's flat-top was gone due to the chemotherapy, he held his head high. Jonathan attended the Venice Film Festival with Joanne as he was one of the judges of the Horizons and Lion of the Future juries. On the lido, Demme was feted with the Persol Tribute to Visionary Talent award. Attending the festival was Clare Peploe, who went alone to say goodbye to her close friend of over forty years.[14] Her husband, Bernardo Bertolucci, had endured back problems and was confined to a wheelchair until his death in 2018. Clare Peploe would be diagnosed with cancer and pass away in 2021.

After returning from Venice, Jonathan filled his time moderating the occasional post-screening interview at the Jacob Burns Film Center, walking his poodles around the neighborhood, and spending time with his family. In late 2015, Jonathan recorded his commentary track for the DVD rerelease of *Caged Heat*. It was an ebullient time for Demme to reflect on his first film, corresponding from his home in Nyack with Erica Gavin and Tak Fujimoto, who were in Los Angeles. "It was as if no time had passed," Gavin recalled. "He made you feel like you knew him your whole life. As famous as he became after *Caged Heat*, he was so down to earth, which is so special and beyond the realm of Hollywood."[15] Before wrapping up the commentary recording, Demme told Gavin about his newfound happiness: "He told me, 'Erica, I'm so happy right now! I'm in remission and living in the country with my family. I'm no longer in Manhattan, I'm living my life and rethinking what I want to do next.' That was the last time I talked to him."[16]

With his hair grown back in a wavy coif, Jonathan could only rest on his laurels for so long until he went back behind the camera. Forty years after *Caged Heat*, he brought his camera back to prison.

Through the nonprofit organization the Hudson Link for Higher Education in Prison, Demme filmed the first TED Talk set inside Sing Sing Penitentiary. The web series captured the various perspectives of prisoners and Sing Sing superintendent Michael Capra, as well as performances that emphasized the importance of community-building within the prison system.[17] Unlike with *Caged Heat*, Demme was fixated on the social commentary and recording it in an impactful manner. He even attended the graduation ceremony for those who didn't let prison impede their thirst for higher knowledge.

21

Eagles and Condors (2016–2022)

Jonathan Demme channeled his energies to the small screen when he was signed on to direct an episode of the Fox crime drama *Shots Fired*. Created by show-running couple and executive producers Reggie Rock Bythewood (the screenwriter behind *Notorious*, the 2009 biopic of slain rapper The Notorious B.I.G.) and Gina Prince-Bythewood (*Love and Basketball*), the series focused on racially motivated shootings in North Carolina. They reached out to Demme with a phone pitch and sent him the script of the first episode. Demme sensed the connection to the systemic racism against people of color and the thin blue line that stretched outside the margins of the script. In February 2012, George Zimmerman shot and killed a Black Miami teenager, Trayvon Martin; two years later, in August 2014, Michael Brown of Ferguson, Missouri, was killed by a police officer, leading to protests captured by national news outlets; in April 2015, Freddie Gray of Baltimore died while in a coma resulting from police brutality—his neck and spine were injured while in the back of a police cruiser.

In the spring of 2016, Jonathan flew down to Mooresville, North Carolina, to shoot a one-hour episode ("Hour Six") of the series. The story unfolds as violence breaks out downtown after the governor, played by Helen Hunt, orders a state of emergency, dispatching police in riot gear to quell the chaos. An armored police tank creeps down the road as the Black community watches with shock and repulsion.

Molotov cocktails are thrown into buildings by people in skeleton masks. "CORPORATE BLOODSUCKERS" is scrawled outside a printing-press building. Wearing his Pokémon pajamas and sitting by the monitors, Demme emphasized to the cast and crew that they were filming an uprising, not a riot.

Demme's camera setups were a mystery to the actors as filming of the uprising was carried out. "Jonathan really created a space for controlled chaos," noted Aisha Hinds, who played a local pastor who tries to calm her parishioners as the violence erupts. "We were so confused, but it served a purpose." Seeing Demme orchestrate the setups and heighten the enthusiasm of the cast impressed Reggie Bythewood: "He wasn't a spring chicken, but Jonathan definitely had a lot of energy."[1] The Bythewoods stood by Demme while he was going through dailies. They were impressed by the work—and not only as executive producers overseeing their series being shot. Sanaa Lathan described Demme as "a magician" when he rallied the cast together after they had blocked some scenes. "Reggie and I immediately made plans that I would come out the first week of his shoot and Reggie would come out the second," Gina Prince wrote in the *Hollywood Reporter*. "We wanted to continue to learn."[2]

Demme flew back to Nyack feeling a sense of personal victory about his work on *Shots Fired*. There was a spring in his step when he walked his daughter Ramona down the aisle in August 2016 and danced with his son-in-law at the reception. According to wedding guest and longtime friend Paul Lazar, "There was this communal warmth between Jonathan and James that really lit the room."[3] In hindsight, the final wedding reception scene in *Ricki and the Flash* that was tarnished by critics could be read as a hopeful foreshadowing of Demme's excitement in preparing for Ramona's wedding.

After the wedding, Demme flew to Toronto for the premiere of *Justin Timberlake + The Tennessee Kids*. Fans screamed for Timberlake as he signed autographs on the red carpet; Jonathan gave the pop star a massive hug, shouting, "We made it!" Catching the attention of fans and paparazzi, Timberlake pulled out his cell phone, directing Jonathan and the throngs of festival attendees in an Instagram video.[4]

The Demme nest was emptying: Ramona had married, and Jos was living in Chicago, studying at the Art Institute and exhibiting paintings on sexuality and ecology at galleries around the city's North Side, not far from where Dodie Rogers Demme had grown up nearly a century before.[5] After graduating from Oberlin College, Brooklyn focused on grassroots organizations in and around Yonkers while spending more time learning how to make movies.[6] Meanwhile, the health problems that Jonathan had tried to keep quiet were reemerging.

When news broke of the mounting protests against building the Dakota Pipeline along Sioux Standing Rock Reservation in Bismarck, North Dakota, Brooklyn approached his father about taking a journey to the Midwest. Initially, Jonathan declined. He was deeply depressed after the November 9 election of Donald Trump as the forty-fifth president of the United States, and his health was declining. The day after the election, Demme had received the Visionaries Tribute award from the DOC NYC film festival and expressed his thanks to his fellow documentarians and producers in the wake of what he considered "the shock" of Trump's electoral win. In a calming speech, he said, "It's not a funeral. It's only hopeless if you've forgotten and pinned your hopes on the Democratic Party. My hopes arise on us; I don't mean documentary people but Americans. I don't think the election changes anybody's personal agenda, and we're still going to push for meaningful progressive change. I'm not impressed by Trump, and I just feel energized."[7]

Jonathan started attending yoga classes at a local studio to quell his anxiety.[8] While there one day, he recalled the Americans he referred to in his speech at the Visionaries Tribute ceremony, as well as Brooklyn's empathy for those at Standing Rock. Demme figured if he wanted to make one last film, why not do it about people trying to make a change for the good?

Jonathan reached out to Stephen Apkon, who had just returned from Standing Rock. As Demme arrived to get recording equipment from the Jacob Burns Film Center, Apkon noticed he was full of energy but showing signs of his illness. Despite this, Jonathan was intent on going to North Dakota: "We had a conversation about what to expect out there, and I was connecting him with people to meet. I know that was a tough shoot for him."[9] Having met up with Tavis Smiley, Demme shot footage for the host's PBS program as he endured snow drifts and arctic winds. Jonathan and Brooklyn stayed at a nearby hotel, basking in the warmth that emanated from the room and from the footage of the protesters standing proud, arms akimbo, as they resisted the local police through nonviolent protest and prayer.

On February 4, 2017, two and a half weeks before his seventy-third birthday, Jonathan made one of his last public appearances at the Walter Reade Theater in Lincoln Center to host the theatrical premiere of *Justin Timberlake + The Tennessee Kids*. He hid his shrinking weight with a heavy plaid coat and baggy military-style pants. He still wore his puka shells around his neck and a black T-shirt with "Reclaim Democracy" printed in big letters. With a relaxed but melancholy sigh, he told filmgoers, "I'm really savoring this moment because we made this film independently. . . . I now want to thank Netflix for agreeing—finally!—with tonight's screening."[10]

Continuing, he talked humbly about having his documentary screened at Lincoln Center, which had premiered his films at the New York Film Festival forty years before. Demme concluded his remarks by thanking editor Paul Snyder, producer Rocco Caruso, and Judge James L. Robart, who famously coined the phrase "Black Lives Matter" after presiding over the case *United States of America v. the City of Seattle*; Robart had recently struck down Trump's executive order barring citizens from seven countries from entering the United States. Jonathan soaked up the energy and revelry at Lincoln Center before driving back to Nyack and starting work on another documentary with Brooklyn about the Split Rock Sweetwater Prayer Camp in Mahwah, New Jersey.

Then suddenly, he was getting sick again. Gary Goetzman was scheduled to fly to England to oversee a production for CNN, but when he heard that Jonathan's health was fading, he had his children handle the project. "Gary said, 'I'll take care of everything,'" Joe Viola recalled. "That was who Gary was and still is; he's selfless like that."[11] Goetzman drove Joanne from Nyack down to Manhattan when Jonathan was recovering from his treatment for heart disease and cancer. After being discharged from the hospital, Demme briefly settled back in Nyack in time for his seventy-third birthday. However, he was barely able to speak. Joe Viola would call every other day to check on him: "He couldn't talk for more than a few minutes. Gary checked him into the hospital the next day."[12]

Demme was originally going to direct a stage-to-screen adaptation of Anna Deavere Smith's off-Broadway play *Notes from the Field* for HBO, but because of his illness, he passed the project over to Kristi Zea. "Just before he died, he handed over the reins for me to direct shooting the play," Zea remembered. "I didn't get the chance to talk to him in any detail about what he wanted me to do. He literally said to Gary, 'Give it to Kristi to do.' It was daunting, terrifying, and sad."[13]

Jonathan received phone calls from his friends. Though short of breath, he tried everything he could to not let his illness affect those who cared for him. Joe Viola called asking when he should fly out to visit him: "He told me, 'Soon, Joe. Soon.' He died the next day. It wasn't the goodbye that I thought would happen. To me, my friendship with Jonathan is a story that will never end."[14] On Wednesday, April 26, 2017, surrounded by friends and family, Jonathan Demme passed away in his sleep; he was seventy-three years old.

A private burial presided over by the immediate family was conducted soon after. One week later, a memorial service was held at St. Mary's Episcopal Church in Harlem, the same church where Bobby Castle served as minister. David Byrne walked to the altar barefoot and performed his 1995 song "Buck Naked" on his acoustic guitar for Jonathan's family and friends. "I couldn't understand at first why that song, until all of a sudden it hit me," Stephen Apkon said. "It was the perfect song for that moment, a perfect JD requiem."[15]

Tributes poured in over social media and through the press after Demme's passing. Martin Scorsese noted the "inner lyricism" of his movies, calling him "my young friend."[16] Jodie Foster cited Demme as her mentor and "champion of the soul."[17] At the Tribeca

Film Festival, before the screening of James Ponsoldt's adaptation of Dave Eggers's *The Circle*, Tom Hanks, who had been friends with Demme since *Philadelphia*, noted, "This is a horrible day." Hanks and his wife, Rita Wilson, recalled seeing *Stop Making Sense* as their first "date film" and remembered the inspiring inclusivity Demme brought to his work.[18]

Two months later, the Connor Theater opened at the Rock and Roll Hall of Fame Museum. The 130-seat theater filled up with spectators watching Demme's seamless homage to the celebrated, musically diverse talents elected into the Hall of Fame.[19] On July 19, 2017, at the Jacob Burns Film Center, glasses were raised by those honoring Jonathan's life and dedication to the local theater before a screening of *Stop Making Sense*.[20] That same day, seventy-one other theaters across the United States, in association with the American Art House, screened the film in honor of Demme. In Croatia, the film was projected outside on Kružna Street in Rijka, known as "the City of Rock." On social media, tributes to Demme and the film were posted under the hashtag #CelebrateDemme.[21] *Stop Making Sense* would garner a new generation of fans when the Talking Heads and A24 theatrically rereleased the film in late 2023.

In March 2018, Brooklyn Demme drove back to the Ramapough Lenape Nation's Split Rock Sweetwater Prayer Camp. It was a time of mourning, prayer, and celebration of his father's life, and Brooklyn took Jonathan's advice: "Get out the camera and start shooting." With his digital camera, Brooklyn began completing the unfinished project he'd started with his father, a documentary on the sovereignty of the Ramapough Lenape Nation's Split Rock Sweetwater Prayer Camp titled *Akuy Eenda Maawehlaang: A Place Where People Gather*. "I find that what grief can offer is bottomless empathy and just jumping in the mix with other people," Brooklyn said in a podcast interview. "I was expecting my dad to be alive for a decade or more longer than he was. Again, it's natural for people to die. For a whole people and culture to die prematurely is a true tragedy."[22]

While America was wrestling with the nationalist rhetoric and civil unrest perpetuated by its forty-fifth president, Brooklyn corresponded with Dwaine Perry, who was chief of the Ramapough Lenape Nation, a Vietnam veteran, and an environmental activist. Their correspondence evolved into documenting Perry's legal fight against the Ramapo Hunt and Polo Club. Interference with the fourteen acres of sacred religious grounds had been commonplace for the Ramapoughs. Noise complaints issued by the wealthy members of the polo club led to frequent visits by the local police and costly citations that affected the tribe's financial well-being.[23]

For Brooklyn, the documentary was an expression of his solidarity with the Lenape Nation in the same way his father documented the jubilation of Haiti's post-Duvalier movement and the resilience of residents in New Orleans after Hurricane Katrina. "With respect to how decisive the presence of the prayer camp is in the local area, mainstream white people think of it in very different terms than our experience by the Ramapough people," Brooklyn said. "The people naysaying their right to pray don't perceive themselves as agents of vicious, age-old terrorism. A deeper intention in positioning myself within the story is to open a door for antagonists to also relate to it and understand through the lens of personal loss the raw value of family continuity."[24]

Brooklyn Demme continues working as an activist and documentarian, marching alongside the Ramapoughs in protest and supporting Chief Perry's debates in the US District Court of New Jersey. His latest project with filmmaker Ashley Dawson examines the history of Nyack's Black community dating back to the seventies. He has since been touring film festivals promoting his first feature film, *Mountain Lion*. "Growing up, my dad would tell aspiring filmmakers, 'All you need is a camera and a story to tell.' Today, with cameras embedded in our cell phones, it's now possible to tell those stories," Brooklyn said. "Just picking up the phone, clicking record, holding it with love, and seeing where it goes."[25]

Indigenous folklore says that the eagle (symbolizing the colonists who came to the Americas) and the condor (representing those immersed in nature and communion with the deceased) will meet in a celebration of reconciliation and healing called *pachakuti*.[26]

THERE'S NO GOING BACK

Jonathan Demme's work, along with that of his family, can be interpreted as a continuous flow of being with the earth while also being with spirit.

Winter snow falls along Rockland County as the nuthatches are perched on the trees. The four-way intersection in downtown Nyack is painted with rainbow colors symbolizing the township's solidarity with the LGBTQ+ movement. Along the rugged roads overlooking the Tappan Zee are American Legion post signs commemorating the Edward Hesdra family, who formed a seminal link in the Underground Railroad in Nyack circa 1855. The mention of Jonathan Demme's name leads to fond smiles and sighs of adoration from the local librarian and restaurateurs.

In a career that spanned nearly five decades, Jonathan Demme was a man of many hats—publicist, screenwriter, producer, director. But to those in his Rockland community and his close circle of friends across the globe, Jonathan Demme was a luminous figure whose ceaseless optimism and upbeat energy are as memorable as the films he made, the causes he fought for, and the stories he loved to tell.

Acknowledgments

Anyone who knows Jonathan Demme would know that he was never one to take sole credit. Similarly, the quintet of academic mentors who guided me over the years deserves recognition: Annette Holba, Tim Miller, Blair Davis, Mark Alberta, and Stephen Ambra.

The service librarians across the United States who helped me find the necessary artifacts to cite and reference Demme's life are the unsung heroes in academia: Catherine Cathers of the Historical Resources and Cultural Arts Department of Coral Gables, Florida; Ani Karagianis of Duke University's Rubenstein Library; Vicki Lynne Glantz at the University of Wyoming's American Heritage Center; Joan Miller, head archivist of the Ogden and Mary Louise Reid Cinema Archives at Wesleyan University; Philip Hallman of the University of Michigan's Screen Arts Mavericks and Makers Collections; and the entire staff of the University of Miami's Richter Library.

Ensuring that I had the great fortune to communicate with those who worked with Jonathan Demme were the agents, band managers, and publicity assistants who went out of their way to help me. Griffen Barchek, Steve Cuden, Eric Dimenstein, Chris Foster, Chelsea Hettrick, Sue Leibman, Nichole Nichols, Hannah Roark, Amanda Uhle, and Karl White were an immense help. Additionally, a special shout-out to The Feelies, who saved the *Something Wild* call sheets, notes, and fun anecdotes.

Those who were part of Jonathan's extended circle of friends have been a great resource for me: Alessandra Bracaglia and Fabien S.

Acknowledgments

Gerard, executive assistants of Bernardo Bertolucci and Clare Peploe's estate. Allen Ferro, Dianne Schroeder Hanks, and Grif Griffis were a delight as they recalled Jonathan's energetic times with Pablo Ferro and Hal Ashby. Christa Fuller was the first person I interviewed, and she is a world-class raconteur like her husband and Jonathan's good friend, Sam Fuller, and she deserves a giant thank-you. My additional gratitude must be shared with Victoria Leacock, Ann Stockdale, Rebecca Eskreis, Robin Fajardo, Jenny Lumet, and Nancy Buirski (1945–2023). Special recognition is extended to the incomparable Joe Viola (1938–2024); an afternoon with him was worth a lifetime of wisdom.

Film scholarship isn't created in a vacuum; it is a communal effort. Steve Vineberg's copy of the *Swing Shift* rough cut was revelatory, as was his 1990 *Sight and Sound* magazine article. Michael Sragow was incredible in sharing his plethora of reportage and production notes as soon as he heard I was writing a book about Jonathan Demme. Brian Iskov was remarkable in sharing his press notes with me from the Venice Film Festival. The good folks at Shadow Distribution in Waterville, Maine, deserve a big thanks for regaling me about Demme's love for the town and their involvement with the release of *Enzo Avitabile: Music Life*. Alan Bisbort, Nick Dawson, Glenn Frankel, Mark Harris, Gillian McCain, Glenn Kenny, and Fred Schruers were as insightful as they were encouraging through my countless emails while writing this book. My line editor and impromptu psychiatrist, Lisa Janssen, did an extraordinary job line editing this book.

The University of Kentucky Press has been a pleasure to work with, and that delight stems from my publisher, Ashley Runyon, and my book editors, Natalie O'Neal and Pat McGilligan, who were as enthusiastic as I was in honoring Jonathan Demme's life. Finally, my sincere acknowledgments are extended to my students and family, who taught me more about the emotional impact of the movies through their insight, activism, and creativity. My brothers, Gavin and Ryan, and my parents, Buddy and Dottie, have put up with my

Acknowledgments

love of film since watching *Philadelphia* as a teenager. I'd also like to honor the memories of my grandparents, Frank, Joanne, Dorothy, and Leo: I'm sure if Jonathan Demme were still around, he would be rolling the camera, filming our family dinners.

Notes

1. Monsieur Demme's Holidays (1944–1959)

1. Nassau County Census Records, New York State Archives (New York, NY), June 1, 1935, 13.
2. World War II draft card.
3. J. Gordon Townley and Claiborne B. Gregory, *Chanticleer* (Durham, NC: Duke University, 1934), 21:277.
4. The Alumni Register of Duke University, February 1934, 40.
5. "Marriage Notices: Dorothy Louise Rogers," *Chicago Tribune*, August 26, 1935, 11.
6. Roy Blount Jr., *Camels Are Easy, Comedy's Hard* (New York: Villard Books, 1991), 79.
7. Robert E. Demme, "Salt Water Safari," *Motor Boating Magazine*, December 1938, 27.
8. Robert E. Demme, "Deep Sea Game Hunting Paradise," *Homer Star*, July 13, 1939, 10.
9. "Least Publicized Club Is—Club of Professional Publicists," *Billboard*, August 9, 1941, 15.
10. Robert E. Demme, "Evolution of the Hellcat," *Skyways*, December 1943, 21.
11. Jonathan Demme and Jenny Lumet, interviewed by David Poland, "DP/30: The Oral History of Hollywood," YouTube, September 17, 2008, https://www.youtube.com/watch?v=En7OtWmsEgM&t=3s.
12. The American Ornithologist's Union, "Membership List of AOU," 1957, xxxi.
13. Author interview with Sylvia Strumpf, January 2022.
14. Michael Henry and Hubert Niogret, "Interview with Jonathan Demme," in *Jonathan Demme Interviews*, ed. Robert E. Kapsis (Jackson: University Press of Mississippi, 2009), 42.

15. Michael Sragow, "Jonathan Demme: On the Line," in Kapsis, *Jonathan Demme: Interviews*, 18.

16. "Agencies: Other Personnel Moves," *Sponsor*, January 10, 1959, 66.

2. The Animal Lover and the *Alligator* (1959–1967)

1 "Woody Kemper Associates," *Broadcasting Magazine*, December 23, 1963, 63.

2. Joseph Gelmis, "Growing Up on Long Island," *Newsday*, May 31, 1998, H23.

3. Hal Hinson, "Master of the Chance Encounter," *Washington Post*, April 22, 1984, F5.

4. Roy Blount Jr., *Camels Are Easy, Comedy's Hard* (New York: Villard Books, 1991), 83.

5. Ibid.

6. Ibid.

7. Max Cea, "Jonathan Demme Interview," *Pink Monkey Magazine*, May 2016, 55.

8. "A History of Overton: Vibrant Early Life Followed by Social and Physical Deterioration," accessed August 8, 2023, https://www.housingissues.org/overtown/hist-his.html.

9. Jan Glidewell, "Born to Be Wild—On Four Wheels," *Tampa Bay Times*, July 3, 1991, 48.

10. Blount, *Camels Are Easy*, 83.

11. Kevin Thomas, "9 Directors Rising from the Trashes" *Los Angeles Times*, December 21, 1975.

12. Grace Wing Bohne, "Lillian Works Hard at Not Being in Control," *Miami Herald*, May 24, 1966, sec. C, 45.

13. "Marquis' Who's Who of American Women," Marquis' Who's Who, 1973, 978.

14. Anthony Loeb, "A Conversation with Jonathan Demme," Columbia College, Chicago Department of Film and Video, 1991, 2.

15. Hinson, "Master of the Chance Encounter."

16. Loeb, "A Conversation with Jonathan Demme."

17. Jonathan Demme, "Best Bet on Campus," University of Florida Digital Collections, *Florida Alligator*, February 24, 1965, 4.

18. Editorial, "Why Not Films at Studio M?" *Coral Gables Times*, June 17, 1965, 6.

19. Jonathan Demme, "*The Hill* Review," *Coral Gable Times*, November 11, 1965.

20. Donald Stoneman, "Filmmaker's Big 'Cut' Came When He Changed Career Plan," *News on Record*, October 22, 1991, 10.

21. The Stuart Byron Papers, May 1967, accessed through the Reid Cinema Archives, Wesleyan University (Middletown, CT), May 2022.

3. A Road Scholar (1968–1970)

1. Author interview with Larry Kaplan, January 2022.

2. "Jonathan Demme: Scene by Scene," *Scene by Scene*, BBC, February 27, 1999.

3. Brian Iskov, "Jonathan Demme Press Junket Interview," Venice Film Festival, September 4, 2008.

4. Stuart Byron papers, March 1967, accessed through the Ogden and Mary Louise Reid Cinema Archives, Wesleyan University (Middletown, CT), May 2022.

5. "Jonathan Demme Interview," *Film at Lincoln Center Podcast*, "Episode #134: From the Archives" (New York, NY), February 2012.

6. "Van Nuys Student Appearing in Play," *Van Nuys News and Valley Green Sheet*, March 18, 1966, 43.

7. Author interview with Evelyn Purcell, February 2022.

8. Author's email correspondence with Evelyn Purcell, February 2022.

9. Ibid.

10. Author interview with Joe Viola, July 2022.

11. Ibid.

12. Adrian Wotton, "*The Guardian* NFT Interview: Jonathan Demme," in *Jonathan Demme: Interviews*, ed. Robert E. Kapsis (Jackson: University Press of Mississippi, 2009), 106.

13. Ibid.

14. Author interview with David Symonds, January 2022.

15. Author interview with Larry Kaplan.

16. Author interview with Joe Viola.

17. Alex Stapleton, *Corman's World: Exploits of a Hollywood Rebel* (A&E IndieFilms, Lionsgate, 2011).

18. Ibid.

19. Ibid.

20. Ibid.

21. Michael Sragow, "Jonathan Demme: On the Line," in Kapsis, *Jonathan Demme: Interviews*, 18.

22. Author interview with Joe Viola.

23. Ibid.

24. Author interview with Evelyn Purcell.

4. A New World (1970–1973)

1. Roman Polanski, *Roman* (New York: Ballantine Books, 1985), 334.
2. Author interview with Joe Viola, July 2022.
3. Ibid.
4. Ibid.
5. Author interview with Evelyn Purcell, February 2022.
6. Michael Blackwood, *Roger Corman: Hollywood's Wild Angel*, Michael Blackwood Productions, documentary, 1978.
7. Author interview with Evelyn Purcell.
8. "*Angels Hard as They Come* Review," *Daily Variety*, August 18, 1971, 15.
9. "*Angels Hard as They Come* Review," *Box Office Magazine*, August 30, 1971, https://www.yumpu.com/en/document/read/30548578/boxoffice-august301971.
10. Author interview with Evelyn Purcell.
11. Author interview with Joe Viola.
12. Ibid.

5. Girls, Guns, and *Shampoo* (1974–1976)

1. Peter R. Breggin and Daniel S. Greenberg, "The Aftermath of Lobotomy—'Partial Murder of the Mind,'" *Sacramento Bee*, March 26, 1972, 93.
2. Christian Blackwood, *Roger Corman: Hollywood's Wild Angel*, Michael Blackwood Productions, documentary, 1978.
3. "Film Production Schedule Ambitious," *Desert Sun*, July 6, 1974, 4.
4. "Buddhist Obon Carnival Will Be Held Sat., Sun," *Independent*, July 24, 1958, 3.
5. Walter V. Addiego, "The Film Has Two Titles: One for Inner Cities, One for Campuses," *San Francisco Examiner*, July 3, 1979, 20.
6. Gary Wrath, "Oscar Nod Not Crucial to Encinitas Man's Long Film Career," *North County Times*, March 26, 1995, 40.
7. Austin Film Festival's *On Story* Podcast, Episode 413, "Greaser's Palace: A Retrospective," July 2014.
8. Author interview with Erica Gavin, March 2023.
9. "Jonathan Demme: Scene by Scene," *Scene by Scene*, BBC, February 27, 1999.
10. Author interview with Erica Gavin.
11. Ibid.

12. Ibid.

13. Author interview with Evelyn Purcell, February 2022.

14. Kevin Thomas, "Upping the Genre of Prison Flicks," *Los Angeles Times*, October 31, 1974.

15. Author interview with Evelyn Purcell.

16. Michael Wolff, "So What Do You Do at Midnight? You See a Trashy Movie," *New York Times*, September 7, 1975, 121.

17. "Jonathan Demme introducing *Harold and Maude* at the Walter Reade Theatre," February 14, 2008, YouTube, https://www.youtube.com/watch?v=Co77MXD3TUE.

18. *Crazy Mama*/New World Pictures publicity brochure, courtesy of William Sandell.

19. Jonathan Demme, audio commentary of *Crazy Mama*, New Concorde, 2002, DVD.

20. Ibid.

21. Ibid.

22. Kevin Thomas, "'Crazy Mama' a Diversion," *Los Angeles Times*, November 5, 1975, 12.

23. "'Mama' Fairish $45,700," *Variety*, November 11, 1975, 14.

24. Kevin Thomas, "Nine Directors Rising from the Trashes," *Los Angeles Times*, December 21, 1975, 58–60.

25. Author interview with Evelyn Purcell.

26. Jonathan Demme, audio commentary of *Fighting Mad*, New Concorde, 2002, DVD.

27. Ibid.

28. "Double Murder Suspect Believed Out of State," *Northwest Arkansas Times*, July 14, 1971, 1.

29. Peter Fonda, audio commentary of *Fighting Mad*, New Concorde, 2002, DVD.

30. Demme, audio commentary of *Fighting Mad*.

31. Ibid.

32. Jonathan Demme, *Fighting Mad* screenplay, February 13, 1975, Jonathan Demme Collection, University of Wyoming, American Heritage Center.

33. Richie Unterberger, "Biography," accessed April 2022, Brucelanghorne.com.

34. Demme, audio commentary of *Fighting Mad*.

35. Ibid.

36. Jeff Freedman, "*Fighting Mad* Review," *Hollywood Reporter*, April 27, 1976, 3.

6. Frequency Issues (1977–1979)

1. Author interview with Evelyn Purcell, February 2022.
2. Ibid.
3. "The Close-Up Episode, #34," *FilmLinc Podcast*, interview conducted at the Walter Reade Theatre (New York, NY), February 2012.
4. Author interview with Bruce McGill, February 2022.
5. "The Close-Up Episode, #34."
6. Ibid.
7. Ibid.
8. Ibid.
9. Mike Wendland, "No Squatter's Rights in CB," *Santa Fe New Mexican*, January 21, 1977, 14.
10. "The Close-Up Episode, #34."
11. Author interview with Bruce McGill.
12. Author interview with Harry Northup, January 2022.
13. Rob Field, "Plugged In," Jonathan Demme Interview, *DGA Quarterly*, Winter 2015, https://www.dga.org/craft/dgaq/all-articles/1501-winter-2015/dga-interview-jonathan-demme.aspx.
14. "The Close-Up Episode, #34."
15. Richard Goldstein, "Artbreaks: Mangle with Care," *Village Voice*, October 31, 1977, 43.
16. "The Close-Up Episode, #34."
17. Guy Flately, "Demme Draws Praise Despite CB Flick's Failure," *Journal Tribune*, November 10, 1977, 25.
18. "Treatment for *The King of the Cannibal Islands* by Jonathan Demme, Hercules Bellville, and Evelyn Purcell—June 12, 1978," the Jonathan Demme Papers (1965–1985), Box 2, the American Heritage Center, Laramie, Wyoming.
19. "On Story 414: Jonathan Demme in conversation with Paul Thomas Anderson at the 2013 Austin Film Festival" (Austin, TX), YouTube, https://www.youtube.com/watch?v=RXT0WOUceak.
20. Author interview with Sandy McLeod, January 2022.
21. Ibid.
22. Carlos Clarens, "Demme Monde," *Film Comment* (September/October 1980), in *Jonathan Demme: Interviews*, ed. Robert E. Kapsis (Jackson: University Press of Mississippi, 2009), 10.
23. Barbara Vancheri, "Producers Break Their 'Silence' on Suspense Film," *Philadelphia Post-Gazette*, March 6, 1990, 21.
24. Author interview with Sandy McLeod.

25. Janet Maslin, "Demme's Newest Film Sets a Record—of Sorts," *New York Times*, May 13, 1979, 41.

26. Author interview with Evelyn Purcell.

27. Maslin, "Demme's Newest Film Sets a Record."

7. Easy Street (1979–1981)

1. Mark Harris, *Mike Nichols: A Life* (New York: Penguin Press, 2021), 330.

2. Author interview with Thom Mount, January 2022.

3. Ibid.

4. Jonathan Demme, *Melvin and Howard* commentary track, Twilight Time, 2019, Blu-Ray.

5. Author interview with Thom Mount.

6. Demme, *Melvin and Howard* commentary track.

7. Ginger Varney and Samir Hachem, "Some Lovely Moments: An Interview with the Director of *Melvin and Howard*," *LA Weekly*, November 13, 1980, 19; Demme, *Melvin and Howard* commentary track.

8. Demme, *Melvin and Howard* commentary track.

9. Author interview with Thom Mount.

10. Author interview with Sandy McLeod, January 2022.

11. Demme, *Melvin and Howard* commentary track.

12. Author interview with Craig McKay, February 2022.

13. "The Close-Up Episode, #34," *FilmLinc Podcast*, interview conducted at the Walter Reade Theatre (New York), February 2012.

14. Vincent Canby, "*Melvin and Howard* Opens Festival Tonight," *New York Times*, September 26, 1980, sec. C, 32.

15. *Melvin and Howard* box office numbers, accessed January 20, 2022, https://www.the-numbers.com/movie/Melvin-and-Howard#more.

16. Bo Goldman's acceptance speech for Best Original Screenplay at the Academy Awards (AMPAS), March 31, 1981.

17. Mary Steenburgen's acceptance speech for Best Actress in a Supporting Role at the Academy Awards (AMPAS), March 31, 1981.

18. Author interview with Bill Million, January 2022.

19. Author interview with Edie Vonnegut, March 2022.

20. Howard Rosenberg, "30 of the Best from an Uneven Collection," *Los Angeles Times*, April 23, 1989, 28.

8. Shift in the Breeze (1982–1983)

1. *Swing Shift* preliminary production information, Warner Bros. Press Release, 1983, 4.

2. Michael Sragow, "Jonathan Demme: On the Line," in *Jonathan Demme: Interviews*, ed. Robert E. Kapsis (Jackson: University Press of Mississippi, 2009), 22.

3. *Swing Shift*, AFI.com, accessed January 2022, https://catalog.afi.com/Catalog/moviedetails/57221.

4. Goldie Hawn, *A Lotus Grows in the Mud* (New York: G. P. Putnam's Sons, 2005), 304.

5. Aiden Kelley, "'Indiana Jones and the Dial of Destiny' Budget Breakdown: Has Indy's Swan Song Officially Flopped?" *Collider*, July 31, 2023, https://collider.com/indiana-jones-and-the-dial-of-destiny-box-office-budget/.

6. Ibid.

7. Sragow, "Jonathan Demme," 22.

8. Ibid., 23.

9. Author interview with Ron Nyswaner, March 2022.

10. Ibid.

11. Ibid.

12. Stephen Farber, "Can Rosie the Riveter Speak to a New Generation?" *New York Times*, May 22, 1983, sec. 2, 21.

13. *Swing Shift* preliminary production information, 6.

14. Hal Hinson, "Master of the Chance Encounter," *The Washington Post*, April 22, 1984, F5.

15. Farber, "Can Rosie the Riveter Speak."

16. Author interview with Sandy McLeod, January 2022.

17. Author interview with Ron Nyswaner.

18. Hawn, *A Lotus Grows in the Mud*, 309.

19. Ibid.

20. Author interview with Chuck Mulvehill, January 2022.

21. *Swing Shift* call sheet, May 19, 1983.

22. Hawn, *A Lotus Grows in the Mud*, 311.

23. Farber, "Can Rosie the Riveter Speak."

24. Hawn, *A Lotus Grows in the Mud*, 313.

25. Author interview with Craig McKay, February 2022.

26. Adrian Wotton, "*The Guardian* NFT Interview: Jonathan Demme," in Kapsis, *Jonathan Demme: Interviews*, 101.

27. Author interview with Sandy McLeod.

28. Jonathan Demme interview, AFI Silver / Docs Festival, Charles Guggenheim Symposium, May 2007.

29. Ibid.

30. Farber, "Can Rosie the Riveter Speak."

31. Steve Vineberg, "Swing Shift: The Unmaking of a Masterpiece?" British Film Institute, accessed July 7, 2022, https://www2.bfi.org.uk/news-opinion/sight-sound-magazine/features/swing-shift-making-of-jonathan-demme-directors-cut-comparison.

32. Ibid.

33. Jonathan Demme interview, AFI Silver / Docs Festival.

34. Author interview with Harry Northup, January 2022.

9. Juggling Act (1983–1984)

1. Lynn Van Matre, "Making 'Sense' with Talking Heads—No Gimmicks, Just Gutty Rock," *Chicago Tribune*, November 25, 1984, sec. 13, 25.

2. David Ehrlich, "'Stop Making Sense' Producer Gary Goetzman Talks the Making of Rock Doc That Changed Concert Movies Forever," Indiewire.com, August 18, 2023.

3. Author interview with Joe Viola, July 2022.

4. Author interview with Sandy McLeod, January 2022.

5. "Bent by Nature: Diedre O'Donoghue and the Lost SNAP Archives," KCRW (Los Angeles, CA), no. 172, November 8, 1984, Podcast.

6. Jonathan Demme interview, AFI Silver / Docs Festival, Charles Guggenheim Symposium, May 2007.

7. Ibid.

8. Author interview with Sandy McLeod.

9. Jonathan Demme interview, AFI Silver / Docs Festival.

10. Jonathan Demme, audio commentary for *Stop Making Sense*, Second Sight, DVD, 2015.

11. "Jonathan Demme introducing *Harold and Maude* at the Walter Reade Theatre," February 14, 2008, YouTube, https://www.youtube.com/watch?v=Co77MXD3TUE.

12. "Bent by Nature."

13. David Denby, "All Quiet on the Homefront," *New York*, April 30, 1984.

14. *At the Movies with Gene Siskel and Roger Ebert*, Tribune Entertainment, April 14, 1984.

15. Jonathan Demme audio commentary of *Fighting Mad*, New Concorde, 2002, DVD.

16. *At the Movies with Gene Siskel and Roger Ebert*, Tribune Entertainment, November 24, 1984.

17. Knight News Service, "Filmmaker Confident His 'Sense' Will Make More Than Cents," *Dayton Daily News*, December 25, 1984, 16.

18. Tina Weymouth, Talking Heads commentary on *Stop Making Sense*, Second Sight, DVD, 2015.

19. David Byrne, Talking Heads commentary on *Stop Making Sense*, Second Sight, DVD, 2015.

20. Jonathan Demme, commentary on *Stop Making Sense*, Second Sight, DVD, 2015.

21. Ibid.

22. Ibid.

23. Hal Hinson, "Master of the Chance Encounter," *Washington Post*, April 22, 1984, F5.

24. "Night-Table Reading Interview with Jonathan Demme," *Vanity Fair*, July 1986, 97.

25. Jonathan Demme interview for the Criterion Collection release of *Something Wild*, recorded at Jacob Burns Film Center, 2012.

26. Roderick Mann, "Jonathan Demme Starts Making Sense with His Career," *Los Angeles Times*, November 11, 1984, 21.

10. Something New (1985–1986)

1. Max Cea, "Jonathan Demme Interview," *Pink Monkey Magazine*, May 2016, 58.

2. Author interview with Mike Medavoy, March 2022.

3. Ibid.

4. Author interview with E. Max Frye, January 2022.

5. Jonathan Demme interview for the Criterion Collection release of *Something Wild*, recorded at JBFC, 2012.

6. Ibid.

7. Ibid.

8. Author interview with E. Max Frye.

9. *Something Wild* call sheet, courtesy of Brenda Sauter.

10. Jonathan Demme interview for the Criterion Collection release of *Something Wild*.

11. Ibid.

12. Fred Schruers, "The Uttmost," *Premiere Magazine*, Special Issue, 8 (1994): 81.

13. Steve Warren, "Opposites Detract," *Bay Area Reporter*, November 13, 1986, 35.

14. Author interview with Sandy McLeod, January 2022.

15. Jonathan Demme interview for the Criterion Collection release of *Something Wild*.

16. Author interview with Bill Million, January 2022.

17. Author interview with Brenda Sauter, January 2022.
18. Author interview with Dave Weckerman, January 2022.
19. Author interview with E. Max Frye.
20. Author interview with Tony Jannelli, December 2022.
21. Jonathan Demme interview for the Criterion Collection release of *Something Wild*.
22. Author interview with Sister Carol East, April 2022.
23. Pauline Kael, "*Something Wild* Review," *New Yorker*, November 17, 1986.
24. Dave Kehr, "*Something Wild* Adds Brilliant Twist to Cliché," *Chicago Tribune*, November 7, 1986.
25. Author's email correspondence with Jeff Daniels, January 2022.
26. Boxofficemojo.com.
27. Patrick Goldstein, "Demme Creates 'Wild' Soundtrack," *News Tribune*, November 28, 1986, 10.
28. *Late Night with David Letterman*, NBC Productions, Worldwide Pants, March 4, 1987.
29. Author interview with Sandy McLeod.
30. Ibid.

11. Second Chances (1987–1989)

1. Author interview with Sandy McLeod, January 2022.
2. Jonathan Demme interview, AFI SilverDocs, June 14, 2007, courtesy of Reelblack.com.
3. Ibid.
4. Author interview with Sandy McLeod.
5. Julie Preston, "Haiti Election Canceled after Voters Are Slain," *Philadelphia Inquirer*, November 30, 1987, 1-A.
6. Fred Schruers, "Jonathan Demme: A Study in Character," *Rolling Stone*, May 19, 1988, 103.
7. Author interview with Paul Lazar, January 2022.
8. Schruers, "Jonathan Demme," 103.
9. Ibid.
10. Author interview with Mark Burns, April 2022.
11. Author interview with Matthew Modine, January 2022.
12. Author interview with Mike Medavoy, March 2022.
13. "Jonathan Demme Interview with Bobbie Wygant," *Bobbie Wygant Archive*, 1988, accessed January 2, 2022, https://www.youtube.com/watch?v=XpEcPs3z2dw.
14. Michelle Pfeiffer, *Inside the Actors Studio* (Season 13, Episode 9), Bravo TV, August 2007.

15. Peter Stone, "Blond Venus," *Interview*, August 1988, 48.
16. Myra Forsberg, "Dean Stockwell's Second Comeback," *Sacramento Bee*, September 20, 1988, F7.
17. Author interview with Kristi Zea, February 2022.
18. Author interview with Bill Todman Jr., February 2022.
19. Author interview with Sister Carol East, April 2022.
20. Author interview with Matthew Modine.
21. Author interview with Kristi Zea.
22. Author interview with Craig McKay, February 2022.
23. Jonathan Demme junket interview, Venice Film Festival, September 4, 2008, courtesy of Brian Iskov.
24. Schruers, "Jonathan Demme."
25. Rita Kempley, "*Married to the Mob* Review," *Washington Post*, August 19, 1988, https://www.washingtonpost.com/wpsrv/style/longterm/movies/videos/marriedtothemobrkempley_a0c9f5.htm.
26. Roger Ebert, "*Married to the Mob* Review," RogerEbert.com, August 19, 1988, https://www.rogerebert.com/reviews/married-to-the-mob-1988.
27. Jonathan Demme, *KONBIT* liner notes, A&M Music, 1989.
28. Ibid.
29. Ibid.
30. Tom Schnabel, "Konbit: Jonathan Demme's Celebration of Haitian Music," KCRW.com, May 3, 2017, https://www.kcrw.com/music/articles/konbit-jonathan-demmes-celebration-of-haitian-music.

12. Dinner with Friends (1990–1992)

1. Joshua Hammer, "Bio: Jonathan Demme," *People*, May 25, 1987, 101.
2. Jill Bernstein, "But Dino, I Don't Want to Make a Film about Elephants . . ." *Guardian*, February 8, 2001, https://www.theguardian.com/film/2001/feb/09/culture.features.
3. Jonathan Demme, *The Silence of the Lambs* commentary track, MGM / The Criterion Collection, DVD, 1998.
4. Anthony Loeb, "A Conversation with Jonathan Demme," Columbia College, Chicago Department of Film and Video, 1991, 18.
5. Barbara Morgan and Maya Perez, eds., *On Story: Screenwriters and Filmmakers on Their Iconic Films* (Austin: University of Texas Press, 2016), 139.
6. Ibid., 140.
7. Demme, *The Silence of the Lambs* commentary track.
8. Author interview with Brooke Smith, January 2022.

9. Ibid.
10. Demme, *The Silence of the Lambs* commentary track.
11. "Principal Photography Begins on Jonathan Demme's 'The Silence of the Lambs' Starring Jodie Foster, Anthony Hopkins and Scott Glenn," *PR Newswire*, November 16, 1989.
12. Jackie Cain, "Pittsburgh Remembers 'Silence of the Lambs' Director," WTAE-TV, April 26, 2017, https://www.wtae.com/article/pittsburgh-remembers-silence-of-the-lambs-director/9567850.
13. Author interview with Kristi Zea, February 2022.
14. Ibid.
15. Ibid.
16. Ibid.
17. Ibid.
18. Ibid.
19. Author interview with Brooke Smith.
20. Demme, *The Silence of the Lambs* commentary track.
21. Author interview with Craig McKay, February 2022.
22. Demme, *The Silence of the Lambs* commentary track.
23. Author interview with Kristi Zea.
24. Author interview with Craig McKay.
25. Author interview with Kristi Zea.
26. "In Conversation with . . . Jodie Foster, on *The Silence of the Lambs*," BFI, YouTube, accessed July 20, 2022, https://www.youtube.com/watch?v=ZETEx_.
27. Ibid.
28. Monica Dorenkamp, "A Sheep in Wolf's Clothing?" *Outweek* 8 (March 6, 1991): 64.
29. Larry Kramer, "Who Killed Vito Russell?" *Outweek* 86 (February 20, 1991): 27.
30. Saskia Baron, dir., "Lambs' Tales," *Late Show Special*, BBC, 1991.
31. Boxofficemojo.com.
32. Shelia Benson, "'Lambs' Dotted with Stunning Performances," *Los Angeles Times*, February 15, 1991.
33. Vincent Canby, "Methods of Madness in 'Silence of the Lambs,'" *New York Times*, February 14, 1991, C-17.
34. Loeb, "A Conversation with Jonathan Demme."
35. Terry Pristin, "How Orion Kept 'Lambs' Alive," *Los Angeles Times*, April 1, 1992.
36. Anthony Heald, *The Silence of the Lambs Anniversary Retrospective*, MGM, 2001, DVD.

13. Angels Crowding Heaven (1992–1995)

1. Amy Taubin, "Still Burning," *Village Voice*, June 9, 1992, 66.
2. Mark Weiss, "Top Director Visits Hudson," *Jersey Journal*, July 24, 1992, E3.
3. Bernard Weintraub, "A Day to Demonstrate Affection for the Stars and Some Dismay," *New York Times*, March 31, 1992, C-13.
4. Jonathan Demme, Best Director Oscar acceptance speech on March 30, 1992, Academy Awards Acceptance Speech Database, https://aaspeechesdb.oscars.org/link/064-8/#:~:text=The%20only%20way%20I%20can,Zea%2C%20Craig%20McKay%20and%20Tommy.
5. "Jonathan Demme Introducing *Harold and Maude* at the Walter Reade Theatre," February 14, 2008, YouTube, https://www.youtube.com/watch?v=Co77MXD3TUE.
6. Author interview with Ron Nyswaner, March 2022.
7. Centers for Disease Control and Prevention, "Update: Mortality Attributable to HIV Infection among Persons Aged 25–44 Years—United States, 1991 and 1992," *Morbidity and Mortality Weekly Report* 42, no. 45 (November 19, 1993): 870.
8. Author interview with Ron Nyswaner.
9. AFI Catalog, *Philadelphia* (1993), accessed June 1, 2023, https://catalog.afi.com/Catalog/MovieDetails/59629?cxt=filmography.
10. Ibid.
11. Ibid.
12. Jonathan Demme, *Philadelphia* commentary track, Sony/TriStar Pictures, DVD, 2005.
13. Jennet Conant, "Tom Hanks Wipes That Grin Off His Face," *Esquire*, December 1, 1993. 82.
14. "Denzel Washington Interview with Bobbie Wygant, 1993," Bobbie Wygant Archive, accessed June 5, 2022, https://www.youtube.com/watch?v=6cQq_9eWQyE.
15. Author interview with Greg Mehrten, February 2022.
16. Ibid.
17. Author interview with Kristi Zea, February 2022.
18. Conant, "Tom Hanks Wipes That Grin."
19. Author interview with Ron Nyswaner, March 2022.
20. Author interview with Kristi Zea.
21. Author interview with Ron Nyswaner.
22. Demme, *Philadelphia* commentary track.
23. Author interview with Greg Mehrten.
24. Demme, *Philadelphia* commentary track.

25. Anthony DeCurtis, "The *Rolling Stone* Interview: Jonathan Demme," in *Jonathan Demme: Interviews*, ed. Robert E. Kapsis (Jackson: University Press of Mississippi, 2009), 95.

26. Author interview with Craig McKay, February 2022.

27. Demme, *Philadelphia* commentary track.

28. David Ansen, "'Tis Not a Jolly Season," *Newsweek*, December 26, 1993, https://www.newsweek.com/tis-not-jolly-season-190784.

29. Janet Maslin, "Tom Hanks as AIDS Victim Who Fights the Establishment," *New York Times*, December 22, 1993, C-15.

30. Larry Kramer, "Philadelphia Sorry," *Chicago Reader*, January 13, 1994, 172.

31. *Philadelphia* box office, accessed January 20, 2022, https://www.the-numbers.com/movie/Philadelphia-(1993)#tab=summary.

32. Author interview with Greg Mehrten.

33. Jane Hall, "'Philadelphia' Story Subject of Lawsuit," *Los Angeles Times*, February 12, 1994.

34. Fred Schruers, "The Uttmost," *Premiere*, Special Issue, 8 (1994): 81.

35. DeCurtis, "The *Rolling Stone* Interview."

36. Tom Hanks, Best Actor Oscar speech, March 21, 1994, Academy Awards Acceptance Speech Database, https://aaspeechesdb.oscars.org/link/066-1/.

37. Robert Demme IMDb page, accessed January 3, 2022, https://www.imdb.com/name/nm9183156/.

38. Martha Gross, "'Philadelphia' Comes to Miami for a Benefit," *South Florida Sun Sentinel*, January 19, 1994, 8E.

39. "Jesse Jackson, 40 Others Arrested in Haiti Protest," UPI Archives, March 15, 1993, https://www.upi.com/Archives/1993/03/15/Jesse-Jackson-40-others-arrested-in-Haiti-protest/2632732171600/.

40. Jonathan Demme, "Jonathan Demme Remembers Robert 'Cousin Bobby' Wilkinson Castle," POV's Documentary Inc., October 2012, http://archive.pov.org/blog/povdocs/2012/12/jonathan-demme-remembers-robert-cousin-bobby- (accessed January 2022).

41. Inscription on Dorothy Rogers Demme's grave at Rockville Cemetery in Rockville, Long Island, New York, author's notes, March 13, 2023.

14. Subways, Galleries, and Storefronts (1996–1997)

1. Tom Hanks interview, "The Making of *That Thing You Do!*" 20th Century Fox, DVD, 2007.

2. Hillary Hughes, "Adam Schlesinger's 'That Thing You Do': One of the Best Fake Songs," Bilboard.com, April 1, 2020, https://www.billboard.com/music/rock/adam-schlesinger-that-thing-you-do-best-fake-song-9348993/.

3. Author interview with Christa Fuller, December 2021.
4. *Subway Stories* ad, *New York*, April 24, 1995, 75.
5. *Ulee's Gold* box office numbers, Boxofficemojo.com, accessed June 5, 2022, https://www.boxofficemojo.com/title/tt0120402/?ref_=bo_rl_ti.
6. Jonathan Demme, "Direct from the Eye: The Jonathan Demme Collection of Self-Taught Art," *Material Culture*, March 2014, 5.
7. Jonathan Demme, Edwidge Danticat, and Pebo Voss, *Island on Fire* (Nyack, NY: Kaliko Press, 1997), 205.
8. Author interview with Kristi Zea, February 2022.
9. Karen Schoemer, "On the Lower East Side with: Jim Jarmusch, Film as Life, and Vice Versa," *New York Times*, April 30, 1992, C-1.
10. Author interview with Robyn Hitchcock, December 2022.
11. "Dramatic Ventures for the Venturesome," *New York Daily News*, July 23, 1982, M7.
12. Author interview with Tony Jannelli, December 2022.
13. Jay Hedblade, "*Storefront Hitchcock* Review," *Chicago Tribune*, November 15, 1998, 7–13.

15. Ghosts at the Door (1997–2000)

1. Kristine Yohe, "Margaret Garner, Rememory, and the Infinite Past: History in *Beloved*," in *Critical Insights: Beloved*, ed. Maureen Ngozi Eke (Hackensack, NJ: Salem Press, 2015), 30.
2. Timothy Greenfeld-Sanders, dir., *Toni Morrison: The Pieces I Am*, Perfect Day Films, 2019.
3. Author interview with Oprah Winfrey, April 2022.
4. Adrian Wotton, "*The Guardian* NFT Interview: Jonathan Demme," in *Jonathan Demme: Interviews*, ed. Robert E. Kapsis (Jackson: University Press of Mississippi, 2009), 104.
5. "*Beloved* Cover Story," *Jet Magazine* 94, no. 21 (October 19, 1998): 64.
6. "The New Recruits: Thandie Newton," *Los Angeles Magazine*, November 1998, 92.
7. Author interview with Oprah Winfrey.
8. Author interview with Joe Viola, July 2022.
9. Roger Ebert, "Winfrey Confronts the Strength and the Spirits of 'Beloved,'" RogerEbert.com, October 11, 1998, https://www.rogerebert.com/interviews/winfrey-confronts-the-strength-and-the-spirits-of-beloved.
10. Author interview with Oprah Winfrey.
11. Oprah Winfrey, *Journey to Beloved* (New York: Hyperion Press, 1998), 135.

12. "A Conversation with Director Jonathan Demme," *The Charlie Rose Show*, Rose Communications, PBS, October 26, 1998.
13. Author interview with Oprah Winfrey.
14. Ibid.
15. Ibid.
16. Author interview with Kristi Zea, February 2022.
17. Author interview with Michael Dennis, April 2022.
18. Ibid.
19. "A Conversation with Director Jonathan Demme," *The Charlie Rose Show*.
20. Kenneth Turan, "Worth All the Begetting," *Los Angeles Times*, October 16, 1998, https://www.latimes.com/archives/la-xpm-1998-oct-16-ca-32890-story.html.
21. Joe Morgenstern, "Oprah Winfrey Can Act, but 'Beloved' Ultimately Fails," *Wall Street Journal*, October 16, 1998, https://www.wsj.com/articles/SB908483651998225000.
22. Author interview with Oprah Winfrey.
23. "ReelBlack.com Talks to Jonathan Demme about New Home Movies," ReelBlack One, YouTube, accessed April 2, 2022, https://www.youtube.com/watch?v=oK6vM8dZJyg.
24. Author interview with Michael Dennis.
25. Letter to Oprah Winfrey from Sidney Lumet dated February 3, 1999, courtesy of the Estate of Sidney Lumet.
26. Author interview with Oprah Winfrey.
27. John Barry, "Movie Director Reunites Family," *Miami Herald*, October 11, 1998, 5B.
28. Leslie Casimir, "Haitian Refugees' Expectations Rise," *Miami Herald*, September 30, 1998, 2B.
29. Robert E. Kapsis, ed., "An Interview with Jonathan Demme: The Agronomist.com," in Kapsis, *Jonathan Demme: Interviews*, 147.
30. Author interview with Edwidge Danticat, June 2022.
31. Kapsis, "An Interview with Jonathan Demme."

16. Losing Control (2000–2004)

1. Scott Tobias, "The Onion A.V. Club Interview with Jonathan Demme," in *Jonathan Demme: Interviews*, ed. Robert E. Kapsis (Jackson: University Press of Mississippi, 2009), 144.
2. *The Truth about Charlie* Publicity Booklet, Universal Pictures, September 2002, 12.

3. Michael Fleming, "Demme, Saxon to Say Adios," *Variety* 379 (July 25, 2000): 16.

4. Mark Cousins, *Scene by Scene*, BBC, February 27, 1999.

5. Michael Fleming, "It's 'Cruelty' for Demme," *Variety*, October 22, 2000, https://variety.com/2000/film/news/it-s-cruelty-for-demme-1117788069/.

6. Jonathan Demme, *The Truth about Charlie* audio commentary track, Universal, 2002, DVD.

7. *The Truth about Charlie* Publicity Booklet, 16–17.

8. Ibid., 14.

9. Tobias, "The Onion A.V. Club Interview," 145.

10. EW Staff, "The Rundown," *Entertainment Weekly*, August 17, 2002, https://ew.com/article/2002/08/17/truth-about-charlie/.

11. Tobias, "The Onion A.V. Club Interview," 145.

12. *The Truth about Charlie* box office information, Box Office Mojo, accessed July 2, 2022, https://www.boxofficemojo.com/title/tt0270707/.

13. Jonathan Rosenbaum, "*The Truth about Charlie*," *Chicago Reader*, October 25, 2022, https://chicagoreader.com/film/the-truth-about-charlie/.

14. Anthony Breznican, "Film-TV Director Ted Demme Collapses, Dies Playing Basketball," *Santa Cruz Sentinel*, January 15, 2002, A-10.

15. "Frederick Rogers Demme," *St. Lucie News Tribune*, April 24, 2002, B3.

16. "Episode 671—Charlie Kaufman Interview," *WTF with Marc Maron*, Podcast, January 11, 2016.

17. Max Cea, "Jonathan Demme Interview," *Pink Monkey Magazine*, May 2016, 61.

18. Richard Freedman, "A Real Man Who Eats Quiche," *Rock Island Argus*, August 8, 1982, 43.

19. Ina Warren, "The Manchurian Candidate: Its Time Is Now—26 Years after Its First Release," *Expositor*, January 14, 1989, 7.

20. "Riveting Remake of Cold War Classic," *Modesto Bee*, July 28, 2004, F-6.

21. Marilyn Beck and Stacey Jenel Smith, "Hollywood: A New 'Candidate,'" *Detroit Free Press*, June 19, 1996, 5D.

22. Amy Wallace, "The Un-Agent Agent," *Los Angeles Magazine*, March 2003, 118.

23. "Antwone Fisher," December 16, 2002, https://www.dga.org/Events/2002/December/Antwone-Fisher.aspx.

24. Author interview with Kristi Zea, February 2022.

25. Bill Mesce Jr., *Overkill: The Rise and Fall of Thriller Cinema* (McFarland: The University of Michigan, 2007), 245.

26. Jonathan Demme, *The Manchurian Candidate* audio commentary track, Paramount, 2004.

27. IMDB.Pro.com.
28. Ibid.
29. Ibid.
30. Author interview with Craig McKay, February 2022.
31. David Thompson, "Mind Control," in Kapsis, *Jonathan Demme: Interviews*, 157.
32. *The Manchurian Candidate* audio commentary track.
33. Ibid.
34. Thompson, "Mind Control," 159.
35. "BMI Woodstock Film Festival Panel," YouTube, September 2009, https://www.youtube.com/watch?v=QI5uIufFBAI.
36. Ibid.
37. Thompson, "Mind Control," 159.
38. "CIA's Final Report: No WMD Found in Iraq," *NBC News*, April 25, 2005, https://www.nbcnews.com/id/wbna7634313.
39. G. Scott Thomas, *Counting the Votes: A New Way to Analyze America's Presidential Elections* (New York: Bloomsbury, 2015), 256.
40. David Ansen, "Review, Seizing the Throne," Newsweek.com, July 25, 2004, https://www.newsweek.com/review-seizing-throne-130909.
41. "Roger Ebert Tells the TRUTH about Manchurian Candidate," The Official Roger Ebert, YouTube, accessed July 2, 2022, https://www.youtube.com/watch?v=AVku54s0_1s.
42. *The Manchurian Candidate*, Box Office Mojo, accessed July 2, 2022, https://www.boxofficemojo.com/release/rl2680653569/.
43. Author interview with Edwidge Danticat, June 2022.

17. Heavy Winds (2005–2006)

1. Sheila Johnston, "Filmmakers on Film: Jonathan Demme on Jared Hess' *Napoleon Dynamite*," *Daily Telegraph*, November 29, 2004, https://www.telegraph.co.uk/culture/film/filmmakersonfilm/3632563/Film-makers-on-film-Jonathan-Demme.html.
2. Peter Keough, "Heart of Gold," *The Boston Phoenix*, February 25, 2010, https://thephoenix.com/boston/movies/97501-heart-of-gold/.
3. Author interview with Stephen Apkon, December 2022.
4. Ibid.
5. Ibid.
6. Kristi Zea at Rivertown Film Society ceremony honoring Jonathan Demme, November 20, 2023.
7. Neil Young, *Waging Heavy Peace* (New York: Penguin/Blue Rider Press, 2012), 303–4.

8. Ibid., 433.
9. Author interview with Ellen Kuras, February 2022.
10. Ibid.
11. Jon Pareles, "Neil Young in Nashville Pondering Mortality," *New York Times*, August 20, 2005, B-7.
12. Ray Waddell, "Rockin' in Music City," *Billboard* 117, no. 36 (September 3, 2005): 27.
13. Matt Crenson, "Experts Expect Katrina to turn N.O. into Atlantis," *Times*, August 29, 2005, 4A.
14. Jonathan Demme, dir., *I'm Carolyn Parker: The Good, the Mad, and the Beautiful*, Clinica Estetico, Jacob Burns Film Center, PBS/P.O.V., 2011.
15. Ibid.
16. Demme, *I'm Carolyn Parker: The Good, The Mad, and the Beautiful* commentary track, Clinica Estetico, Jacob Burns Film Center, PBS/P.O.V., 2011.
17. Ibid.
18. Stacey Plaisance, "Demme Delves Into New Orleans Devastation," *Central New Jersey Home News*, May 28, 2007, E4.
19. Jonathan Demme, *Jimmy Carter: Man from Plains* commentary track, Sony Pictures Classics, 2007.
20. Ibid.
21. Ibid.
22. Ibid.
23. Ibid.
24. Ibid.
25. Brian Iskov, *Rachel Getting Married* press junket interview in Venice, Italy, September 4, 2008.

18. A Creative Marriage (2007–2009)

1. Brian Iskov, *Rachel Getting Married* press junket notes, September 4, 2008, Courtesy of Brian Iskov.
2. Ibid.
3. David Poland, "DP/30—Demme and Lumet on Rachel Getting Married," *DP/30: The Oral History of Hollywood*, YouTube, https://www.youtube.com/watch?v=En7OtWmsEgM.
4. Iskov, *Rachel Getting Married* press junket notes.
5. Ibid.
6. "*Capote* Box Office Numbers," Box Office Mojo, accessed June 3, 2022, https://www.boxofficemojo.com/release/rl2118682113/.

Notes to Pages 168–174

7. Brian Iskov, *Rachel Getting Married* press junket interview, September 4, 2008.
8. Ibid.
9. Neda Armian, "*Rachel Getting Married* Q&A with Cast and Crew at the Jacob Burns Film Center," *Rachel Getting Married*, Blu-Ray Special Features, Sony Pictures Classics, 2009.
10. Ibid.
11. Iskov, *Rachel Getting Married* press junket notes.
12. Ibid.
13. Jonathan Demme, "Q&A with Cast and Crew at the Jacob Burns Film Center," *Rachel Getting Married*, Blu-Ray Special Features, Sony Pictures Classics, 2009.
14. Jonathan Demme, *Rachel Getting Married* commentary track, Sony Pictures Classics, 2009.
15. Jonathan Demme, Opening remarks for *Neil Young: Trunk Show* at the IFC Theater in New York City, April 20, 2015.
16. Stuart Kemp, "Demme Replaces Scorsese on Bob Marley Documentary," *Reuters / Hollywood Reporter*, May 21, 2008, https://www.reuters.com/article/film-marley-dc/demme-replaces-scorsese-on-bob-marley-documentary-idUSN2245013920080522.
17. Author interview with Sister Carol East, April 2022.
18. Colleen Barry, "Dealmaking Is More Informal at Venetian Fest," *Toronto Star*, September 2, 2009, https://www.thestar.com/entertainment/dealmaking-is-more-informal-at-venetian-fest/article_e3b6b8b6-dba9-57b6-a59b-80e2d9d3a24d.html.
19. Iskov, *Rachel Getting Married* press junket notes.
20. Demme, Opening remarks for *Neil Young: Trunk Show* at the IFC Theater.
21. *Rachel Getting Married*, BoxOfficeMojo.com, accessed June 2, 2023, https://www.boxofficemojo.com/title/tt1084950/?ref_=bo_se_r_1.
22. A. O. Scott, "From Rehab, Wreaking Her Havoc," *New York Times*, October 3, 2008, E1.
23. Rodrigo Perez, "Jonathan Demme Says Bob Marley Documentary on Hold, but Not Necessarily over for Him," *Playlist*, October 5, 2009, https://theplaylist.net/exclusive-jonathan-demme-says-bob-20091005/.
24. Author interview with Sister Carol East.
25. Dave Itzkoff, "'Zeitoun' as Cartoon: Demme Plans Animated Film of Eggers Book," *Arts Beat: The New York Times Blog*, October 28, 2009, https://archive.nytimes.com/artsbeat.blogs.nytimes.com/2009/10/28/zeitoun-as-cartoon-demme-plans-animated-film-of-eggers-book/.

26. Email correspondence with Dave Eggers, April 2022.
27. Cain Burdeau, "Police: Katrina Hero Plotted Ex-Wife's Murder," *Sentinel Tribune*, August 11, 2012, 20.
28. Email with Dave Eggers.

19. Burning Desires (2010–2013)

1. Jordan Raup, "Jonathan Demme's Arcade Fire Documentary That Never Was," *Film Stage*, February 25, 2010, https://thefilmstage.com/jonathan-demmes-arcade-fire-documentary-that-never-was/.
2. John Griffin, "For Demme, Young Is a Rock Standard-Bearer," *Gazette*, May 8, 2010, E7.
3. David Sims, "Remembering Jonathan Demme," *Atlantic*, April 26, 2017, https://www.theatlantic.com/entertainment/archive/2017/04/remembering-jonathan-demme/524391/.
4. Wesley Morris, "Celebrating Demme, a Director for Our Times," *Boston Globe*, February 28, 2010, N10.
5. Artists-Studios.com, "Joanne Howard," accessed January 29, 2024, https://artists-studios.com/joanne-howard.
6. Dan Cox, "Demme Heads to U," *Variety*, December 19, 1996.
7. Rob Weinert-Kendt, "Drawn Off-Screen and Off-Broadway," *Los Angeles Times*, May 4, 2010, D5.
8. Ibid.
9. Joe Dziemianowicz, "Demme Debuts with 'Week' Effort," *New York Daily News*, May 5, 2010, 38.
10. Linda Winer, "A Family Gathers to Share Some Pain," *Newsday*, May 7, 2010, B17.
11. "Friends of the Apollo," Oberlin College and Conservatory, accessed May 2, 2022, https://www.oberlin.edu/life-at-oberlin/museum-and-the-arts/apollo/friends.
12. Greg Kot, "An Unexpected 'Journey,'" *Daily Press*, July 15, 2012, 2.
13. Mark Kermode, *Kermode and Mayo's Film Review*, BBC Radio 5 Broadcast, December 14, 2012, https://www.youtube.com/watch?v=BWw2_Bsif4U.
14. "Jonathan Demme at DOC NYC 2011 on the Song 'Ohio' from his film *Neil Young Journeys*," YouTube, accessed July 2, 2022, https://www.youtube.com/watch?v=gowhziGpb7Q.
15. "Jonathan Demme Interview—Occupy Wall Street 2011," YouTube, accessed June 4, 2022, https://www.youtube.com/watch?v=y3lCKSwSkTo.
16. "Much Loved—Apresentação por Nabil Ayouch e Jonathan Demme," YouTube, https://www.youtube.com/watch?v=logSD_3DGkM.

17. "Jonathan Demme on Oberlin on YouTube," Oberlin College and Conservatory YouTube Page, accessed January 5, 2022, https://www.youtube.com/watch?v=ZY2NJOnkJHM.

18. *"Enzo Avitabile: Music Life.* Jonathan Demme in Conversation with John Shaefer," filmed November 10, 2012, at DocNYC at the IFC in New York City, YouTube https://www.youtube.com/watch?v=9r_iffLe7Bg.

19. Ibid.

20. Jonathan Demme, "Jonathan Demme Remembers Robert 'Cousin Bobby' Wilkinson Castle," POV's Documentary Inc., October 2012, http://archive.pov.org/blog/povdocs/2012/12/jonathan-demme-remembers-robert-cousin-bobby- (accessed January 2022).

21. "*Song One* Shooting Schedule and Anecdotes," Sundance 2014 Press Booklet.

22. Ibid.

23. Christopher Wallenberg, "Rebuilding 'The Master Builder' for Stage, then Screen," *Boston Globe*, September 14, 2014, N10.

24. "Jonathan Demme in Conversation with David Edelstein for the Criterion Collection Release of *A Master Builder*," DVD, 2013.

25. Ibid.

26. Ibid.

27. Ibid.

28. "Wallace Shawn in conversation with David Edelstein for the Criterion Collection Release of *A Master Builder*," DVD, 2013.

29. BoxOfficeMojo.com.

30. Peter Keough, "*A Master Builder* Review," *Boston Globe*, September 16, 2014, G9.

31. Author interview with Sandy McLeod, January 2022.

20. Flash and Dance (2014–2015)

1. Brett Walton, "Water Law: $105 Million Settlement in Water Pollution Lawsuit between Swiss Company and U.S. Communities," *Circle of Blue*, June 1, 2012, https://www.circleofblue.org/2012/world/water-law-105-million-settlement-in-water-pollution-lawsuit-between-swiss-company-and-u-s-communities/.

2. "The Making of *Ricki and the Flash*," Sony/TriStar Pictures, 2015, DVD.

3. Author interview with Stephen Apkon, December 2022.

4. Steve Harvey, "Recording Ricki and the Flash Live," Mixonline.com, September 14, 2015, https://www.mixonline.com/recording/recording-ricki-and-the-flash-live.

5. *Ricki and the Flash* call sheet, July 2014.

6. Box Office Mojo, accessed June 7, 2022, https://www.boxofficemojo.com/release/rl1047299585/.

7. The Associated Press, "*Ricki and the Flash* Review: Meryl Streep and Daughter Charm," *Denver Post*, August 5, 2015, https://www.denverpost.com/2015/08/05/ricki-and-the-flash-review-meryl-streep-and-daughter-charm/.

8. Glenn Kenny, "*Ricki and the Flash* Review," RogerEbert.com, August 7, 2015, https://www.rogerebert.com/reviews/ricki-and-the-flash-2015.

9. "The Art of Performance: A Conversation with Jonathan Demme," 2016 Toronto International Film Festival, TIFF Talks/YouTube, https://www.youtube.com/watch?v=MmyMRSRbRus.

10. Max Cea, "Jonathan Demme Interview," *Pink Monkey Magazine*, May 2016, 60.

11. Jann S. Wenner, *Like a Rolling Stone: A Memoir* (New York: Little, Brown, 2022), 514.

12. Nikki Delamotte, "Rock & Roll Hall of Fame Captivates the Senses with Debut of Connor Theater," Cleveland.com, June 29, 2017, https://www.cleveland.com/entertainment/2017/06/rock_hall_captivates_the_sense.html.

13. Cea, "Jonathan Demme Interview," *Pink Monkey Magazine*, May 2016, 60.

14. Email correspondence with Fabian S. Gerard, May 2022.

15. Author interview with Erica Gavin, December 2022.

16. Ibid.

17. "The Hudson Link for Higher Education in Prison," December 2014 Events, accessed December 1, 2022, https://hudsonlink.org/timeline-moment/december-2014/.

21. Eagles and Condors (2016–2022)

1. "Mack Wilds, Sanaa Lathan, DeWanda Wise, and Aisha Hinds Join Us at the Roundtable to Look Into Hour 6 of Shots Fired," Facebook video, April 26, 2017, https://m.facebook.com/ShotsFiredonTV/videos/1889994374574973/?locale2=ps_AF.

2. Gina Prince-Bythewood and Reggie Rock Bythewood, "'Shots Fired' Creators Remember Jonathan Demme as a Collaborative 'Magician,'" *Hollywood Reporter*, April 26, 2017, https://www.hollywoodreporter.com/tv/tv-news/shots-fired-creators-remember-jonathan-demme-as-a-collaborative-magician-997928.

3. Author interview with Paul Lazar, January 2022.
4. "Justin Timberlake + The Tennessee Kids: Jonathan Demme TIFF 2016 Movie Premiere Arrival," ScreenSlam, accessed March 14, 2023, https://www.youtube.com/watch?v=s5cC_2RS-ag.
5. "DATE-DATE-DATE; 5/6," Visualist, accessed March 14, 2023, http://www.thevisualist.org/tag/jos-howard-demme/.
6. "Sundance 2021 Beyond Film Programming: Jacob Burns Film Center," https://burnsfilmcenter.org/virtual-events/sundance-2021-beyond-film-programming/, accessed March 14, 2023.
7. "DOC NYC 2016 Visionaries Tribute—Lifetime Achievement Award, Jonathan Demme," DOCNYCFest YouTube Page, accessed March 14, 2023, https://www.youtube.com/watch?v=zx_SCnGmWyE.
8. Author interview with Brooke Smith, January 2022.
9. Author interview with Stephen Apkon, December 2022.
10. "Jonathan Demme / JT intro," Keith Uhlich's YouTube Page, accessed March 14, 2013, https://www.youtube.com/watch?v=BuS48xA3T98.
11. Author interview with Joe Viola, July 2022.
12. Ibid.
13. Author interview with Kristi Zea, February 2022.
14. Author interview with Joe Viola.
15. Author interview with Stephen Apkon, December 2022.
16. "Hollywood Remembers Jonathan Demme: 'Purest, Most Loving and Talented,'" *Deadline*, April 26, 2017, https://deadline.com/2017/04/jonathan-demme-hollywood-reaction-alec-baldwin-1202077746/.
17. Ibid.
18. "Tom Hanks Remembers Jonathan Demme," ET Canada|Facebook, April 27, 2017, https://www.facebook.com/ETCanada/videos/tom-hanks-remembers-jonathan-demme/1415255358521447/.
19. "Jonathan Demme's Short, Final Film Takes Center Stage at Rock Hall," *Deadline*, June 29, 2017, https://deadline.com/2017/06/jonathan-demme-power-of-rock-experience-rock-and-roll-hall-of-fame-1202122149/.
20. Peter D. Kramer, "Raising a Glass to Demme at Jacob Burns," *Journal News*, Lohud.com, July 20, 2017, https://www.lohud.com/story/entertainment/movies/2017/07/20/raising-glass-demme-jacob-burns/495591001/.
21. "Najbolji Koncertni Film «*Stop Making Sense*» u Kružnoj Ulici" ["Croatia Screening of *Stop Making Sense*"], *Art Kino*, July 19, 2017, https://www.art-kino.org/en/novosti/najbolji-koncertni-film-stop-making-sense-u-kruznoj-ulici.
22. "Interview with Brooklyn Demme," *Faith in Farming* Podcast, Episode 34, February 2020.

23. Robert Brum, "Nyack's Brooklyn Demme Films Ramapough Nation's Struggle," accessed January 1, 2022, https://www.lohud.com/story/news/local/rockland/ramapo/2018/09/27/brooklyn-demme-ramapough-nation-film/1256814002/.

24. "Interview with Brooklyn Demme."

25. Ibid.

26. "Prophecy of the Eagle and the Condor: Ancient Healing Ways for Modern Times," Workshops, Esalen Center for Theory and Research, June 2022, https://www.esalen.org/workshops/prophecy-of-the-eagle-the-condor-ancient-healing-ways-for-modern-times-06202022.

Index

Abraham, F. Murray, 114
Abrahams, Jim, 184
Abu Ghraib prison abuses, 152
Academy Awards and nominations: *Melvin and Howard*, 53; *Philadelphia*, 122; *The Silence of the Lambs*, 111, 114
"Accumulation with Talking Plus Water Motor" (Brown), 82
Accused, The (Kaplan, 1998), 98
actors and casting: in *Beloved*, 132–35; in *Caged Heat*, 26; in *Citizens Band*, 37–38; in *Crazy Mama*, 31–32; in *Last Embrace*, 44–46; in *The Manchurian Candidate*, 150, 151; in *Married to the Mob*, 88–89; in *Melvin and Howard*, 48–49; in *Philadelphia*, 114–16; in *Rachel Getting Married*, 167–69; in *Ricki and the Flash*, 185–86; in *The Silence of the Lambs*, 98–100; in *Something Wild*, 77, 100; in *Swing Shift*, 59–60
Adams, Glen, 81
Adaptation (Jonze, 2002), 148, 150
Adebimpe, Tunde, 169
Adventures of Robin Hood, The (1938), 2
Agronomist, The (Demme, 2003), 143, 156–57, 176
Agronomist's Wife, The, 176

Aguirre, the Wrath of God (Herzog, 1972), 49
AIDS. *See* AIDS/HIV crisis
Airplane! (Abrahams / Zucker Brothers, 1980), 184
Akuy Eenda Maawehlaang: A Place Where People Gather (Demme [Jonathan and Brooklyn], 2019), 196
Alda, Alan, 44
Alden, William Tracy, 1–2
Ali (Mann, 2001), 145–46
Allen, Dede, 51
Allen, Irving, 16
Allen, Woody, 75, 82
All That Jazz (Fosse, 1979), 44
All the President's Men (1976), 48
Almodóvar, Pedro, 115, 168
Altamont concert (1969), 22, 44
Altman, Robert, 171
Amadeus (Forman, 1984), 75
Amend, Kate, 164
American Beauty (Mendes, 1999), 140
American Graffiti (Lucas, 1973), 38
American International Pictures, 17
American Society of Cinematographers (ASC), 33
American Zoetrope, 21
Amistad (Spielberg, 1997), 138
Anderson, Paul Thomas, 21, 145, 169, 181

Index

... *And Justice for All* (Jewison, 1979), 60
Andy Hardy series (Seitz), 17
Angels Hard as They Come (Viola, 1971), 20–22, 32
Ansen, David, 120, 155
Antwone Fisher (Washington, 2002), 150
Apkon, Stephen, 157, 186, 195
Apocalypse Now (Coppola, 1979), 23
Arbus, Amy, 90
Arcade Fire (band), 176
Aristide, Jean-Bertrand, 141, 142, 181
Aristide, Roland, 141
Arkoff, Samuel Z., 17
Armian, Neda, 163, 168, 180
Armitage, George, 33
Arnold, Moxley, 1
Artists Entertainment Complex (AEC), 26
Ashby, Hal, 30, 33, 46, 57, 158; comparison with Demme, 75; death of, 112; film editing system of, 70
At Risk (Hoffman), 113
Attenborough, Richard, 44
Atwood, Colleen, 90
Autobiography of Malcolm X, The, 13
Avitabile, Enzo, 180–81
Aviv, Rachel, 185
Away We Go (Mendes, 2009), 175, 178
Aznavour, Charles, 146
Azzolini, Davide, 180

Bach, Johann Sebastian, 104
Bacon, Francis, 105
Badham, John, 42
Badlands (Malick, 1973), 26
Baker, Ginger, 16
Balaban, Bob, 126
Ball, Lucille, 13
Ballad of Cable Hogue, The (Peckinpah, 1970), 48
Band, The, 67

Banderas, Antonio, 115
Banks, Russell, 94
Barker-Froyland, Kate, 181–82
Barrett, Syd, 128
Basquiat, Jean-Michel, 146
Basquiat (Schnabel, 1996), 146
Bauer, Steven, 78
Bava, Mario, 26
Beah: A Black Woman Speaks (Hamilton, 2004), 141
Beasts of the Southern Wild (Zeitlin, 2012), 140
Beatles, The, 129, 142
Beatty, Warren, 30, 51, 57
Beautiful Girls (1996), 126
Becker, Harold, 88
Beckett, Andrew, 113
Before the Devil Knows You're Dead (Lumet, 2007), 166
Begley, Ed, Jr., 37
Being John Malkovich (1999), 148
Being There (1979), 80
Bellboy, The (Lewis, 1960), 6
Bellville, Hercules, 20, 27, 40, 42, 175
Beloved (Demme, 1998), 132–41, 145, 166; casting for, 132–35; critical reception of, 138; relation to Morrison's novel, 135–36
Beloved (Morrison novel), 131
Benson, Sheila, 108
Ben Tzur, Shye, 181
Berg, Jeff, 164
Berlin Film Festival, 108
Bernhard, Sandra, 83
Berry, Chuck, 18
Bertolucci, Bernardo, 27, 34, 46, 74, 86, 133, 189–90
Besieged (Bertolucci, 1998), 133
Beyond the Valley of the Dolls (Meyer, 1970), 26, 38
Bick, Jerry, 56, 57
Big Bad Mama (Carver, 1974), 31
Big Dance Theatre, 86
Big Doll House, The (Hill, 1971), 26

Index

Big Heat, The (Lang, 1953), 4
Billy Jack (1971), 33
Bing, Steve, 173
Bissett, Shane, 179
Black, Louis, 54–55
Black Mama, White Mama (Romero, 1973), 23
Black Orpheus (Camus, 1959), 5, 187
Black Panthers, 29, 110
Blade Runner (Scott, 1982), 73
Blake, Andre B., 117
Blaxploitation films, 29
Blondell, Kathryn, 61, 62
Bloody Mama (Corman, 1970), 31
Blossom, Roberts, 37, 48
Blow (Ted Demme, 2001), 148
Blue (Jarman, 1993), 119
Blue Velvet (Lynch, 1986), 89
Body Double (De Palma, 1984), 76
Bogdanovich, Peter, 31
Bogosian, Eric, 83
Boogie Nights (Anderson, 1997), 145, 146
Boone, David, 55
Botas, Juan, 121
Bound for Glory (Ashby, 1976), 75, 139
Bourne Supremacy, The (Greenglass, 2004), 155
Bowers, Geoffrey, 121
Bowie, David, 79
Boxcar Bertha (Scorsese, 1972), 18
Boys in the Band, The (Friedkin, 1970), 45
Boyz N the Hood (Singleton, 1991), 112
Bozman, Ron, 178
Brady Bunch, The (ABC TV series, 1969–1974), 14
Bragg, Billy, 128
Bramon, Risa, 77
BRC Imagination Arts, 189
Bregman, Marin, 26
Brickman, Paul, 38–39

Bride Wore Black, The (Truffaut, 1968), 13, 45
Broccoli, Albert R. "Cubby," 14
Brokeback Mountain (Lee, 2005), 167
Brooks, Albert, 184
Brooks, James L., 76, 90
Brooks, Mel, 31
Brown, Garrett, 118
Brown, Juanita, 26, 28
Brown, Tisha, 82
Bucket of Blood, A (Corman, 1959), 17
Buddy Holly Story, The (1978), 48
Bullock, Sandra, 139
Bundy, Ted, 103
Burns, Mark, 87, 88
Busey, Gary, 48
Bush, George W., 149, 155, 164, 174
Busia, Akosua, 132
Bustin' Loose (1981), 60
Byrne, David, 67, 72, 73, 188; at Demme's memorial service, 195; Oscar for co-scoring *The Last Emperor*, 93
Byron, Stuart, 10, 13
Bythewood, Reggie Rock, 191, 192

Cage, Nicolas, 148
Caged (Cromwell, 1950), 25
Caged Heat (Demme, 1974), 25–30, 61, 88, 101, 187, 190
Cain, James M., 125
Cale, John, 29
Caliban Films, 20
Callender, Colin, 125
Camus, Marcel, 5
Canby, Vincent, 52, 108
Canned Heat (band), 187
Cannes Film Festival, 110
Capote (Miller, 2005), 168
Capote, Truman, 74
Capra, Frank, 111
Capra, Michael, 190
Carey, Philip, 33

231

Index

Carpenter, John, 59
Carter, Jimmy, 42, 162–65
Caruso, Rocco, 194
Carver, Steve, 31
Casper (Silberling, 1995), 138
Cassavetes, John, 43
Castle, Edie (paternal grandmother of Jonathan Demme), 3
Castle, Bobby, 110, 116, 171, 181, 195
CBGB's (New York), 53, 79
Celluloid Closet, The (Russo), 107
Chair vs. Ruth Snyder, The (Fuller), 125
Chapman, Ben, 39
Chappaqua (Rooks, 1966), 157
Charade (Donen, 1962), 144, 145
Chavannes, Etienne, 127
Cher, 88
Cherry, Harry & Raquel! (Meyer, 1969), 38
Chesney, Kenny, 180
Chicago Blues (documentary, 1970), 26
Chinatown (1974), 46, 64
Chitty Chitty Bang Bang (1968), 14
Chorus Line, A, 45
Chungking Express (Wong Kar-Wai, 1994), 144
Cimino, Michael, 57
Cinderella Man (Howard, 2005), 168
Cinesound Productions, 14
Circle, The (Eggers), 196
Citizens Band (Demme, 1977), 36–37, 39–43, 48, 51, 68, 156; Demme's struggle with Paramount over, 40–41, 150, 153; Jimmy Carter as supporter of, 42, 162
Citron, Neil, 186
civil rights, 13
Clancy, Tom, 151
Clarens, Carlos, 44
Clark, Candy, 37, 41
Clarke, Shirley, 31

Cleaver, Eldridge, 13
Clinica Estetico (Esthetic Clinic), 79, 87, 97, 121, 127, 178; financial struggles of, 145; Les Freres Parents at offices of, 94–95; Jorobado mascot, 93; origin of name, 74; production deal with Universal Pictures, 126
Clinton, Bill, 120, 123
Clockwork Orange, A (Kubrick, 1971), 25
Cocoanuts, The (1929), 9
Coconut Grove (Black community in Miami), 7
Cody, Diablo, 185
Coffy (Hill, 1973), 26
Collective for Living Cinema (New York), 55
Collins, Roberta, 26
Color Purple, The (Walker, 1982), 133
Columbia Pictures, 57, 58, 146
Columbo (NBC TV series), 43, 125
Coming Home (Ashby, 1978), 57, 75
Complex Sessions, The (Demme, 1994), 124–25, 158
Condon, Richard, 149, 153
Conformist, The (Bertolucci, 1970), 27, 34, 93
Connection, The (Clarke, 1961), 31
Continental Drift (Banks), 94
Cooper, Chris, 148
Coppola, Francis Ford, 18, 21, 23, 125
Coppola, Sofia, 140
Corman, Gene, 32
Corman, Julie, 31, 32
Corman, Roger, 17–18, 22, 53, 73, 98, 156; biker film and, 20–21; *Caged Heat* and, 26, 30; *Crazy Mama* and, 31, 32, 33; in *Philadelphia*, 116, 125; *Rachel Getting Married* and, 171; in *The Silence of the Lambs*, 125; social activism and, 139
Costa-Gavras, 42

Index

Costner, Kevin, 59, 112
Cotten, Joseph, 106
Cousin Bobby (Demme, 1992), 110–11, 123, 143, 162
Cousins, Mark, 12, 28
Crazy Horse (band), 49, 158, 171
Crazy Mama (Demme, 1975), 31–33
Crimes of the Heart (Henley), 60, 177
Crisp, Quentin, 117
critics, 54–55; on *Angels Hard as They Come*, 22; on *Beloved*, 138; on *Caged Heat*, 29; on *Citizens Band*, 41; on *Crazy Mama*, 32; on *Fighting Mad*, 35; on *The Manchurian Candidate*, 155; on *Married to the Mob*, 94; on *A Master Builder*, 184; on *Melvin and Howard*, 52; on *Philadelphia*, 120–21; on *Rachel Getting Married*, 173; on *Ricki and the Flash*, 187; on *The Silence of the Lambs*, 107–8; on *Something Wild*, 81–82; on *Stop Making Sense*, 71–72; on *Swing Shift*, 71; on *The Truth about Charlie*, 147
Crocodile Dundee (Faiman, 1986), 82
Cromwell, John, 25
Cronenberg, David, 112
Cronenweth, Jordan, 39, 68, 70, 73
Cry-Baby Killer (1958), 17
Cuban Missile Crisis, 7, 149
Cuevas, Manuel, 159
Curtis, Tony, 40
Curtiz, Michael, 2, 4

Dahmer, Jeffrey, 108
Dalí, Salvador, 159
Dallas Buyers Club (Vallée, 2013), 113
Daly, Robert, 64
Dancing with Shiva. See *Rachel Getting Married* (Demme, 2008)
D'Angerio, Alan, 90
Daniel, Lee, 55
Daniels, Jeff, 76, 82, 89

Daniels, Lee, 140
Danticat, Edwidge, 131, 142
D'Antoni, Philip, 45
Dark Knight (Nolan, 2008), 173
Dash, Julie, 126
Davis, Andrew, 26
Dawson, Ashley, 197
Day, Lisa, 70
Day-Lewis, Daniel, 114
Dean, Howard, 163
"Death of a Salesman" (Miller play), 184
"Deep Sea Game Hunting Paradise" (Robert Demme), 2–3
Defiant Ones, The (Kramer, 1958), 23
de Klerk, Frederik Willem, 86
De Laurentiis, Dino, 98
Dementia 13 (Coppola, 1963), 18
Demme, Brooklyn (second-born child of Jonathan), 106, 125, 171, 178; Bobby Castle's influence on, 181; at Marrakesh Film Festival (2012), 180; Split Rock documentary completed by, 196–97; Standing Rock Reservation protests and, 193, 194
Demme, Dorothy "Dodie" Louise Rogers (mother of Jonathan), 2, 4, 11, 193; death of, 123; in *Married to the Mob*, 92; in *Philadelphia*, 116, 123; struggles with alcohol, 8, 167
Demme, Frederick "Rick" Alexander (brother of Jonathan), 2, 3, 4, 8, 148
Demme, Jonathan: battles with studios and distributors, 188; book publishing venture, 127; Corman and early career of, 17–36; death of, 195–96; directorial debut, 25–30; in London, 15–16; in Los Angeles, 20–24; memorial tributes to, 195–96; as producer, ix, 33, 35, 124

Index

Demme, Jonathan, awards: Oscar for *The Silence of the Lambs*, 109, 111–12, 114, 167; Persol Tribute to Visionary Talent, 189; Silver Bear for Best Director, 108; Visionaries Tribute award, 193–94

Demme, Jonathan, family and personal life, 1–5, 97, 127; activities of grown children, 193; affair with Peploe, 46; battle with esophageal cancer, 176, 189; death of Robert Demme, 122–23; death of Utt and, 121–22; decline and end of marriage to Purcell, 36–37, 43, 46, 47; Demme as baseball fan, 137; folk art collection of, 127, 172; marriage to Howard, 87; marriage to Purcell, 19; musical tastes, 29, 53, 60, 93, 128; theater interest of, 54, 86, 128, 182–83

Demme, Jonathan, films of: *The Agronomist* (2003), 143, 176; *Akuy Eenda Maawehlaang: A Place Where People Gather* (completed by Brooklyn, 2019), 196; *Caged Heat* (1974), 25–30, 61, 88, 101, 187; *The Complex Sessions* (1994), 124–25, 158; *Cousin Bobby* (1992), 123, 143, 162; *Crazy Mama* (1975), 31–33; *Enzo Avitabile: Music Life* (2012), 181; *Fighting Mad* (1976), 31, 33–35, 38, 49, 100; *A Gifted Man* (TV series, pilot episode, 2011), 177–78; *Haiti Dreams of Democracy* (1988), 84–86, 94, 142, 172; "Hour Six" (*Shots Fired* episode, 2016), 191–92; *I'm Carolyn Parker* (2011), 161–62, 170, 174, 185; *Jimmy Carter: Man from Plains* (2007), 163–65, 169; *Justin Timberlake + The Tennessee Kids* (2016), 188, 192, 194; *Last Embrace* (1979), 43–46, 51, 81, 149; *The Manchurian Candidate* (2004), 149–55, 166, 186; *Married to the Mob* (1988), 87–92; *A Master Builder* (2013), 183–84; *Melvin and Howard* (1980), 47–55, 58, 67, 115, 118; *Neil Young: Heart of Gold* (2006), 158–60, 166, 171, 179, 188; *Neil Young Journeys* (2011), 178–79; *Neil Young: Trunk Show* (2009), 171–72, 173; *The Night of the Living Feelies* (unrealized), 54, 78, 95–96; *Philadelphia* (1993), 112; *Rachel Getting Married* (2008), 167–73, 177, 181–82; *Ricki and the Flash* (2015), 185–89, 192; *Right to Return* (TV miniseries, 2007), 162; *Something Wild* (1986), 75–82, 87, 89, 93, 94, 100; *Stop Making Sense* (1984), 68–74, 81, 83, 129–30, 188, 196; *Storefront Hitchcock* (1998), 129–30, 145; *SUBWAYStories: Tales from the Underground* (Demme et al., TV movie, 1997), 126; *The Truth about Charlie* (2002), 151; *What's Motivating Hayes* (2015), 185; *Who Am I This Time?* (*American Playhouse* episode, 1982), 54. See also *Beloved*; *Citizens Band*; *Silence of the Lambs, The*; *Stop Making Sense*

Demme, Jonathan, quotes and opinions: on Avitabile, 181; on becoming a father, 87; on *Beloved*, 132, 138–39; on cinema and filmmaking, 5, 16, 27, 60–61; on civil rights, 13; on Corman, 18; on ghosts and spirits, 137–38; on Haiti, 85, 142; on Jimmy Carter, 163–65; on *The Manchurian Candidate*, 151, 153; on *Melvin and Howard*, 49; on presidential election (2016), 193; on psychosurgery in prisons, 25; on

Index

The Silence of the Lambs, 102, 104; on *Something Wild*, 76–77, 78, 80–81; on *Stop Making Sense*, 69, 70–71; on *Swing Shift*, 58–59; on the Vietnam War, 12; on women, 3; on working in television, 165
Demme, Jonathan, youth of: birth (1944), 3; enthusiasm for cinema, 4–5, 7; in Florida, 6–11; interest in animals, 6–7, 8; on Long Island, 3–5; military service, 8; in New York City, 10, 12–14
Demme, Jos (third-born child of Jonathan), 123, 166, 171, 193
Demme, Peter Castle (brother of Jonathan), 4
Demme, Ramona (first-born child of Jonathan), 96, 97, 98, 166, 178; birth of, 87; marriage of, 193
Demme, Robert Eugene (father of Jonathan), 1–3, 5, 110; death of, 122–23; divorce and second marriage of, 8, 11; as publicist for Fontainebleau Hotel, 6
Demme, Ted (nephew of Jonathan), 126, 148
Dennis, Michael J., 137, 139
De Palma, Brian, 76, 88
De Passe, Suzanne, 50
Dern, Bruce, 17
Dern, Laura, 99, 178
Dershowitz, Alan, 163
Deschanel, Caleb, 21
Devil in a Blue Dress (Franklin, 1995), 124
Devil Wears Prada, The (Frankel, 2006), 181
DGA (Directors Guild of America), 43, 67–68
Dickerson, Ernest, 112
Didion, Joan, 39
Diller, Barry, 41, 125
Dixon, Mort, 50
DOC NYC film festival, 193

Doe, John, 77
Dog Day Afternoon (Lumet, 1975), 26, 166
Dominique, Jean, 86, 141–43
Donen, Stanley, 72, 144, 145
Donner, Richard, 133
D'Onofrio, Vincent, 100
Dorenkamp, Monica, 107
Douglas, Gordon, 4
Douglas, John, 100
Dowd, Nancy, 56–57, 58, 59, 64
Downey, Robert, Sr., 42
Dracula (1931), 103
Drake, Nick, 128
Dummar, Lynda, 48
Dummar, Melvin, 47
Dunne, Griffin, 139
Duvalier, François (Papa Doc), 84, 142, 143
Duvalier, Jean-Claude (Baby Doc), 84, 94
Dylan, Bob, 34

East, Sister Carol, 81, 89, 91, 92, 169, 172, 173–74
Eastmond, Barry, Jr., 171
Ebert, Roger, 71, 72, 94, 155
Edelstein, David, 182
Ed Sullivan Show (TV program), 14
Edwards, Blake, 9, 145
Edwards, Jonathan, 2
Edwards, Marjorie, 2
Edwards, Tracy, 108
Eggers, Dave, 174, 175, 196
Eggleston, William, 90
Ehle, Jennifer, 178
Eisner, Michael, 56, 57
Elephant Man, The (Lynch, 1980), 99
Elias, Alex, 37
Elise, Kimberly, 134, 151
El Shaffir, Amir, 165
Elvis (Carpenter, 1979), 59
Embassy Pictures, 10, 99
Englund, Bryan, 32

235

Index

Enlightened (HBO series, White and Dern), 178
Enzo Avitabile: Music Life (Demme, 2012), 181
Eon Productions, 14
Equitable Art Gallery (New York), 127
Erin Brockovich (Soderbergh, 2000), 178
Et Moi, Je Suis Belle (Dominique, 1962), 143
Everyman (Boone), 55
"Evolution of the Hellcat" (Robert Demme), 3
Extreme Prejudice (Milius), 74
Eyewitness (Hough, 1970), 16

Fab 5 Freddy, 169
Fahrenheit 9/11 (Moore, 2004), 155
Faiman, Peter, 82
Fajardo, Robin, 122
Falk, Peter, 43
Fall, The (band), 106
Fame (Parker), 90
Family Week (Henley), 177, 182
Farber, Stephen, 62, 65
Far from Vietnam (Godard, Ivens, Klein, Lelouch, Resnais, Varda, 1967), 12, 149
Fast and the Furious, The (1954), 17
Fast Food Nation (Linklater, 2004), 178
Fatal Attraction (Lyne, 1987), 112
Fat Bernie's Environmental Living, 20, 27
Father Goose (Nelson, 1964), 7
Fats Domino, 18
Favreau, Jon, 173
Feelies, The (band), 53–54, 78–79, 95–96
feminism, second-wave, 56, 57, 66, 97, 98, 99
Ferrara, Abel, 126
Ferro, Allen, 119

Ferro, Pablo, 70, 72, 119
Fields, Freddie, 36, 37, 39, 40, 150, 153
Fighting Mad (Demme, 1976), 31, 33–35, 38, 49, 100
Filmmakers United against Apartheid, 86
film noir, 4, 64
Fincher, David, 188
Fisk, Jack, 21
Fisk University Jubilee Singers, 159
Fitzpatrick, Tony, 87
Florida Alligator (University of Florida newspaper), 9
Fly, The (Cronenberg, 1986), 112
Fly Me (Santiago, 1973), 23
Flynn, Errol, 2
Fonda, Henry, 14, 33, 123
Fonda, Peter, 17, 33, 34, 35, 126
Ford, John, 145
Forman, Milos, 75, 76, 111
Forrestal, James A., 3
Fosse, Bob, 15, 44, 45
Foster, Jodie, 98–99, 102–3, 110, 112, 195
Fountains of Wayne (band), 124, 153
Franco, Gino, 33, 35
Frankel, David, 181
Frankenheimer, John, 149, 151, 152
Franklin, Carl, 124
Frantz, Chris, 72, 73
Freedman, Jeff, 35
French Connection, The (Friedkin, 1971), 45
Freres Parents, Les (Haitian band), 94–95
Fresson, Bernard, 12
Friedkin, William, 45
Frye, E. Max, 76, 80, 81
Fujimoto, Tak, 26–27, 178; *Beloved* and, 134, 135, 139; *Caged Heat* and, 28, 190; *Fighting Mad* and, 33; *The Manchurian Candidate* and, 151; *Married to the Mob* and, 90, 91; *Melvin and Howard* and,

236

Index

49; *Philadelphia* and, 118; *The Silence of the Lambs* and, 103, 104; *Something Wild* and, 78; *Swing Shift* and, 61; *The Truth about Charlie* and, 146
Fuller, Christa, 31
Fuller, Samuel, 30–31, 125
Full Metal Jacket (Kubrick, 1987), 88, 100

Galvin, Tim, 106
Garner, Margaret, 131, 134
Gavin, Erica, 26, 27, 28, 190
Gazzara, Ben, 43
Gein, Ed, 102
Gelfman, Samuel, 26
Gerardo, Vinnie, 80
Get Carter (1971), 17
Gibson, Angus, 126
Gibson, Mel, 155
Gifted Man, A (TV series, 2011–2012), 177
Gimme Shelter (documentary, 1970), 44, 67
Ginger Baker's Air Force (band), 16
GLAAD (Gay and Lesbian Alliance against Defamation), 107, 109
Glenn, Scott, 33, 100
Glover, Danny, 132, 133
Godard, Jean-Luc, 12
Godfather, The (1972), 64
Goetzman, Gary, 14, 20, 46, 67, 124; *Caged Heat* and, 27; Demme's declining health and, 194–95; in *Married to the Mob*, 93; in music industry, 60; in *Philadelphia*, 116; *Ricki and the Flash* and, 186–88
Goin' South (1979), 49
Goldfinger (1964), 6
Goldman, Bo, 47, 53, 58, 59
Goodbye Charlie (Minnelli, 1964), 7
Goodfellas (Scorsese, 1990), 90, 101
Graham, Bob, 141
Grant, Cary, 145, 147

Grant, Susannah, 177–78
Gray, Spalding, 82, 83
Grease 2 (Birch, 1982), 88
Green, Al, 73
Greengrass, Paul, 155
Greenwood, Jonny, 181
Gregory, Andre, 182, 183, 184
Gridlock'd (1997), 133
Grier, Pam, 23, 26
Griffis, Grif, 112
Griffith, Melanie, 76, 77, 78, 89
Grosbard, Ulu, 45
Guay, Richard, 126
Guess Who's Coming to Dinner (Kramer, 1967), 134
Gummer, Mamie, 185, 187
Guthrie, Woody, 139
Gypsy Joker gang, 22

Hackman, Gene, 97
Hagerty, Julie, 184
Haitian Refugee Fairness Act, 141
Haitian Revolution, 133
Haiti Dreams of Democracy (Demme, 1988), 83, 84–86, 94, 142, 172
Haiti: Killing the Dream (Perry and Kean, 1992), 141
Haiti: Three Visions, 127
Haley, Alex, 139
Hamilton, Guy, 6
Hamilton, LisaGay, 137, 141, 146
Hammett, Dashiell, 74
Handcarved Coffins (Capote), 74
Handle with Care. See Citizens Band (Demme, 1977)
Hanks, Tom, 114, 122, 124, 187, 196
Hannibal (Scott, 2001), 148
Hansen, Brian, 55
Hanson, Curtis, 24
Harder They Come, The (Henzell, 1973), 30
Harlan County, U.S.A. (Kopple, 1976), 35
Harold and Maude (Ashby, 1971), 30

Index

Harpo Pictures, 132
Harrington, Curtis, 33
Harris, Ed, 59, 60, 66
Harris, Emmylou, 159
Harris, Thomas, 97, 108
Harrison, Jerry, 72, 73
Harry, Debbie, 93
Hart, Moss, 45
Harvey, Laurence, 150
Hathaway, Anne, 167–68, 170, 171, 172, 173, 181–82
Havoc (Kopple, 2005), 167
Hawn, Goldie, 55, 59, 61–64, 65, 69; lobbying of studios to make *Swing Shift*, 57, 58; role as producer on *Swing Shift*, 63; romance with Kurt Russell on set of *Swing Shift*, 62, 66, 71
Hawn-Sylbert Productions, 58
Hayes, Tyrone, 185
Hays Code, 152
HBO Films, 125
Heald, Anthony, 109
Heartburn (Nichols, 1986), 186
Heaven's Gate (Cimino, 1981), 57
Heche, Anne, 126
Hedblade, Jay, 130
Heidnik, Gary, 103
Hell's Angels gang, 22
Help, The (Taylor, 2011), 140
Henderson, Ray, 50
Henley, Beth, 54, 60, 177
Henzell, Perry, 30
Hepburn, Audrey, 145
Hepburn, Katharine, 99
Herrera, Hayden, 74
Herrmann, Bernard, 105
Herzog, Werner, 49
Hesdra, Edward, 198
High Noon (Zinnemann, 1952), 163
Hill, George Roy, 54
Hill, Jack, 26
Hill, The (Lumet, 1965), 10
Hinds, Aisha, 192

Hines, Gregory, 126
Hinson, Hal, 74
Hired Hand, The (Fonda, 1971), 34
Hitchcock, Alfred, 45, 81, 105, 106, 182
Hitchcock, Robyn, 128, 129, 169
Hitchcock/Truffaut (Truffaut, 1966), 13, 148
HIV/AIDS crisis, 112, 113, 116, 119, 122
Hoffman, Alice, 113
Hoffman, Dustin, 180
Hollywood, 26, 46, 57–58
Hollywood Reporter, 35
Holocaust (NBC miniseries, 1978), 51
Holt, Ednah, 72
Hopalong Cassidy (TV series, 1952-1954), 4
Hopkins, Anthony, 99, 102–3, 110
Hopkins, Billy, 77
Hopper, Edward, 96
Horovitz, Israel, 126
Hot Box, The (Viola, 1972), 22–23
"Hour Six" (Demme, *Shots Fired* TV drama, 2016), 191–92
Household Saints (Savoca, 1991), 126
Houston, Thelma, 60
Howard, Joanne (second wife of Jonathan Demme), 86–87, 91, 112, 127–28, 189, 195
Howard, Ron, 31, 168
HSFA Ltd., 15
Hudson Link for Higher Education in Prison, 190
Hughes, Howard, 47, 48
Hunt, Helen, 191
Hunter, Holly, 60, 65
Hunter, Meredith, 22
Hurricane, The (Jewison, 1999), 150
Hurricane Katrina (2005), 161–62, 174, 196
Hurricane Sandy (2012), 181

Ibsen, Henrik, 182
Ice Storm, The (Lee, 1997), 140

Index

ICM (International Creative Management), 149, 164
Idaho Transfer (Fonda, 1973), 34
I'm Carolyn Parker: The Good, the Mad, and the Beautiful (Demme, 2011), 161, 170, 174, 185
Incredible Melting Man, The (Sachs, 1977), 42
Incredible Shrinking Woman, The (Schumacher, 1981), 60
"Inside Women's Prison" (Kellogg), 25
International Alliance of Theatrical Stage Employees, 10
Interview with the Vampire: The Vampire Chronicles (Jordan, 1994), 133
In the Heat of the Night (Jewison, 1967), 133–34
Into the Night (Landis, 1984), 89
Intruder, The (Corman, 1962), 139
Iraq War, 153, 154
Iron Man (Favreau, 2008), 173
Irwin, Bill, 169, 170
Isaak, Chris, 93
It Happened One Night (Capra, 1934), 111
Ivens, Joris, 12
Ivory, James, 133

Jackson, Jesse, 123
Jacob Burns Film Center, 157, 165, 186, 190, 193, 196
Jannelli, Tony, 80, 129, 159
Jarman, Derek, 119
Jean-Baptiste, Edgar, 127
Jefferson in Paris (Ivory, 1995), 133
Jewison, Norman, 60, 133–34, 150
JFK (Stone, 1991), 108–9
Jimmy Carter: Man from Plains (Demme, 2007), 163–65, 169
Joffé, Roland, 82
Johansen, David, 93
Johnson, Don, 78

Jones, Mel, 169–70, 174
Jones, Robert C., 57
Jonze, Spike, 148, 175
Jordan, Neil, 133
Joseph, Gonzales R., 156–57, 176
Joseph, Jasmin, 127
Journey to Beloved (Winfrey), 135
Juice (Dickerson, 1992), 112
Julia (1977), 48
Julian, Kyria, 170
Juno (Reitman, 2007), 185
Junun (Anderson, 2015), 181
Justin Timberlake + The Tennessee Kids (Demme, 2016), 188, 192, 194

Kael, Pauline, 41, 71, 81, 107
Kahlo, Frida, 74
Kaleidoscope (UK band), 16
Kaliko Press, 127
Kaplan, Jonathan, 98
Kaplan, Larry, 12, 16
Kaufman, Charlie, 148
Kaufman, Donald, 148
Kaufman, Philip, 60
Kean, Katharine, 141
Keaton, Diane, 54
Kehr, Dave, 81
Keighley, William, 2
Keir, Andy, 129
Kellogg, Virginia, 25
Kennedy, John F., assassination of, 7
Kenny, Glenn, 187
Kent State shootings (1970), 179
Kermode, Mark, 179
Kern, Gail (sister-in-law of Jonathan Demme), 8
Kidman, Nicole, 139
Kilday, Gregg, 108
Killing Fields, The (Joffé, 1984), 82–83
Kilman, Julian "Buzz," 7, 9
King of the Cannibal Islands, The (1978), 42
Kino Lorber, 180
Klein, William, 12

Index

Kleinbard, Alexa, 77
Kline, Kevin, 76, 185, 187
KONBIT: Burning Rhythms of Haiti (compilation album), 94–95
Kopple, Barbara, 35, 167
Kramer, Larry, 107, 121
Kramer, Stanley, 23, 134
Krim, Arthur, 75
Kubrick, Stanley, 25, 88
Kuras, Ellen, 159

Lachel, Christian, 189
Lahti, Christine, 59–60, 71
Landis, John, 89
Landlord, The (Ashby, 1970), 30
Lang, Fritz, 4
Lange, Jessica, 88
Langhorne, Bruce, 34–35, 49, 60, 64, 71
Lansing, Sherry, 149, 150
LA riots (1992), 110
LaRoche, John, 148
Last Detail, The (Ashby, 1973), 30
Last Embrace (Demme, 1979), 43–46, 51, 81, 149
Last Emperor, The (Bertolucci, 1987), 93
Last King of Scotland, The (MacDonald, 2006), 174
Last Picture Show, The (Bogdanovich, 1971), 31
Last Waltz, The (Scorsese, 1978), 53, 67
Lathan, Sanaa, 192
Lazar, Paul, 86, 89, 170, 192
Leachman, Cloris, 31, 32
Leary, Denis, 126
Lee, Ang, 140, 167, 171
Lee, Spike, 76, 114
Lee Myung-se, 144
Lelouch, Claude, 12
Le Mat, Paul, 37–38, 39, 41, 42, 48, 49
Lenny (Fosse, 1974), 15
Leonardo, Jr. (Oshatz), 55

Leone, Sergio, 48
Lethal Weapon series, 133
Let It Be (Lindsay-Hogg, 1970), 129
Let's Spend the Night Together (Ashby, 1983), 70
Letterman, David, 82
Levine, Joseph E., 10, 99, 122–23
Levine, Ted, 100, 146
Lewis, Jenny, 187
Lewis, Jerry, 6
LGBTQ+ rights, 13, 113–14, 115, 117, 120
Liautaud, Georges, 127
Life Is Beautiful (Benigni, 1998), 138
Lindsay-Hogg, Michael, 129
Linklater, Richard, 55, 178
Linson, Art, 52
Lion in Winter, A (1968), 99
Liotta, Ray, 77
Little, Cheryl, 141
Little Man Tate (Foster, 1991), 112
Little Shop of Horrors, The (Corman, 1960), 17–18
Littleton, Carol, 152
Live 1970 (concert filmed for German television), 16
Long Day's Journey into Night (Lumet, 1962), 48
"Long Day's Journey Into Night" (O'Neill play), 184
Lookin' to Get Out (Ashby, 1982), 70
Lorimar, 70
Lost in America (Brooks, 1985), 184
Louverture Films, 133
Lou Ye, 144
Love and Basketball (Prince-Bythewood, 2000), 191
Lowry, Lynn, 35
Lucas, Craig, 168
Lucas, George, 38, 41, 58
Lucasfilms, 58
Lugosi, Bela, 103
Lumet, Jenny, 166–67, 171
Lumet, Sidney, 10, 123, 140, 166

Index

Lynch, David, 21, 89, 99
Lyne, Adrian, 112

Mabry, Lynn, 72
MacDonald, Kevin, 174
Mack, Connie, 141
Magic (Attenborough, 1978), 44
Malcolm X (Lee, 1992), 114
Malick, Terrence, 21, 26, 138
Malle, Louis, 183
Manchurian Candidate, The (Demme, 2004), 149–55, 166, 169, 186
Manchurian Candidate, The (Frankenheimer, 1962), 149, 152, 153
Mandela (Gibson and Menell, 1996), 126
Mandela, Nelson, 86
Manigat, Leslie, 86
Mann, Michael, 145
Marathon Man (1976), 64
Marcos, Ferdinand, 23
Marin County Courthouse shooting (1970), 29
Markland, Ted, 34
Markov, Margaret, 23
Marley, Bob, 81, 172, 173, 175
Marrakesh Film Festival, 180
Married to the Mob (Demme, 1988), 87–94, 103
Marshall, Garry, 167
Marx Brothers, 9
Maslansky, Paul, 16
Maslin, Janet, 120–21
Master Builder, A (Demme, 2013), 183–84
Master Builder, A (Ibsen play), 182–84
Maxwell's (Hoboken, New Jersey), 53
May, Elaine, 63
Maysles Brothers, 44
McDonald, Audra, 186
McGill, Bruce, 37, 40

McKay, Craig, 51, 63, 92, 104, 107; on Demme's irritability on set of *The Manchurian Candidate*, 152; on Springsteen's song for *Philadelphia*, 120
McLeod, Sandy, 43–44, 46, 50, 54, 74, 184; *Haiti Dreams of Democracy* and, 84, 85; *Last Embrace* and, 44, 45; on making of *Swing Shift*, 63; *Something Wild* and, 77, 78; *Stop Making Sense* and, 68; *Swimming to Cambodia* and, 83
McMasters, Rick, 101
McQueen, Steve, 140
Medavoy, Mike, 75, 88, 89, 97, 113
Medium Cool (Wexler, 1969), 26
Mehrten, Greg, 115–16, 117, 119, 121
Meininger, Frédérique, 146, 147
Meisner, Sanford "Sandy," 48
Melville, Herman, 42
Melvin and Howard (Demme, 1980), 47–55, 58, 67, 115, 118
Mendes, Sam, 140, 175, 178
Menell, Jo, 85, 126
Mercer, Glenn, 53, 79
Meyer, Russ, 26, 28, 38
Miami Blues (Armitage, 1990), 33
Midnight Cowboy (Schlesinger, 1969), 45
Mighty Joe Young (1949), 4
Milestone Films, 180
Milius, John, 32, 74
Miller, Arthur, 184
Miller, Bennett, 168
Miller, Kathleen, 33
Miller, Warren, 28
Million, Bill, 53, 78–79
Minnelli, Vincente, 7
Miracle Worker, The (Penn, 1962), 133
Mitchell, Joni, 73
Modine, Matthew, 88, 91, 92–93
Monda, Antonio, 180
Monette, Paul, 114

Index

Monsieur Hulot's Holiday (Tati, 1953), 5
Montas, Michèle, 142
Moore, Michael, 155
Morel, Pierre, 146
Morgenstern, Joe, 138
Morricone, Ennio, 34–35
Morrison, Toni, 131–32, 134, 135–36
Mosley, Walter, 131
Most, Donny, 31–32
Motels, The (band), 80
Mount, Thom, 47–48, 50, 52
Mountain Lion (Brooklyn Demme, 2024), 197
Moving On (D'Antoni, 1974–1976), 45
Mozambique Liberation Front, 93
Mr. Dead and Mrs. Free (play), 128
"Mr. Tambourine Man" (Dylan song), 34
Mudd Club (New York), 54
My Dinner with Andre (Malle, 1981), 183

Nagin, Ray, 161
Naked Kiss, The (Fuller, 1964), 30
Namphy, Henri, 84, 86, 95
Napier, Charles, 37, 38, 45–46, 90, 105
Naples Film Festival, 180
Napoleon Dynamite (2004), 156
National Recording Studios sound effects library, 43–44
Neil Young: Heart of Gold (Demme, 2006), 158–60, 166, 171, 179, 188
Neil Young Journeys (Demme, 2011), 178–79
Neil Young: Trunk Show (Demme, 2009), 171–72, 173
Nelson, Ralph, 7
Netflix, 188, 194
Network (Lumet, 1976), 166
Neville Brothers (band), 95
Newman, Christopher, 102

Newman, Colin, 103
Newman, Paul, 86
Newman, Robert, 149
New Sounds (Shaefer, WNYC program), 180
Newton, Thandiwe, 132, 133, 145, 147
New Wave, American, 57
New Wave, French, 148
New World Pictures, 18, 20, 23, 87, 106, 144; AEC and, 26; *Caged Heat* and, 29, 30; Corman family and, 32; *Crazy Mama* and, 31; *Melvin and Howard* and, 47–48
New York, New York (Scorsese, 1977), 60
New York Dolls (band), 93
New York Film Festival, 12, 52, 149, 194
Nichols, Mike, 47, 48, 59, 88, 183, 186
Nicholson, Jack, 17, 49, 53
Nicholson, Jim, 17
Nightmare on Elm Street 4, A: The Dream Master (Harlin, 1988), 94
Night of the Living Dead, The (Romero, 1968), 54
Nolan, Christopher, 173
Northup, Harry, 33, 37, 116
Notes from the Field (Smith off-Broadway play), 195
Notorious (2009), 191
Notorious B.I.G., 191
Novecento [1900] (Bertolucci, 1976), 139
Nowhere to Hide (Lee Myung-se, 1999), 144
Nuñez, Victor, 35, 126
Nyack (New York), 96, 124, 176–77, 195; connections to social justice causes, 198; Demme's idyllic life in, 131
Nyswaner, Ron: *Philadelphia* and, 112–14, 115, 117, 118, 121; *Swing Shift* and, 57, 58, 59, 60, 64

Index

Occupy Wall Street movement, 179–80
Ochs, Phil, 49
O'Donoghue, Deirdre, 70
Olivier, Laurence, 99
Once Upon a Time in the West (Leone, 1968), 48
One and Only, Genuine, Original Family Band, The (1968), 59
One Day in September (MacDonald, 1999), 174
One Flew Over the Cuckoo's Nest (Forman, 1975), 75, 111
One Foot on a Banana Peel, the Other in the Grave (documentary), 116, 121
O'Neill, Eugene, 48, 184
Operation Desert Storm, 151
Orchid Thief, The (Orlean), 148
Ordinary People (Redford, 1980), 53
Oriolo, Joe, 138
Orion Pictures, 75, 80, 97, 99, 121; bankruptcy of, 113, 145; revival of Demme's career after *Swing Shift* and, 130
Orlean, Susan, 148
Orphans (Pakula, 1987), 88
Oshatz, Lorrie, 55
O'Toole, Peter, 99
Overtown (Black community in Miami), 7

Pacino, Al, 26, 60
Pakula, Alan J., 88
Palestine: Peace Not Apartheid (Carter, 2006), 162–63
Paramount Pictures, 10, 26, 37, 125, 149; *Citizens Band* and, 40, 41, 42, 150, 153; *The Manchurian Candidate* and, 154; *Swing Shift* and, 56, 57
Paris, Texas (Wenders, 1984), 89
Parker, Alan, 90
Parker, Carolyn, 161–62, 170

Parker, Trey, 154
Park Joong-Hoon, 144, 146
Parks, Gordon, 29
Parson, Annie-B, xiv, 86
Parsons, Gram, 159
Passion of the Christ, The (Gibson, 2004), 155
Peckinpah, Sam, 48
Pe De Boi (samba band), 91
Pelosi, Nancy, 163
Penn, Arthur, 133
People vs. Anderson (California), 25
Peploe, Clare, 27, 46, 74, 189–90
Peploe, Mark, 74
Peretz, Susan, 65
Perez, Rosie, 125
Perić, Suzana, 154, 165
Perry, Dwaine, 197
Perry, Frank, 39
Perry, Hart, 141
Pfeiffer, Michelle, 88–89, 90, 91, 92–93, 94, 98
Philadelphia (Demme, 1993), 93, 112–23, 125, 150; Academy Awards won by, 122; controversy surrounding, 121; musical score, 119–20
Phillips, Don, 47, 52
Phillips, Michael, 184
Picker, David V., 37
Pierre, Andre, 127
Platt, Ben, 186
Platt, Marc, 113, 185, 186
Play It as It Lays (Didion, 1972), 39
Playtone Productions, 124, 186–87
Pleskow, Eric, 75
Poe, Edgar Allan, 18
Polanski, Roman, 20, 40
Ponsoldt, James, 196
Pontecorvo, Gillo, 180
Portman, Rachel, 154
Postman Always Rings Twice, The (Cain novel), 125
Practical Magic (Dunne, 1998), 139

Index

Pran, Dith, 82–83
"Prayers from the Burned-Out City" (Castle), 181
Precious: Based on the Novel "Push" by Sapphire (Daniels, 2009), 140
Presley, Elvis, 6, 59, 159
Price, Vincent, 26
Prince-Bythewood, Gina, 191
Princess Diaries, The (Marshall, 2001), 167
Prine, John, 34
Private Benjamin (1980), 55, 58
Prophete, Ernst, 127
Pryor, Richard, 60
Psycho (Hitchcock, 1960), 105
Publicity Club of New York, 3
Public Theatre (New York), 83, 89
Punch-Drunk Love (Anderson, 2002), 145
Purcell, Evelyn (first wife of Jonathan Demme): *Caged Heat* and, 26, 27, 29; on *Citizens Band*, 36, 38; on Corman, 21, 24; divorce from Demme, 46, 47; on *Fighting Mad*, 33; film career ambitions, 35, 36; in London, 14, 15; in Los Angeles, 20; on marriage to Demme, 19; *Melvin and Howard* and, 51; as producer, 26, 27
Purl, Linda, 31
Purple Rose of Cairo, The (Allen, 1985), 75, 76
Putney Swope (Downey, 1969), 42
Pyne, Daniel, 151

Q Lazzarus, 82
Queen Latifah, 54
Quinn, Declan, 96, 159, 163, 170, 183, 188

race relations, in United States, 13, 43
Rachel Getting Married (Demme, 2008), 167–73, 177, 181–82
Radio Haiti, 141–42
Radiohead (band), 181
Raging Bull (Scorsese, 1980), 53
Ragtime (Forman, 1981), 76
Raiders of the Lost Ark (Spielberg, 1981), 57–58
Rajasthan Express (musical ensemble), 181
Ramapough Lenape Nation, 196, 197
Rarely Seen Cinema series, 157
Rashomon (Kurosawa, 1950), 19, 20
Ratner, Brett, 148
Rawlings, David, 165
Reagan, Ronald, 163
Red Dragon (Ratner, 2002), 148
Redford, Robert, 53
Red Harvest (Hammett), 74
Reds (Beatty, 1981), 51, 57
Ref, The (1994), 126
Reid, Ella, 28
Reit, Seymour, 138
Reitman, Jason, 185
Resnais, Alain, 12
Rice, Jonathan, 187
Rich, Matty, 112
Richards, Beah, 133–34, 141
Ricki and the Flash (Demme, 2015), 185–89, 192
Ridgely, Robert, 115
Right Stuff, The (Kaufman, 1983), 60
Right to Return: New Home Movies from the Lower 9th Ward (Demme, TV miniseries, 2007), 162
Rivertown Film Society, xiii
Riviera Theatre (Miami), 7
Robards, Jason, 48, 49–50, 53, 115, 119
Robart, James L., 194
Robbins, Tim, 146
Roberts, Elliot, 171
Robinson, Smokey, 60
Roche, Jim, 77, 78, 170
Rock and Roll Hall of Fame museum (Cleveland), 189, 196

Index

Rockland County (New York), 96, 131, 155
Rodd, Marcia, 37
Rolling Stones, 49, 52; Altamont concert (1969), 22, 44; in *Gimme Shelter*, 44, 67; in *Let's Spend the Night Together*, 70
Romero, Eddie, 23
Romero, George A., 54
Rooks, Conrad, 157
Roots (Haley, ABC TV miniseries, 1977), 139
Rosas, Rick, 186, 189
Rose, Charlie, 137
Rosenberg, Howard, 54
Ross, Diana, 53
Rossellini, Roberto, 13
Roud, Richard, 41
Rove, Karl, 149
Rowan and Martin's Laugh-In (NBC TV series, 1968–1973), 58
Rowley, Isaiah, 110
Royal Wedding (Donen, 1951), 72
Rudin, Scott, 121, 149, 150
Ruehl, Mercedes, 89, 90
Rugoff, Don, 41–42
Run Lola Run (Tykwer, 1998), 144
Russell, Kurt, 59, 71
Russell, Rosalind, 59–60
Russo, Vito, 107
Ryan, Meg, 98

Sachs, William, 42
Salt, Waldo, 57
"Salt Water Safari" (Robert Demme, 1938), 2
Saltzman, Harry, 14
Sandler, Adam, 139
San Sabastian Film Festival, 173
Santiago, Cirio H., 23
Sarandon, Susan, 54, 88
Sarris, Andrew, 147
Saturday Night Fever (Badham, 1977), 42

Sauter, Brenda, 79
Saving Private Ryan (Spielberg, 1998), 138
Savoca, Nancy, 126
Saxon, Ed, 90, 116, 124, 125, 129, 148; as independent producer, 178; *Something Wild* and, 76, 78; split with Demme, 145
Scales, Steve, 72, 116
Schatzberg, Jerry, 44
Scheider, Roy, 44, 45
Scherschel, Frank, 102
Schlesinger, Adam, 124
Schlesinger, John, 45
Schmidt, Steve, 145
Schnabel, Julian, 146
Schoedsack, Ernest B., 4
Schreiber, Liev, 150
Schruers, Fred, 87
Schumacher, Joel, 60
Scorsese, Martin, 18, 53, 76, 98, 172, 195
Scott, A. O., 173
Scott, Ridley, 73, 148
Sears, Henry, 3
Sears, Mary, 3
Seduction of Joe Tynan, The (Schatzberg, 1979), 44
Seitz, George B., 17
Sellers, Peter, 9, 80
Semel, Terry, 64
Sendak, Maurice, 98
September 11, 2001, terrorist attacks, 149
Serpico (Lumet, 1973), 26, 166
Seven-Ups, The (D'Antoni, 1973), 45
Shaber, David, 44
Shadow of a Doubt (Hitchcock, 1943), 106
Shafransky, Renée, 83
Shaft (Parks, 1971), 29
Shakespeare in the Park, 38
Shakey Pictures, 158
Shakur, Tupac, 133

Index

Shampoo (Ashby, 1975), 30, 58
Shawn, Wallace, 182
Sheen, Martin, 83
Sherman, Gary, 16
Shock Corridor (Fuller, 1963), 30
Shoot the Moon (Parker), 90
Shore, Howard, 105, 119
Shot in the Dark, A (Edwards, 1964), 9
Shulman, Adam, 181, 182
Shutter Island (Scorsese, 2010), 172
Shyamalan, M. Night, 155
Silberling, Brad, 138
Silence of the Lambs, The (Demme, 1991), 97, 101–9, 125, 138, 175, 183; Academy Awards won by, 111–12, 114, 167; casting for, 98–100; controversy surrounding, 107, 108–9, 110; critical reception of, 107–8; as feminist film, 98, 99, 101; parallel editing in, 105; referenced in *The Truth about Charlie*, 147
Silence of the Lambs, The (Harris novel), 97, 101
Silkwood (Nichols, 1983), 59
Simon, Carly, 66
Sinatra, Frank, 6, 11, 116, 149
Sinclaire, Crystin, 28
Singleton, John, 112
Siskel, Gene, 71
Slaughterhouse-Five (Hill, 1972), 54
Sleeps with Angels album (Young), 125
Small Tragedy (Lucas), 168
Smith, Anna Deavere, 169, 170, 195
Smith, Brooke, 100, 103–4
Smith, Cheryl "Rainbeaux," 26
Smith, Will, 145
Snyder, Paul, 194
Snyder, Ruth, 125
social activism, Demme's commitment to, 65, 123, 198; audiences and, 139; carried on by Brooklyn, 196–97; feminism, 63, 66, 106; humanitarian efforts in Haiti, 141–43, 197; Occupy Wall Street movement and, 179–80; Sing Sing TED Talk and, 190; Standing Rock Reservation protests and, 193; Vietnam War protests, 12–13, 179
Social Network, The (Fincher, 2010), 188
Soderbergh, Steven, 177–78
Something Wild (Demme, 1986), 75–82, 87, 89, 93, 94; casting for, 77, 100; location scouting for, 101; *Rachel Getting Married* compared to, 167
Song One (Barker-Froyland, 2013), 181, 182, 187
Sony Pictures Classics, 168, 178
Sothern, Ann, 31
Soul on Fire (Cleaver), 13
soundtracks/music scores: *Beloved*, 154; *Caged Heat*, 29; *Fighting Mad*, 34–35; *The Manchurian Candidate*, 169; *Married to the Mob*, 93; *Melvin and Howard*, 49, 51–52; *Philadelphia*, 119–20; *The Silence of the Lambs*, 104, 106; *Something Wild*, 78–80, 81; *Swing Shift*, 60, 64, 66; *The Truth about Charlie*, 148, 154
South Africa, apartheid in, 86, 93
South Park (Comedy Central animated series), 154
Spacek, Sissy, 31
Speed of Light (Hansen), 55
Spider's Stratagem, The (Bertolucci, 1970), 93
Spielberg, Steven, 43, 57, 125, 133, 138
Split Rock Sweetwater Prayer Camp (Mahwah, New Jersey), 194, 196
Springfield, Rick, 186
Springsteen, Bruce, 119, 120, 122, 124
Squat Theatre (New York), 128

Index

Squyres, Tim, 171
Sragow, Michael, 58
Stallone, Sylvester, 79, 105
Stan, Sebastian, 185
Star 80 (Fosse, 1983), 15
Star Trek (NBC TV series, 1966–1969), 38
Star Wars (Lucas, 1977), 41
Steele, Barbara, 26
Steenburgen, Mary, 48–49, 53, 59, 115
Stewart, Jimmy, 88
Stockwell, Dean, 89, 92, 93, 152
Stone, Matt, 154
Stone, Oliver, 76, 108
Stone, Peter, 144
Stop Making Sense (Demme, 1984), 68–74, 75, 81, 83, 129–30, 188, 196
Stopwatch Gang, The, 177
Storaro, Vittorio, 139
Storefront Hitchcock (Demme, 1998), 129–30, 145
Straight Out of Brooklyn (Rich, 1991), 112
Strasberg, Lee, 60
Streep, Meryl, 59, 148, 150, 152, 185–86, 187
Strugatz, Barry, 87, 88
Strumpf, Sylvia, 4
Studio 54 (New York), 54
Studio M Playhouse (Miami), 9–10
Sturges, Preston, 33
Subject Was Roses, The (Grossbard, 1968), 45
SUBWAYStories: Tales from the Underground (Demme et al., TV movie, 1997), 126
Sum of All Fears, The (Clancy novel), 151
Sumpter, Rachell, 175
Sundance Film Festival, 144
Sutherland, Donald, 53
Suzhou River (Ye Lou, 2000), 144
Sweet Sweetback's Baadasssss Song (Van Peebles, 1971), 29
Swimming to Cambodia (Gray), 82, 83
Swing Shift (Demme, 1984), 55, 56–66, 74, 130; *Beloved* compared with, 136; critics' reception of, 71; Demme's loss of creative control over, 62–66, 69; musical score, 60; reshoots for, 63, 68
"*Swing Shift*—a Tale of Hollywood" (Vineberg, 1991), 65–66
Sylbert, Anthea, 58, 63
Sylbert, Richard, 37, 56, 58, 153
Symonds, David, 16

Talking Heads (band), 54, 67, 68–74, 80. See also *Stop Making Sense* (Demme, 1984)
Tally, Ted, 97–98, 110
Tanen, Ned, 53
Tati, Jacques, 5
Taubin, Amy, 107, 110
Tawil, Zafer, 170
Taxi Driver (Scorsese, 1976), 98
Taxi to the Dark Side (2007), 174
Taylor, Tate, 140
Team America: World Police (Trey and Stone, 2004), 154
Teigh-Bloom, Murray, 44
television, 4, 17, 45, 120, 126, 165, 191; Demme's TV directorial debut, 125; made-for-television films, 16, 54, 59, 67, 139; in *The Manchurian Candidate* films, 153; Netflix streaming and, 185; relation to cinema, 125; Saxon's work in, 178
Terms of Endearment (Brooks, 1983), 76, 90, 97
Terror, The (Corman, Coppola, Hale, 1963), 18
That Thing You Do! (Hanks, 1996), 124
Them! (Douglas, 1954), 4
There Will Be Blood (Anderson, 2007), 169

Index

Thin Red Line, The (Malick, 1998), 138
13th Man, The (Teigh-Bloom novel), 44
Thomas, Kevin, 29
Thompson, David, 152
Thunderball (1965), 14
Tie Me Up! Tie Me Down! (Almodóvar, 1989), 115
Timberlake, Justin, 187–88
Tobolowsky, Stephen, 65
Todd, Marcia, 38
Todman, Bill, Jr., 90–91
Tony Rome (Douglas, 1967), 11
Topaz (Hitchcock, 1969), 81
Toronto International Film Festival, 173
Towne, Robert, 57, 64
Tragedy of a Ridiculous Man (Bertolucci, 1981), 158
Travers, Peter, 147
Trial and Error (Hill, 1962), 9
Tribeca Film Festival, 195–96
TriStar, 113, 121
True Love (Savoca, 1989), 126
Truffaut, François, 13, 45, 147
Trump, Donald, 193
Truth about Charlie, The (Demme, 2002), 144–49, 151
Trying Times (PBS TV series), 177
TV on the Radio (band), 169
12 Angry Men (Lumet, 1957), 123, 166
12 Years a Slave (McQueen, 2013), 140
Twentieth Century Fox, 17, 113, 124
2046 (Wong Kar-Wai, 2004), 168
Tykwer, Tom, 144
Typee (Melville novel), 42

Ulee's Gold (Nuñez, 1997), 35, 126–27, 130
Underground Railroad, 198
United Artists (UA), 12, 14, 26, 44, 57, 75
United Haitian Filmmakers collective, 143
United States of America v. the City of Seattle, 194
Universal Pictures, 52, 126
Ustinov, Peter, 53
Utt, Kenneth, 44–45, 78, 129; death of, 121–22; *Married to the Mob* and, 90–91, 92; in *Philadelphia*, 116; photo displayed in Demme films, 147, 152

Vallée, Jean-Marc, 113
Van der Graaf Generator (band), 16
Van Peebles, Melvin, 29
Vanya on 42nd Street (Malle, 1994), 183
Varda, Agnès, 12
Variety (1983), 82
Variety (trade publication), 32, 145
Vawter, Ron, 86, 115, 116, 119, 122
Velvet Underground (band), 29
Venice Film Festival, 52, 172, 189
Vertigo (Hitchcock, 1958), 45
Vevo-YouTube Concert Series, 180
Vida, Vendela, 175
Vietnam War, 8, 23, 57, 110, 179
Village, The (Shyamalan, 2004), 155
Village Voice, 10, 13, 41, 110
Vineberg, Steve, 65, 66
Viola, Joe, 15, 16, 17, 20, 32, 46; on *Angels Hard as They Come*, 20; *Beloved* and, 134; Corman and, 18–19, 20–21; Demme's declining health and, 195; at Demme's marriage to Purcell, 19; as DGA member, 67–68; on *The Hot Box*, 22–23; *SUBWAYStories* and, 126
Virgin Suicides, The (Coppola, 1999), 140
Vision Quest (Becker, 1985), 88
Vitale, Joe, 186, 187
Vixen (Meyer, 1968), 26
Volver (Almodóvar, 2006), 168

Index

Vonnegut, Edie, 54
Vonnegut, Kurt, 54
Von Richthofen and Brown (1971), 17, 18

Wahlberg, Mark, 146
Walken, Christopher, 45
Walker, Alice, 133
Ward, Fred, 60
Warner Brothers, 26, 55, 58, 62, 63, 65, 67
Washington, Denzel, 114–15, 122, 124, 150
Waterboy, The (1998), 139
Watkins, Michael, 33
Watts, Brandon, 179–80
Weckerman, Dave, 79
Wedgeworth, Ann, 37, 38–39
Weir, Alex, 72
Welch, Gillian, 165
Welles, Orson, 145
Wenders, Wim, 89
Wenner, Jann S., 189
Wexler, Haskell, 26, 139
Weymouth, Tina, 72, 73
What about Bob? (Oz, 1991), 184
What Is the What (Eggers), 174
What's Motivating Hayes (Demme, 2015), 185
Where the Wild Things Are (Jonze, 2009), 175
Whiskey A-Go-Go (Los Angeles), 53
White, Mike, 178
White Dog (Fuller, 1982), 125
Whitman, Stuart, 32
Who Am I This Time? (Demme, 1982), 54
"Who Am I This Time?" (Vonnegut, 1961), 54
Who's Afraid of Virginia Woolf? (Nichols, 1966), 183
Wide Blue Road, The (Pontecorvo, 1957), 180

Wild Angels, The (Corman, 1968), 18–19
Wilkinson, Bob, 52
Williams, Tennessee, 31
Wilson, Patrick, 178
Wilson, Rita, 196
Wilson, Trey, 100
Winfrey, Oprah, 131–32, 133, 135–36, 140, 141
Winged Victory (Hart), 45
Winger, Debra, 169
Winters, Shelley, 31
Witches of Eastwick, The (Miller, 1987), 88
Witt, Kathryn, 15–16, 116
Wolper, David L., 139
"women in jeopardy" films, 23, 98
Wong Kar-Wai, 144, 168
Wooster Group, 82, 83, 86, 115
World War II, 3, 56, 58
Worrell, Bernie, 72, 186, 187
Wright, Jeffrey, 146
Writers Guild of America, 64
Wurtzel, Stuart, 186

X (punk band), 77

Yaniz, Lillian (stepmother of Jonathan Demme), 8, 11
Yankee Doodle Dandy (1942), 4
Yo! MTV Raps (MTV, 1988–1995), 89, 126
Young, Neil, 119, 120, 124–25, 159–60, 171; collaborations with Demme, 158–60, 166, 171–72, 173, 178–79, 186; *Greendale* rock opera, 158; *Prairie Wind* album, 158, 159. See also *Neil Young: Heart of Gold*; *Neil Young Journeys*; *Neil Young: Trunk Show*
Young Adult (Reitman, 2011), 185
Young Frankenstein (Brooks, 1974), 31
You Only Live Twice (1967), 14

Index

Yours, Mine and Ours (1969), 14, 59
YouTube, 180

Z (Costa-Gavras, 1969), 42
Zea, Kristi, 90, 91, 92, 101, 105; on camera movements in *Silence of the Lambs*, 101–2; on layout of *Philadelphia* scenes, 116–17; *The Manchurian Candidate* and, 150, 153; *Notes from the Field* and, 195; *Philadelphia* and, 118; photos of Ed Gein's house studied by, 102
Zeitlin, Benh, 140
Zeitoun, Abdulrahman, 174, 175
Zinnemann, Fred, 163
Zucker Brothers, 184
Zulu (1964), 10
Zwerin, Charlotte, 44

About the Author

David M. Stewart is a published scholar and film journalist and has been writing about movies since he was a high school senior. He worked on the set of the film *The Diary of a Teenage Girl* (2015) and did research for the documentary *Hal* (2018). His work can be seen in *Air Mail*, the *Film Stage*, the *Arts Fuse*, and PleaseKillMe.com. He teaches film and media studies at Emerson College, Plymouth State University, and Southern New Hampshire University. He lives outside of Boston.

X/Instagram Handle: filmnerddave

Screen Classics

Screen Classics is a series of critical biographies, film histories, and analytical studies focusing on neglected filmmakers and important screen artists and subjects, from the era of silent cinema through the golden age of Hollywood to the international generation of today. Books in the Screen Classics series are intended for scholars and general readers alike. The contributing authors are established figures in their respective fields. This series also serves the purpose of advancing scholarship on film personalities and themes with ties to Kentucky.

Series Editor   Patrick McGilligan

Books in the Series
Olivia de Havilland: Lady Triumphant
   Victoria Amador
Mae Murray: The Girl with the Bee-Stung Lips
   Michael G. Ankerich
Harry Dean Stanton: Hollywood's Zen Rebel
   Joseph B. Atkins
Hedy Lamarr: The Most Beautiful Woman in Film
   Ruth Barton
Rex Ingram: Visionary Director of the Silent Screen
   Ruth Barton
Conversations with Classic Film Stars: Interviews from Hollywood's Golden Era
   James Bawden and Ron Miller
Conversations with Legendary Television Stars: Interviews from the First Fifty Years
   James Bawden and Ron Miller
They Made the Movies: Conversations with Great Filmmakers
   James Bawden and Ron Miller
You Ain't Heard Nothin' Yet: Interviews with Stars from Hollywood's Golden Era
   James Bawden and Ron Miller
Charles Boyer: The French Lover
   John Baxter
Von Sternberg
   John Baxter
Hitchcock's Partner in Suspense: The Life of Screenwriter Charles Bennett
   Charles Bennett, edited by John Charles Bennett
Hitchcock and the Censors
   John Billheimer
The Magic Hours: The Films and Hidden Life of Terrence Malick
   John Bleasdale
A Uniquely American Epic: Intimacy and Action, Tenderness and Violence in Sam Peckinpah's The Wild Bunch
   Edited by Michael Bliss

My Life in Focus: A Photographer's Journey with Elizabeth Taylor and the Hollywood Jet Set
    Gianni Bozzacchi with Joey Tayler
Hollywood Divided: The 1950 Screen Directors Guild Meeting and the Impact of the Blacklist
    Kevin Brianton
He's Got Rhythm: The Life and Career of Gene Kelly
    Cynthia Brideson and Sara Brideson
Ziegfeld and His Follies: A Biography of Broadway's Greatest Producer
    Cynthia Brideson and Sara Brideson
Eleanor Powell: Born to Dance
    Paula Broussard and Lisa Royère
The Marxist and the Movies: A Biography of Paul Jarrico
    Larry Ceplair
Dalton Trumbo: Blacklisted Hollywood Radical
    Larry Ceplair and Christopher Trumbo
Warren Oates: A Wild Life
    Susan Compo
Helen Morgan: The Original Torch Singer and Ziegfeld's Last Star
    Christopher S. Connelly
Improvising Out Loud: My Life Teaching Hollywood How to Act
    Jeff Corey with Emily Corey
Crane: Sex, Celebrity, and My Father's Unsolved Murder
    Robert Crane and Christopher Fryer
Jack Nicholson: The Early Years
    Robert Crane and Christopher Fryer
Anne Bancroft: A Life
    Douglass K. Daniel
Being Hal Ashby: Life of a Hollywood Rebel
    Nick Dawson
Bruce Dern: A Memoir
    Bruce Dern with Christopher Fryer and Robert Crane
Intrepid Laughter: Preston Sturges and the Movies
    Andrew Dickos
The Woman Who Dared: The Life and Times of Pearl White, Queen of the Serials
    William M. Drew
Miriam Hopkins: Life and Films of a Hollywood Rebel
    Allan R. Ellenberger
Vitagraph: America's First Great Motion Picture Studio
    Andrew A. Erish
Jayne Mansfield: The Girl Couldn't Help It
    Eve Golden
John Gilbert: The Last of the Silent Film Stars
    Eve Golden
Strictly Dynamite: The Sensational Life of Lupe Velez
    Eve Golden
Stuntwomen: The Untold Hollywood Story
    Mollie Gregory
Jean Gabin: The Actor Who Was France
    Joseph Harriss

Yves Montand: The Passionate Voice
    Joseph Harriss
The Herridge Style: The Life and Work of a Television Revolutionary
    Robert Herridge, edited and with an introduction by John Sorensen
Otto Preminger: The Man Who Would Be King, updated edition
    Foster Hirsch
Saul Bass: Anatomy of Film Design
    Jan-Christopher Horak
Lawrence Tierney: Hollywood's Real-Life Tough Guy
    Burt Kearns
Hitchcock Lost and Found: The Forgotten Films
    Alain Kerzoncuf and Charles Barr
Pola Negri: Hollywood's First Femme Fatale
    Mariusz Kotowski
Ernest Lehman: The Sweet Smell of Success
    Jon Krampner
Sidney J. Furie: Life and Films
    Daniel Kremer
Albert Capellani: Pioneer of the Silent Screen
    Christine Leteux
A Front Row Seat: An Intimate Look at Broadway, Hollywood, and the Age of Glamour
    Nancy Olson Livingston
Ridley Scott: A Biography
    Vincent LoBrutto
Mamoulian: Life on Stage and Screen
    David Luhrssen
Maureen O'Hara: The Biography
    Aubrey Malone
My Life as a Mankiewicz: An Insider's Journey through Hollywood
    Tom Mankiewicz and Robert Crane
Hawks on Hawks
    Joseph McBride
John Ford
    Joseph McBride and Michael Wilmington
Showman of the Screen: Joseph E. Levine and His Revolutions in Film Promotion
    A. T. McKenna
William Wyler: The Life and Films of Hollywood's Most Celebrated Director
    Gabriel Miller
Raoul Walsh: The True Adventures of Hollywood's Legendary Director
    Marilyn Ann Moss
Veit Harlan: The Life and Work of a Nazi Filmmaker
    Frank Noack
Harry Langdon: King of Silent Comedy
    Gabriella Oldham and Mabel Langdon
Mavericks: Interviews with the World's Iconoclast Filmmakers
    Gerald Peary
Charles Walters: The Director Who Made Hollywood Dance
    Brent Phillips

Some Like It Wilder: The Life and Controversial Films of Billy Wilder
    Gene D. Phillips
Ann Dvorak: Hollywood's Forgotten Rebel
    Christina Rice
Mean . . . Moody . . . Magnificent! Jane Russell and the Marketing of a Hollywood Legend
    Christina Rice
Fay Wray and Robert Riskin: A Hollywood Memoir
    Victoria Riskin
Lewis Milestone: Life and Films
    Harlow Robinson
Michael Curtiz: A Life in Film
    Alan K. Rode
Ryan's Daughter: The Making of an Irish Epic
    Paul Benedict Rowan
Arthur Penn: American Director
    Nat Segaloff
Film's First Family: The Untold Story of the Costellos
    Terry Chester Shulman
Claude Rains: An Actor's Voice
    David J. Skal with Jessica Rains
June Mathis: The Rise and Fall of a Silent Film Visionary
    Thomas J. Slater
Horses of Hollywood
    Roberta Smoodin
Barbara La Marr: The Girl Who Was Too Beautiful for Hollywood
    Sherri Snyder
Lionel Barrymore: Character and Endurance in Hollywood's Golden Age
    Kathleen Spaltro
Buzz: The Life and Art of Busby Berkeley
    Jeffrey Spivak
Victor Fleming: An American Movie Master
    Michael Sragow
Aline MacMahon: Hollywood, the Blacklist, and the Birth of Method Acting
    John Stangeland
My Place in the Sun: Life in the Golden Age of Hollywood and Washington
    George Stevens, Jr.
There's No Going Back: The Life and Work of Jonathan Demme
    David M. Stewart
Hollywood Presents Jules Verne: The Father of Science Fiction on Screen
    Brian Taves
Thomas Ince: Hollywood's Independent Pioneer
    Brian Taves
Picturing Peter Bogdanovich: My Conversations with the New Hollywood Director
    Peter Tonguette
Jessica Lange: An Adventurer's Heart
    Anthony Uzarowski
Carl Theodor Dreyer and Ordet: *My Summer with the Danish Filmmaker*
    Jan Wahl

Wild Bill Wellman: Hollywood Rebel
    William Wellman Jr.
Harvard, Hollywood, Hitmen, and Holy Men: A Memoir
    Paul W. Williams
The Warner Brothers
    Chris Yogerst
Clarence Brown: Hollywood's Forgotten Master
    Gwenda Young
The Queen of Technicolor: Maria Montez in Hollywood
    Tom Zimmerman